PSYCHOLOGY'S
OCCULT DOUBLES

PSYCHOLOGY'S OCCULT DOUBLES

Psychology and the Problem of Pseudoscience

Thomas Hardy Leahey
and
Grace Evans Leahey

Nelson-Hall nh **Chicago**

LIBRARY OF CONGRESS CATALOGING IN PUBLICATION DATA

Leahey, Thomas Hardy.
  Psychology's occult doubles.

  Bibliography: p.
  Includes index.
  1. Occult sciences. 2. Psychical research.
3. Phrenology. 4. Cults. 5. Psychology—Methodology.
I. Leahey, Grace Evans. II. Title.
BF1409.5.L43 1983   133   82-24635
ISBN 0-88229-717-1

Manufactured in the United States of America

10 9 8 7 6 5 4 3 2

The paper in this book is pH neutral (acid-free).

Contents

Preface

We live in a time when strange beliefs flourish like tropical insects. Most of us are puzzled about why people should cleave to nonsense; we should also be puzzled by why we think it is nonsense. Especially important in this regard are belief systems that pretend to be sciences but are called pseudosciences by established scientists. The pseudosciences challenge us to examine what science is and what are its claims, promises, and limits. Perhaps more than any other intellectual institution, science shapes the lives of everyone in the world today. Yet despite science's dominance, occult beliefs flourish. Why?

Our book is an attempt to answer this question by examining several pseudosciences, primarily of the nineteenth century. That century witnessed the final destruction of the classical-medieval world view by modern science, and it also witnessed the growth of popular pseudosciences: phrenology, mesmerism, spiritualism, and psychical research. So to understand the roots of contemporary occult beliefs and pseudosciences (parapsychology, therapeutic cults), we must look to the nineteenth century. As a science whose bona fides is often questioned, psychology plays a central role in modern pseudoscience. Psychology has its fringe fields and peculiar practitioners, and it is often looked on with skepticism by natural sciences. Yet as Martin Gross has pointed out in his *Psychological Society* (New York: Touchstone Books, 1978), modern America's new theology is psychology; scientific therapy has replaced worn-out religion. In an age when the natural sciences are established beyond question and people look to psychologists for answers to their problems, it is psychology that spawns pseudosciences and therapeutic cults.

Our aim in this book is to understand why pseudosciences exist, why they attract followers, why they are rejected. We will also study the traditional grounds for distinguishing between science and pseudoscience, to see how far they are justified and what role they have played in the historical rejection of "real pseudosciences," if such there be. Finally, we will reflect on the nature of science, its relation to human cognitive and emotional needs, and how far it may go in replacing other human endeavors such as religion and art.

Although each of us has read everything in this book, certain parts were primarily written by one or the other of us. T.H.L. wrote chapters 1, 3, 4, 5, 7, 9, and the astrological part of chapter 2. G.E.L. wrote the Introduction, chapters 6 and 8, and the alchemical part of chapter 2.

Acknowledgments

Material has been reprinted with permission from the following sources:

Chart entitled "Comparative Table of Faculties" from Howard Davis Spoerl, "Faculties vs. Traits: Gall's Solution," *Character and Personality* (now *Journal of Personality*) 4 (1935-36): 222. Copyright 1935, Duke University Press, Durham, N.C.

Schematic depiction of Gall's theory of phrenology from Robert M. Young, *Mind, Brain, and Adaptation in the Nineteenth Century* (Oxford: At the Clarendon Press, 1970), p. 36.

"Powers and Organs of the Mind." Frontispiece to J. C. Spurzheim, *Phrenology* (Philadelphia: J. B. Lippincott, 1908).

Mesmer's twenty-seven propositions of mesmerism from Franz Anton Mesmer, Dissertation on the Discovery of Animal Magnetism (1779). Translation from the French in Maurice M. Tinterow, *Foundations of Hypnosis* (Springfield, Ill.: Charles C Thomas, 1970), pp. 54–56. Courtesy of Charles C Thomas, Pub., Springfield, Ill.

Translation from the French in Vincent Buranelli, *The Wizard from Vienna* (New York: Coward, McCann and Geoghegan, 1975), p. 118. Copyright 1975 by Vincent Buranelli. Reprinted by permission of McIntosh and Otis, Inc.

Robert Darnton, *Mesmerism and the End of the Enlightenment in France* (Cambridge, Mass.: Harvard University Press, 1968), pp. 70, 79, 80, 124.

Translation from the French in Frank Podmore, *From Mesmerism to Christian Science* (New Hyde Park, N. Y.: University Books, 1936), p. 76. Reprinted by arrangement with Lyle Stuart, Inc.

M. Lamar Keene, *The Psychic Mafia* (New York: St. Martin's Press, 1976), pp. 60, 65, 76, 132–34, 153, 301, 302–3. Reprinted by permission of St. Martin's Press, Inc. Macmillan & Co., Ltd.

J. B. Priestley, *English Journey* (London: William Heinemann, 1934), pp. 158–59, 161. Reprinted by permission of William Heinemann Ltd.

H.R. Ellis-Davidson, *The Road to Hel* (Cambridge, Eng.: Cambridge University Press, 1943).

Magnus Magnusson and Hermann Palsson, eds., *The Vinland Sagas* (Baltimore: Penguin Books, 1965), pp. 81–83. Copyright © Magnus Magnusson and Hermann Palsson, 1965. Reprinted by permission of Penguin Books Ltd.

C. R. Snyder and R. J. Shenkel, "The P. T. Barnum Effect," *Psychology Today* 8 (1975): 52–54. Copyright 1975, Ziff-Davis Pub. Co.

Joseph Banks Rhine, *New Frontiers of the Mind* (New York: Farrar and Rinehart, 1937), pp. 20–21. Reprinted by permission of Louisa E. Rhine.

William Simms Bainbridge, *Satan's Power* (Berkeley and Los Angeles: University of California Press, 1978), pp. 205, 208, 219–20. Copyright 1978 by The Regents of the University of California. Published by the University of California Press.

Introduction

The Occult Marketplace

Do you desire esoteric knowledge of hidden truths—for which Dr. Faustus sold his soul? Today such secrets are available to anyone with the interest and a few dollars to spare. Lost continents, ancient astronauts, the occult power of pyramids, fortune tellers, and character readers abound, and astrology columns appear in almost every newspaper. There follow some gleanings from the occult marketplace of this scientific twentieth century.

In a randomly chosen issue of *The Star*, one of the large tabloid weeklies, twenty ads appeared under "Astrology" in the classified ad section, of which these are representative:

> **SISTER JACQUELIN,** Spiritual healer. Helps all problems of Life! Free question. Phone . . .
> **REV. MARY** can help you through all problems. Love, health, alcohol, nature, business, bad luck, evil . . .
> **MYSTIC POWER.** Gain money, love, luck. Write . . .

In addition, the book department was offering a "**GIANT NEW** occult catalog! Magic, voodoo, witchcraft, astrology, herbs, talismans, incense. Send $2. . . ." The "Psychic" department offered "**SUC-CEED! PUT** your unrealized psychic powers to work! Psychic formulas for success! $1.00. . . ." Other departments offered: "**LEARN DYNAMIC** mind powers. Make dreams come true! Cassette instruction. . . ." and "**HYPNOTIZE STRANGERS** in 30 seconds! Most powerful hypnotic device ever created. . . . Only $3 each. . . ."

One of the feature stories in the same issue (May 13, 1980) is headlined "**TERRIFIED FAMILY CLAIMS: GHOSTS KILLED OUR PETS.**" (Other interesting stories could be written about Terrified Family Claims: Pets Killed Our Ghosts, or Terrified Ghosts Claim: Family Killed Our Pets) The story concerns a typical case of poltergeisting in a London house, very like the occurrences at the home of the Fox sisters, one hundred and fifty years ago, that started Spiritualism (see chapter 5). Ghosts of former inhabitants of the house talk through the two daughters of the family, turn over the furniture, yell obscenities, etc.

So if you think table-turning, rapping Spiritualism is out of date, think again. We are not so rational that we can escape hope and fear any better than our ancestors could.

There are many other places besides the tabloids where the occult flourishes. *Teacher* magazine, in 1978, carried an article in which a teacher suggested that students be grouped for class work by their astrological signs.[1] In Salt Lake City, Utah, an alchemy school offered, at least as recently as 1972, a two-week course on how to turn lead into gold.[2] The University of California at Berkeley gave Isaac Bonewits a B.A. in magic studies,[3] and advanced degrees in parapsychology are now given by the University of Edinburgh, Cambridge, Surrey, and the University of London.[4] Forty percent of the students in a New Zealand University believe they themselves possess psychic powers.[5]

Reverend Willard Fuller of Louisiana, an ordained Southern Baptist preacher, claims a special mission to repair teeth. "If God can put silver or gold in a mountain, He can put it in your mouth!" To work his miracle cures, he holds the patient's jaw and roars, "Lord, heal these teeth! For Jesus' sake!"[6]

A sign saying "Shoplifting Plays Hell with Your Karma" is on display in Eleanore Person's Hermetic Workshop in Los Angeles. There you can buy aerosol spray cans of incense, along with such other preparations as *yohimbé,* a supposed aphrodisiac. Other spray cans contain tannis root, used for its awakening powers in all the best mummy movies, and High John the Conquerer Bath Spray, based on an old voodoo love drug. This interest in voodoo is also evident in the two brands of voodoo dolls for sale, into which believers stick pins. Still another voodoo item is guaranteed black cat bone, used for cursing enemies.[7]

The occult is alive and well and living next door.

PART ONE

The Nature
of Pseudoscience

One

Pseudoscience and Psychology

The wizard patrols the room. The walls are decorated with lush drapes and mysterious symbols; the air is filled with music and incense. People wait hopefully, some standing near needles protruding from a large tub of water. Suddenly, the wizard fixes his gaze on a woman and points his iron wand. She goes into a state of mindless frenzy and is taken to a room lined with mattresses. There her seizure, and the affliction that brought her to see the wizard, will pass away.

This scene was frequently repeated in a Parisian clinic on the eve of the French Revolution, an upheaval inspired by the science of the Age of Reason. Paris was in the grip of the mesmeric mania. People from all walks of life sought out the "Wizard of Vienna," Franz Anton Mesmer, hoping he could cure their physical and mental afflictions. Mesmer set up a clinic in Paris where he held his "seances," hypnotizing and manipulating his clients to health.

Mesmer was a physician and proposed a theory of hypnotism that he felt was just as scientific as any other theory of the day. But established French science was skeptical, considering Mesmer a charlatan. A commission was appointed to investigate Mesmer's practices and cures; its chairman was one of the greatest scientists of the day, Benjamin Franklin. The commission concluded that Mesmer's theories were false, that his techniques were occult rather than scientific, and that his appeal was to human gullibility rather than to reason. Mesmerism was labeled a pseudoscience, nonsense masquerading as science.

Who was correct, Mesmer or his critics? If mesmerism was false science, why did it attract adherents and how did it gain testimonials from patients both rich and poor? If Mesmer was a fraud, why did he persistently seek to be investigated by the official medical establishment? Why was Mesmer denounced for his incorrect ideas while others' errors were treated simply as honest mistakes?

The episode of mesmerism illustrates the problem of pseudoscience. Can true science be separated from false? How do scientists and others in fact make such distinctions? Are their criteria purely rational and disinterested, or do historical, sociological, and psychological factors play a part? To seek answers to these questions, we will investigate psychology's "occult doubles," those branches of psychology that seem to cross the line between science and pseudoscience.

WHAT IS PSEUDOSCIENCE?

It would be generally agreed that the various sciences and would-be sciences can be arranged along a continuum of scientific status with physics as the prototype, for its scientific status is secure and unchallenged. At the other end of this continuum are enterprises calling themselves sciences, that are looked on with suspicion and are frequently accused of insincerity, charlatanry, and fraud. These fields are the clear pseudosciences; their prototype is astrology. In between the clear-cut sciences and clear-cut pseudosciences are other disciplines with pretensions to science that are taken seriously but not so seriously as to protect them from charges of confusion or outright fraud.

Psychology is an interesting case because it seems to sit astride the line between science and pseudoscience. Some of its branches, such as psychophysics and much of the research on animal and human learning, seem securely scientific in their pursuit of testable hypotheses and use of rigorous experimentation. Other areas, such as personality theory and social psychology, display a certain hesitance in claiming the mantle of science. Still other areas are embroiled in controversy, defended as scientific by their proponents and attacked as pseudoscience by their antagonists. Psychoanalysis and especially parapsychology, for example, are frequently under attack and seem to occupy the pseudoscience end of the scientific continuum.

In a time when many people aspire to the almost priestly title of "scientist'' and many studies to the almost religious appellation of ''science,'' the problem of sorting out science from pseudoscience is important. Yet the disinterested study of pseudoscience has been neglected in recent years, even while pseudosciences are regularly denounced and defended. Few have tried to study the conditions or characteristics that make a field scientific or pseudoscientific, or that lead some people to damn pseudosciences while others praise them. The problem of pseudoscience may be illuminated by the study of some neglected branches of psychology, those that form the anomalous group that sits on the border of science and pseudoscience.

THE PHILOSOPHICAL ANSWER: POPPER'S DEMARCATION CRITERION

As a young philosopher in post–World War I Vienna,[1] Karl Popper was interested in a number of apparently scientific theories—Marx's theory of history, Freud's psychoanalysis, Adler's individual psychology, and Einstein's theory of relativity. While the last of these received often dramatic confirmations and seemed securely scientific, Popper became disenchanted with the others and began to wonder why they seemed not to be scientific while Einstein's theory was.[2]

Popper was able to exclude certain superficially obvious answers to his question. Simple, observable truth was not the answer, for it was not yet clear to what extent relativity would prove true, and, historically, sciences have often been wrong while myths contain grains of truth. Most scientists separated true from false science by claiming that science rests on observation and generalization from observation, that is, on induction, while pseudoscience does not. But Popper saw that this distinction was untenable, for both psychoanalysts and astrologers observe nature, and both appeal to observation for confirming instances.

It was in fact the ability of Marxists, Freudians, Adlerians, and astrologers to amass confirming evidence that suggested Popper's solution. He saw that any economic news could be interpreted as consistent with Marxism; that any case history could be interpreted within a Freudian or Adlerian scheme; that any daily event could be reconciled with your horoscope. Speaking of Freudian and Adlerian psychology, Popper said: ''I could not think of any human behavior which could not be interpreted in terms of either theory. It was precisely this fact—that they always fitted, that they were always confirmed—which in the eyes of their admirers constituted the strongest argument in favor of these theories. It began to dawn on me that this apparent strength was in fact their weakness."[3]

In contrast, Einstein's theory committed itself to precise and risky predictions. It said that certain things such as the curving of light rays in a gravitational field, should occur while others should not. Like the social science theories and astrology, Einstein's theory could be observationally confirmed, but unlike them it could be observationally *refuted.* With respect to relativity, there were physical events that could not be interpreted in terms of the theory. Should light rays not curve passing by the sun, the theory would stand refuted.

Thus Popper formulated his demarcation criterion for separating the sciences from the pseudosciences: "The criterion of the scientific status of a theory is its falsifiability, or refutability, or testability."[4] Unlike some other philosophers,[5] Popper was careful not to conclude that pseudosciences were necessarily unimportant nonsense, saying only that they were not truly scientific. This point is often overlooked; given the tremendous prestige of science, to call something unscientific may be to dismiss it entirely. Later, Popper himself tended to do just that when he identified science with critical thinking and pseudoscience with dogmatism.

Popper's account has insight and persuasiveness. He cuts away certain preconceptions about science and pseudoscience and proposes a rational, plausible distinction between the two. His analysis of the nature of science and of the failings of pseudoscience is still widely influential even though Popper propounded it fifty years ago.[6] But this analysis does contain certain serious flaws, which have resulted in modifications to Popper's view.

The most sophisticated revision of Popper's ideas is that worked out by Imre Lakatos.[7] Lakatos observes two serious weaknesses in Popper's simple account of falsifiability as the criterion of scientific status. First, observational refutation is not as straightforward as it first appears. When a theory is put to experimental test and its predictions fail, scientists generally criticize the experiment rather than the apparently refuted theory. The possibility is always open that an experiment was misconceived or misperformed or failed to consider important information. In fact, if a theory has been generally successful, experimental "refutations" are normally attributed to poor method. Natural-science students become painfully aware of this fact of life. Despite close attention to the procedures given in their laboratory manuals, their experiments do not always come out "right." The teacher then flunks the student, not the established theory.

The second failing of Popper's ideas is that theories resist refutation until better ones are available. For more than eighty years, physicists knew that Newton's laws failed to correctly describe the orbit of Mercury. But they did not count this failure as a refutation of Newton until Einstein's theory proved able to explain the anomalous orbit. As Lakatos points out, the history of science shows that the struggle for scientific progress is not between a single theory and possibly refuting data, but between two (or more) theories and data that refute one and confirm the other.

Scientific theories, then, are highly resistant to refutation. Scientists can take refuge from contrary experimental results by criticizing the results instead of the theory—at least until a better theory is available. As Lakatos concludes, "Tenacity of a theory against empirical evidence [is] an argument for rather than against regarding it as 'scientific'."[8] There is, therefore, a kind of valuable scientific dogmatism, for, as Lakatos argues, quoting Popper against himself, "Without it we could never find out what is in a theory—we should give the theory up before we had a real opportunity of finding out its strength."[9] Lakatos also remarks that in one respect Popper's criterion of falsification allows crackpot ideas to count as science, for in many instances they are easily refuted. The medieval belief that walnuts, because of their similarity to the brain, could cure brain diseases is easily proven false; yet few would call it a scientific hypothesis.

The demarcation between science and pseudoscience now seems even fuzzier. Science is dogmatic; its theories resist refutation. Lakatos proposes a new, more pragmatic and historically accurate demarcation criterion. Saying that no single theory can be called scientific or pseudoscientific, he suggests that we evaluate something larger, a "research program." A research program consists of a "hard core" of fundamentally unfalsifiable ideas that guide scientists in their investigations of nature. It tells them which lines of investigation are likely to be fruitful and which are not. Around this hard core is constructed a "protective belt" of specific hypotheses, consistent with the hard core, that are tested through observation and experiment. Inconsistent data call for replacement of the suspect protective hypothesis with new ones consistent both with the hard core and with existing information. These new hypotheses should also make new predictions. The hard core is extremely difficult to replace, and will be given up only under severe stress.

Lakatos argues that "It is a succession of theories [within a research program] and not one given theory which is appraised as scientific or pseudoscientific."[10] More specifically, Lakatos's "account implies a new criterion of demarcation between 'mature science,' consisting of research programs, and 'immature,' consisting of a mere patched up pattern of trial and error."[11]

To illustrate his new demarcation criterion, Lakatos, like Popper, contrasts Marx and Freud with the natural sciences. In a good natural-science research program, empirical and theoretical progress is made. That is, hypotheses are proposed, tested, and retained or replaced, and at each step of the way a new hypothesis must not only explain the data at hand, but also must commit itself to predicting new facts. Scientific research therefore accumulates facts at the same time as it makes risky predictions. In Marxism and Freudianism, on the other hand, we do find hard cores giving a general sketch of their respective fields and methods of investigation, but they "unfailingly devise their actual . . . theories in the wake of facts without, at the same time, anticipating others."[12] That is, their hypothese are entirely ad hoc, resolving only current difficulties without pointing towards anything new.

Lakatos has liberalized Popper's demarcation criterion by admitting that there is dogmatism in science and by recognizing the part played by the historical dimension in evaluating scientific and pseudoscientific theories. Both accounts, however, remain rational and philosophical. Lakatos has not abandoned the notion that scientific theories are open to disproof. Instead, he has only stretched the act of falsification over time. He shares with Popper the fundamental belief that scientific change is a rational process with its own explicible logic. Lakatos strives to preserve the boundary between science and pseudoscience as a hard one that can be drawn philosophically, ignoring historical, sociological, and psychological factors.

Yet in admitting history, however rationally reconstructed, and dogmatism, however qualified, to the study of science, Lakatos undermines the entire rationalist enterprise. For we are given no clear criterion that would serve to separate scientific from pseudoscientific dogmatism. Aside from generalities, we are not told how to distinguish progressive change from degenerative change. As Lakatos sometimes acknowledges, these are decisions that must be made by a scientific community of human beings, who may differ on what accounts as progress, on what is admirable persistence and what is obstinate dogmatism. It is out of the interplay of ideas within a human scientific community that decisions about scientific progress and maturity are made, and pure philosophy is incapable of describing this interplay.

THE SOCIAL-PSYCHOLOGICAL APPROACH: KUHN'S PARADIGMS

In 1958 Thomas S. Kuhn, a physicist turned historian of science, was struck by the same difference that had interested Karl Popper, namely the serious difference between the social and natural sciences.[13] From his own training, Kuhn knew that natural scientists argue about specific problems of research: how to modify this or that concept, how to interpret this or that finding. Now he was "struck by the number and extent of the overt disagreements between social scientists about the nature of legitimate scientific problems and methods." The practice of natural science "normally fails to evoke the controversies over fundamentals that today often seem endemic among, say, psychologists or sociologists."[14] Kuhn decided that natural scientists accept, often unconsciously and unquestioningly, a conceptual framework, or paradigm, that decides fundamental issues for the scientific community, freeing its members from the confusions of debate so that they may concentrate on specific empirical puzzles capable of solution. Kuhn's conception leads him to draw the line between science and pseudoscience quite differently from Popper.

In the history of the mature sciences, Kuhn distinguishes normal science, the typical activity of most scientists at most times, from scientific revolutions, which change the scientific paradigm, the conceptual framework and unconscious presuppositions shared by scientists engaged in routine experimentation. During periods of normal science, aspiring scientists are brought into a certain scientific tradition with its own precepts, rules, and directions for conduct that are rarely open to debate. A student accepts these traditions or he does not become a certified scientist. Learning this tradition, or paradigm, is much like the socialization of a child, and, like culture, a paradigm governs a scientist's behavior in ways of which he or she is only dimly, if at all, aware. A paradigm, then, constitutes a value system or ideology. Consequently, explanation of scientific progress "must, in the final analysis, be psychological or sociological,"[15] not just philosophical.

The job of a scientist doing normal science is to solve puzzles about how nature operates, while keeping his hypotheses consistent with the established body of scientific knowledge embodied in the paradigm. Kuhn's use of the term "puzzle solving" is most important. A scientific puzzle is a piece of nature's behavior that remains unexplained and challenges the cleverness of the scientist. This challenge is like a crossword puzzle—the scientist assumes that a solution exists, a solution that fits the rules already learned. If your answer to a crossword puzzle clue does not fit, you blame yourself. You do not assume that the puzzle is insoluble in principle or that the rules of crossword puzzles that you have learned are invalid. Similarly, in normal science only a scientist's "personal conjecture is tested. If it fails the test, only his own ability not the corpus of current science is impugned."[16] Put another way, during normal science a paradigm is applied to nature, not tested by it.

During periods of revolutionary science, when a new paradigm is competing with an old one, the onus of failure shifts from investigator to theory. Some puzzles resist solution over and over, which may cause scientists to feel uneasy with their tradition. Persistent crises of this sort may give rise to a new and radical theory, the beginning of a new paradigm, that solves the puzzle by breaking traditional rules. If the new theory is sufficiently successful, it will attract a new generation of scientists who launch a new tradition with its own, frequently new, puzzles for its own normal science. Such change does not happen easily, however. Like all established traditions, scientific paradigms are conservative. Scientists dogmatically resist crisis and revolution until radical change is forced upon them by intensifying crises.

Apart from these two forms of scientific work, Kuhn distinguishes a third kind of human intellectual activity, characteristic of philosophy and of the social sciences: Popper's tradition of critical discussion in which basic and fundamental issues are contested by members of rival intellectual schools. Kuhn says this sort of fundamental confusion is characteristic of a science before it acquires a paradigm. When a field becomes a science it leaves such arguments behind, for acceptance of a paradigm by a scientific community settles the fundamental issues by creating a consensus that precludes these arguments except in times of crisis or revolution. Kuhn's thesis stands "Sir Karl's [Popper's] view on its head: it is precisely the abandonment of critical discourse that marks the transition to a science."[17]

We may now formulate Kuhn's demarcation criterion. He agrees with Popper that psychoanalysis and Marxism are not sciences, but his extended discussion of astrology, a favorite Popperian example of pseudoscience, shows that he draws the line differently from Popper or Lakatos. Popper pictures astrology as vague and irrefutable, escaping refutation by making itself untestable and thereby unscientific. Kuhn, however, shows that historically astrology did make predictions, usually of natural disasters,[18] many of which did not come true: "Astrology cannot be barred from the sciences because of the form in which its predictions were cast."[19] Nor were its protective hypotheses in any way different from those used by scientists to protect the hard core of their research programs.

Kuhn argues that astrology is a craft, not a science (cf. psychoanalysis), that failed to achieve a paradigm and a puzzle-solving tradition: "they had no puzzles to solve and therefore no science to practice."[20] Astrologers were divided into mutually critical groups, and in this respect resemble philosophers and social scientists rather than scientists.[21] Kuhn suggests that astrology's failure lay in its excessive complexity; "There were too many potential sources of difficulty, most of them beyond the astrologer's knowledge, control, or responsibility. Individual failures were correspondingly uninformative, and they did not reflect on the competence of the prognosticator in the eyes of his professional compeers."[22] Astrology failed to achieve normal science.

Not only that, but Kuhn further suggests that "without puzzles . . . astrology could not have become a science, even if the stars had, in fact, controlled human destiny."[23] This suggestion is both startling and revealing. We have come to think of science as the search for truth, but, if Kuhn is correct, science is defined, not by whether it seeks truth, but by the kinds of practices followed by a scientific community. Thus, the search for truth may be scientific or nonscientific, and what we call science is defined by sociological and historical, not philosophical, considerations. The same conclusions would apply to pseudoscience and the occult.

Kuhn's view of astrology receives substantial support from the massive researches of Lynn Thorndike into astrology and other magical systems of thought.[24] Thorndike argues that the idea of universal natural law was not invented by modern science but rather was the very basis of astrology. Astrologers believed that the heavenly bodies exert causal influences over events on earth, a belief that is not magical, that is postulating supernatural influences, but only incorrect. Thorndike objects to those historians who do astrology the "grave injustice" of ignoring its faith in universal, uniform, cosmic laws and its use of mathematics in formulating these laws.

But historians do commit this injustice. So did Popper, a great philosopher and student of scientific history. This indicates that there is more to the study of pseudoscience than has yet been suggested. Myths accrete around pseudosciences that acute study often fails to dispel. There seems to be a desire on the part of philosophers and historians to dismiss certain ideas as rubbish. Unreflective scientists do this even more frequently, finding it easy to devalue ideas they do not like by labelling them pseudoscientific. Reflective philosophers find it harder to make such judgments and struggle to formulate a demarcation criterion that will neatly shear off pseudoscience from true science. As with Popper and astrology, however, the shearing may be done by distorting the pseudoscience. If Kuhn is at all correct, we can hope to locate the source of this desire to eliminate and distort pseudoscience in the social-psychological structure of the scientific community itself.[25]

AN APPROACH THROUGH THE OCCULT

We have found that it is difficult to draw any formal line between science and pseudoscience. Kuhn's arguments indicate that whatever line exists is more sociological and psychological than philosophical, and may well not be rational. All these demarcation criteria, however, overlook the fact that historically the line between science and pseudoscience has been drawn sharply and forcefully. Pseudoscience, to scientists, is more than simple error—it is sin.

Isaac Newton exemplifies this view of pseudoscience as a shameful activity. The scientific revolution took place in the seventeenth century, and its great hero was Sir Isaac Newton. Newton and those who followed him created the scientific style, and, by negative implication, the pseudoscientific style as well. Yet recent studies of the scientific revolution have shown that it was shot through with pseudoscientific, occult elements hushed up by later generations of scientists and historians. Newton himself wrote more on alchemy than he did on physics, a fact his successors found shameful. His literary executor, Thomas Pellet, wrote "Not fit to be printed" on Newton's alchemical manuscripts; Samuel Horseley's edition of Newton's *Opera Omnia* (Complete Works) deleted them without mention; and Newton's nineteenth-century biographer conceded that Newton copied "the most contemptible alchemical poetry."[26] These reactions are not those of disinterested critical thinkers who have detected refutable hypotheses in Newton's work. Rather, they are the reactions of members of a social community whose value system has been violated by their hero.

Newton's alchemy was not just incorrect, it was contemptible; it was not just criticized and forgotten, it was rejected and suppressed. Alchemy survived for many years as an underground movement, a mystical and scientifically rejected double of chemistry. The historian James Webb calls such rejected but surviving ideas the occult, existing in the occult underground and opposing, while reflecting and sometimes influencing, an intellectual establishment.[27]

Webb's approach to pseudoscience is related to Kuhn's but is broader. Kuhn focuses on the scientific community, but loses sight of the larger intellectual community of which it is a part. Just as the traditions of science—its paradigm—shape research, so broader intellectual traditions must shape the scientific tradition. To be occult, an idea need not be mystical or magical, true or false; the occult is made up of all ideas that are rejected by the official, established culture. Pseudoscience offends the values of the dominant intellectual tradition and so meets with vehement rejection, distortion, and, where possible, simple repression. Yet at the same time occult ideas exert a powerful hold on many members of our culture. Occult ideas do continue to live, albeit secretly. Pseudoscience offends some people deeply; it fascinates others just as deeply. The paradox of the occult, of pseudoscience, is this Janus face. It says that Western culture is at war with itself, for profoundly different systems, paradigms perhaps, animate the occult enthusiast and the occult iconoclast.

PSEUDOSCIENCE AND PSYCHOLOGY

To draw the line between science and pseudoscience, although difficult, is valid and important. It is indeed hard to do; we have seen how pseudoscience sometimes resembles science and vice versa. But some distinction is valid, for clearly physics is a science and prognostication from moles on the body is not. The psychophysicist S. S. Stevens once said that just because the difference between night and day is not sharp does not mean that the difference does not exist. Our task is to locate and describe the boundary between science and pseudoscience, however fuzzy it may be. Understanding this distinction is important because today science is important, and we should fear false scientists. Should astrologers testify to Congress along with physicists and economists? Should they testify in criminal trials as psychiatrists and pathologists do? Should astrology qualify for research grants as an established science? Should astrologers regulate the lives of Aquarians and Moon Children? Should the Pentagon continue to spend $6 million a year to develop "psychotronic weapons" and pay $400 a month to Washington's "Madame Zodiac" for her plots of Soviet submarine movements?[27] To some, these questions may be easy to answer, while others may find some of them difficult. Economists, for example, have not been obviously successful at managing the political economy. How then do economists differ from astrologers? If we are to follow the advice of scientists, we should try to find out which claimants are indeed scientific.

What we suggest is that, precisely because psychology straddles the boundary between science and pseudoscience, a study of psychology's occult doubles will prove illuminating. By occult doubles we mean those psychological movements that have been rejected by established psychology but that survived nevertheless, at least for a time. Because they have been rejected, psychologists and official historians ignore them, but they form a dark, unconscious side of establishment psychology. By examining these occult doubles, and the reasons for their rejection by some and attraction for others, we hope to throw light on the development and nature of orthodox science as well as those of its rejected relations.

Psychology's relationship to the occult and pseudoscience is especially close. It is no accident that Golden Fleece awards tend to go to research projects in the social sciences. Sen. William Proxmire (who presents these awards for the month's biggest waste of government research money) does not pretend to understand quarks and quasars; he does pretend to understand love and sex. People have strong and tenaciously held ideas about human nature, which psychology has not dislodged. Many of these ideas are systematized and taught by occult movements from astrology to scientology, and these movements often have more popular appeal than orthodox psychology. Moreover, the borderline is blurred between that psychology which everyone accepts as scientific and that which is pseudoscientific and potentially occult.

Many experimentalists regard psychoanalysis as magical mumbo jumbo, while some humanists reject it as unfeelingly scientific. Indeed, in some circles to call something ''scientific'' is to label it unacceptable. Occultists can form their own establishment, which rejects traditional science. This occult establishment may embrace many of psychology's odder theories and therapies.

Psychology's continuing relationship with the occult is nicely illustrated by William Bainbridge,[29] who has shown how a neo-Adlerian therapy group slowly evolved into a satanic cult. But even as a cult it retained something of science and psychology. Its theology expressed a complex theory of personality types and interpersonal relations, and the theory changed in order to improve its fit to observed behavior. The cult also designed a personality test given to potential members to uncover their personality structure.

In subsequent chapters of this book we will examine a number of psychology's occult doubles. In chapter 2 we will outline two models to guide us in our approach to rejected science, two of natural science's important occult doubles, astrology and alchemy. As we probe psychology's doubles we will be able to see in what ways, if any, the development of psychology and its doubles resembles the development of chemistry and astronomy and their doubles. But we will narrow the range of our investigation to four of psychology's historically most important occult doubles. The vogue for two of these, phrenology and mesmerism, has passed, but the other two, psychical research and psychological-religious cults, are currently both fashionable and controversial. These movements will occupy our attention in Part Two.

Phrenology, the topic of chapters 3 and 4, began as Franz Joseph Gall's earnest and scientific attempt to deduce brain structure from observable behavior and cranial shape, but it was quickly and vehemently rejected by the physiological establishment largely on philosophical grounds. The experiments that claim to refute phrenology were provoked by it and were in fact largely irrelevant to it. But phrenology became an occult success after this rejection. In America especially, phrenology became something of a pseudoscientific religion during the nineteenth century; its teachers, the brothers Fowler, dispensed advice to potential mates and read the character of job applicants for employers.

Phrenology admirably suited the American temper; it was atheoretical, rested more on external observation than on introspection, urged the improvement of humanity, and sought practical results usable by fiancees, businessmen, and governments. Phrenology played a part in the early careers of several contributors to orthodox psychology, such as Herbert Spencer, and was touted as the psychology of the future by Alfred Russel Wallace, codiscoverer of evolution.

Nevertheless, phrenology was occult from its earliest days. Gall's original proposals offended the empiricist, associationist, and dualist dogmas of French physiology, and phrenology never recovered from its initial rejection. Later on, its very popularity probably ensured the distaste of academic psychologists. Of course Gall's ideas were empirically disproven, but as with Newton's alchemy, there is more in psychologists' rejection of phrenology than the discarding of error; there is positive abhorence. But phrenology flourished for the same reasons American psychology flourished; it is one of psychology's occult doubles.

We have already met mesmerism briefly and will consider it further in chapter 5. It is a particularly important movement because it was, at least in its beginnings, a product of the Enlightenment, itself a product of the scientific revolution and a constant antagonist of superstition. Mesmerism, however, with its outré séances and emotional trances, is a symptom of the end of the Age of Reason and of the start of the romantic worship of the irrational. We will find that physicians who used mesmerism to treat the ill became pariahs to their colleagues, and that hypnotism, the valuable kernel established science extracted from mesmerism, has never lost its occult aura.

An interesting case on the borderline of the occult has existed since psychology's birth. This field, parapsychology—or, as it used to be called, psychical research—will be considered further in chapters 6 and 7. Nothing has so persisted despite continued rejection than psychical ideas ranging from the positively crackpot to the conservatively statistical. Psychical research attracted William James (and some physical scientists) as alchemy did Newton—a fact many established psychologists would rather ignore. Today, parapsychologists vehemently assert their claim to scientific status, while others just as vehemently deny it. Again, more than the possibility of error is involved, for the rhetoric of the debate is not the same as that between the learning theories of E. C. Tolman and Clark Hull. Even the debate between B. F. Skinner's behaviorism and Carl Rogers's humanism is not carried on with the same heat as skeptics' attacks on parapsychology. It cannot be the methods of the parapsychologists that are at issue, for they have taken pains to use established scientific procedures since the beginning. Parapsychologists even keep up with trends in mainstream experimental psychology. Some parapsychologists use operant procedures to train ESP and use information-processing mechanisms to explain it. Clearly we must look for sociological and psychological factors to account for the forceful rejection of parapsychology by academics, although psychical research has mirrored establishment psychology since the beginning of both fields.

In the last chapter of Part Two we will look at some of the more psychologically oriented religious cults. Like parapsychology, religion has always offered help to the troubled, but some modern religious cults purport to use "scientific" techniques to improve their devotees. This was true of the cult described by Bainbridge and of its parent cult, Scientology. These movements are often rejected not only by science but also by the political establishment, but they exert an enormous attraction for large numbers of troubled people.

In our concluding chapter we will pull together the separate threads of our investigation to answer several important questions. Is there any nonhistorical way to separate science and pseudoscience, as philosophers want to believe, or is repression into the occult underground a unique event for each pseudoscience? Why do pseudosciences persist despite their rejection? Why are many pseudosciences rejected more as intellectual sins than as simple errors? Can science grow out of pseudoscience? Can a science degenerate into a pseudoscience? What can the study of the occult tell us about "mainstream" intellectual history?

Two

Doubles of Natural Science: Alchemy and Astrology

There are occult doubles of the natural sciences, and especially in recent years they have received increased and sympathetic treatment by historians of science. In particular, the assessment of the role of occult traditions during the Renaissance and the scientific revolution has been revised, so that these movements are no longer seen as sharp and absolute breaks with the medieval past. Rather they are seen as arising from, and gradually overthrowing, the mystical-cum-proto-scientific past.

The magical world view that the scientific revolution displaced, creating the enlightened world of reason as well as the underground of the occult, gave a general picture of the cosmos that shaped peoples' thought and perception through the Middle Ages. It gave meaning and order to the world for medieval people, but it was incompatible with the scientific world view triumphant in Isaac Newton's (1642–1727) *Principia Mathematica* (1687). Two ancient sciences, alchemy and astrology, embodied that world view and they became pseudosciences as their scientific doubles flourished. Since the history of these natural pseudosciences has been well studied, we shall describe them briefly here, for they exemplify the occult mind and may provide models for our study of psychology's less-well-known doubles.

ALCHEMY

"Not fit to be printed" was scrawled on the wrapper of Newton's alchemical papers by Thomas Pellet, who examined the papers for Newton's family soon after the scientist's death.[1]

> David Brewster, Newton's nineteenth-century biographer, ad-
> mitted that Newton had copied "the most contemptible alchemical
> poetry" and had annotated "the obvious productions of a fool and
> a knave."[2]

> Newton's interest in the art was neither a youthful frolic nor an
> aberration of senility. It fell squarely in the middle of his scientific
> career, spanning the time of most of the achievements on which his
> reputation rests. Whereas other studies [including his calculus,
> mechanics, and optics] could rivet his attention only briefly, al-
> chemy held it without a major interruption for nearly thirty years.
> . . . Newton's records reveal that in the spring of 1686, before the
> final copy of the *Principia* had been completed, he interrupted its
> composition to work in the [alchemical] furnaces.[3]

What was this alchemical art that could fascinate a genius such as
Newton while, at the same time, disgusting his admirers? The popular
image of the alchemist has always been that of a crazy wizard or an outright fraud—someone who believed he could make gold out of lead—or
who duped others into supporting him in style while he pretended to
make gold out of lead. Why would anyone, especially anyone as intelligent as Newton, fall for such a con game?

Precisely because it was not a con game. While there were many charlatans who preyed on others' greed and gullibility—just as there were
priests who sold fake relics and pardons—fraud was no more necessary
to alchemy than to Roman Catholicism. Both were mystical world
views that answered the real human need for spirituality. The Church
was established and alchemy was occult; however, both drew on the
mystical Neoplatonic outlook that became a part of Western culture during the late Roman era. Saint Augustine worked Neoplatonism into the
obscure, messianic Jewish cult of Christianity, giving this religion the
philosophical underpinnings necessary to the conversion of Roman gen-
tiles.[4]

At about the same time, some philosophers in Greco-Roman Egypt
were developing the Hermetic doctrines of alchemy out of the same basic Neoplatonism. The Egyptians credited their ideas to Hermes Tris-
megistus, who was supposed to have written the doctrines on the Emerald Tablet. This Hermes was mythical, a combination of the Greek god

Hermes and the Egyptian god Thoth, both gods of writing. Much of the doctrine of Neoplatonism is summarized in the second aphorism of the Emerald Tablet: "What is below is like that which is above, and what is above is like that which is below. . . ."[5] or more concisely, "As above, so below." This means that there are correspondences between all things on different levels of existence. Thus the body of man (the microcosm) mirrors the universe (the macrocosm)—man is small (micro) cosmos. Thus too, all parts of the larger cosmos, having sexual divisions like ours, can grow and propagate as we do, and, most important, are alive as we are. Also, all these mirroring levels influence each other. Thus, those suffering from melancholy, or having a saturnine disposition, had received too much of the influence of Saturn. To cure the melancholy they were told to surround themselves with the gems, plants, herbs, animals, and people belonging to Jupiter (Jove) or Venus. A talisman bearing Jupiter's image and gem would make you jovial by drawing down to you the healthful influences of that planet.[6] You, the gems, plants, etc. and the star all partake of the same essence but on different levels.

This Neoplatonist assumption is basic to both alchemy and astrology. Its system of correspondences was carefully sorted out. For example, gold equals Christ the King, or any earthly king, or the lion, king of the beasts, or Leo, king of the astrological beasts in the heavens. By manipulating any one of these equated items, you could affect the others. As Plotinus, founder of Neoplatonism, put it: "How are enchantments produced? By community of feeling, through the natural concord of like principles and contrariety of unlike, and through the variety of the many powers which go to make up the one world-animal."[7]

This idea of correspondences is at once beautifully simple and monstrously complex. In essence it says that all of the cosmos is alive and interrelated; everyone has a place in the web of life. The ramifications of this beautifully simple idea, however, are indeed complex. All the planets, parts of the body, jewels, and metals had each their own equations. All the world and everything in it made sense and fitted into place with a comforting, and elating, precision.

To the modern reader, however, it is more likely to seem a bedeviling confusion. Again, how could Newton have believed this gibberish?

To answer this question we must consider another basic tenet of the Hermetic world view: All above and all below is made of one spiritual substance, which exists in varying states of purity and degrees of perfection, from the etherial planets to heavy lead. This was the basis of Hermetic physics and chemistry.[8]

This physics starts with the orthodox, Aristotelian elements—earth, air, fire, and water—which corresponded to the four human temperaments or humors—melancoly, sanguine, choloric, and phlegmatic. To the orthodox list of these four elements, the Hermeticists added the quintessence, literally the fifth essence or element. It is also called *prima materia,* or "first matter." It is "the Beginning of all things, a confused mass . . . which is neither moist nor dry, not earth nor water, not light nor darkness, not air nor fire." It is a spiritual matter, "ontologically located between the four elements and pure immateriality."[9] It is the breath of the universe, or the spirit, that joins the body and soul. The planets are made of this *prima materia* in its pure form. On earth, however, it is " 'clogged in heavy matter,' and is never free and visible." Yet "it is omnipresent, and he who can free this fifth element from the matter it inhabits shall hold in his hand the creative power with which God has endowed the world of matter,"[10] This fifth element was the Philosopher's Stone or the Elixir, or to use two of the forty-nine names Newton listed under "prima matter" in his *Index Chemicus,* chaos and the dark abyss.[11]

Thus the individual and the universe, the microcosm and the macrocosm, all above and all below, were united by this quintessence, this breath and spirit of the cosmos. This concept of cosmic union underlies all the alchemical correspondences and manipulations.

But what were these manipulations? What was Newton doing when he took time off from writing the *Principia* to work at the furnaces? The answer to this question takes us back to the Egyptians, but this time to somewhat more mundane Egyptians, the goldsmiths. Only somewhat more mundane, however, for the refining process was a closely guarded, priestly secret, accompanied by magical incantations. This refining process came to be seen as analogous to the refining of the soul. Analogous to, or even identical with, the refining of the soul.[12]

Alchemy always had this dual aspect—retorts, furnaces, and chemical recipes on the one hand, and a mystic searching for the soul's perfection and union with God on the other. Synesius, in the fourth century A.D., described the philosopher's stone as a "living light which illuminates every soul that has seen it . . . the spirit that nourishes and animates all things . . . the quintessence . . . that is our stone . . . is nothing other than our glorious soul, which we extract from its mine (the body, or the human being), which alone produces it.''[13] When the adept finally made gold, the figure of Christ would appear in his retort;[14] that is, he would then be at one with God.

These two aspects of alchemy may seem completely different to the modern mind—one aspect is chemistry, the other is mysticism. To us these two studies seem as separate and distinct as astronomy and astrology. To the alchemist, however, they were inextricably bound together. The chemical reactions were predicted on the basis of the spiritual theory, and faults in the alchemist's spiritual state would hinder the experiments.[15] Thus, although Newton and many other alchemists did chemical experiments, they were not working within a materialistic, chemical paradigm. Their paradigm, and indeed their whole world view, was profoundly mystical.

At its most basic, the alchemical theory said that the adept would get the quintessence if he removed the four terrestrial elements from an earthly substance. Mercury was considered the closest of all earthly substances to the *prima materia*. This belief is reflected in the element's archaic name, quicksilver—literally "living silver"—the closest thing on earth to the living gold the alchemists sought. Even in a thoroughly modern materialistic chemical laboratory, mercury looks strange. Shiny silver that shimmers and wobbles, that sloughs off dirt just as the alchemists sought to remove all dross and fecal matter, all earthly substances, from their gold and their souls.

This quicksilver was refined by fire and water, with much distillation, calcification, and dissolution, to remove the earthly elements and render it back into its original, pure form as *prima materia*. If the adept then added some goldlike substance to this *prima materia,* he should get gold. Sulfur, being of a yellow color, was used for this pigmentation. Then salt was added to stabilize, or fix, the mixture.

As fits the system of correspondences, this process was sexually described. The Man (sulfur) married the Woman (mercury) to propagate gold. In a further refining process the volatile (female) spirit of mercury, that is, the evaporating moisture that rose during purification when the mercury was heated, was united with the fixed (male) mercury, which stayed in the bottom of the retort, to form the alchemical hermaphrodite (Hermes plus Aphrodite), the symbol of perfect and complete union.

This is the alchemists' metallurgical theory at its most basic. It is based in part on the Aristotelian assumption that all matter is animate, all tending towards its perfection. As the acorn tends towards the oak, so all metals tend towards gold. The alchemist only speeds up the process. Aristotle, however, had been transmuted by Neoplatonism—perfection had taken on a spiritual rather than a biological meaning. In Aristotle's system, an oak is only more developed than an acorn, not spiritually higher. Oaks and acorns inhabit the mundane sphere, as did Aristotle. The alchemists, however, took his four elements and his ideal of growth and transmuted them into spiritual gold, the basis of a mystical chemistry of the soul.

Newton came under the influence of Platonists as an undergraduate at Cambridge.[16] By the 1660s he was copying alchemical treatises, which he got from several other Cantabrigian alchemists such as Foxcroft and Hartlib. Foxcroft translated the "Chemical Wedding," an alchemical Rosicrucian poem. There was little intellectual activity in seventeenth-century Cambridge, and Newton seems to have had few close friends outside the alchemical circle. Loneliness may well have been a part of the reason he first became interested in alchemy, but, as his later attempts at Biblical exegesis show, Platonism probably filled some spiritual need that naturalistic mechanics ignored.

It might seem impossible to reconcile Newton's mechanics with a mystical world view, but Henry More, one of the Cambridge Platonists, illustrated how such a union can be achieved. More "welcomed the mechanical philosophy for its clear distinction of body and spirit . . . which served a religious end, for by showing the limitations of matter, it demonstrated the necessity of spirit."[17] Action and planning, More felt, required a better explanation than mere matter in motion. Thus, even starkly materialistic mechanics can be made to bolster a mystical, Neoplatonist world view.

Newton worked on alchemy the whole time he was at Cambridge. He collated all the alchemical works he could find, listing the chemical name, synonyms, and poetic names he found for each alchemical substance and process. He compiled his findings in the *Index chemicus,* which was more than one hundred pages long and contained 879 headings. This list was not just his notes. Although it was not meant to be published, it was written for his fellow alchemists. Newton was sure all major alchemists were doing the same work, behind the profusion of images, all working on the same subject, within the same paradigm and "publishing" their findings in treatises circulated among themselves.

As far as Newton was concerned, then, the alchemists were doing what Kuhn calls normal science. In 1678 he started doing his own experiments, which he continued until 1696, when he went to London as warden of the mint after the publication of the *Principia*. In 1681 he thought he had succeeded:

> May 18. I perfected the ideal solution . . . two equal salts carry up Saturn. Then he carries up the stone and joins with malleable Jupiter [tin, which probably joins with sophic sal ammonica] and that in such proportion that Jupiter grasps the scepter. Then the eagle carries Jupiter up. Hence Saturn can be combined without salts in the desired proportions so that fire does not predominate. At last mercury sublimate and sophic sal ammoniac . . . shatter the helmet and the menstrum carries everything up.

A few days earlier "a series of experiments investigating the volitizing virtue" had culminated in one in which a sublimate of copper (*Venus volens*) had carried up lead.

> May 10, 1681. I understood that the morning star is Venus and that she is the daughter of Saturn and one of the doves . . . .

And a few years later he had full confirmation of his art: "Friday May 23 [1684]. I made Jupiter fly on the wings of the eagle."[18] The rest of the time he was at Cambridge, he wrote treatises about these experiments.

Saturn is lead; Jupiter (Jove) is tin; Venus is copper.[19] The dove is a state of regeneration following death or dissolution.[20] This state of dissolution comes before the eagle, the fixed volatile,[21] the alchemical hermaphrodite, the Elixir, the Philosopher's Stone. Thus, to the extent that his terms can be interpreted, Newton apparently believed he had achieved his goal.

In the process, however, he had also killed it. His approach to this mystical chemistry seems to have been mundanely chemical, as the chemical equivalents given in his *Index chemicus* reveal. In the end, his materialistic mechanics seem to have conquered his mystical leanings. "Remorselessly Newton's measurements bound and confined the free spirit" of alchemical symbolism.[22] For the active principle of alchemy Newton substituted mechanical attraction: "The forces of attraction and repulsion between particles of matter, including gravitational attraction . . . were primarily the offspring of alchemical active principles. They were offspring transformed, however. The alchemical active principle was an entity capable of being separated from the mass it animated. It was seed to be planted in passive soil, a yeast added to dough. Newton's forces could have no separate existence, however.'' This perfect union of two principles was not achieved by the alchemist, in fact. "It was a brute fact of nature effected by God in the creation. . . .'' The essence of an attraction, in contrast to an active principle, was its quantitative definition whereby it might fit into the structure of rational mechanics.'' "The alchemical spirit, the quintessence or the spirit of the universe, had become the force of modern science.''[23]

After Newton moved to London and was accepted into the normal science community of the Royal Society, he lost interest in alchemy. Perhaps he realized that through his science "he had embraced Truth, albeit in a somewhat homlier form from the enchanting Venus he had pursued.''[24]

While Newton pursued the scientific aspect of alchemy's dual nature, his contemporary, John Donne (1572–1631), was pursuing the symbolic aspect. Donne was a courtier, poet, soldier, and, later, Dean of St. Paul's. He had a low opinion of practicing alchemists:

> . . . such gold as that wherewithall
> Almighty *Chymiques,* from each minerall
> Having with subtle fire a soul out pulled;
> are dirtely and desparately gulled.[25]

Clearly Donne the courtly wit did not believe that alchemists could make gold. Those who believed they could, wasting whatever real wealth they had on the endeavor, were only led on by false hopes, or conned by fraudulent alchemists.

On the other hand, the mystical symbolism of alchemy fascinated Donne. His most serious love poetry is imbued with alchemical imagery. Just as Newton was on a quest for doves and eagles, so was John Donne. This quest is most evident in "The Canonization," one of Donne's most important poems. This poem claims that the lover, the speaker (possibly Donne himself) and his lady, are so perfectly united, by their admittedly sexual love, that they will serve as a sainted pattern of love for other earthly lovers, despite their previous rejection by the world.

> For Godsake hold your tongue, and let me love
> Or chide my palsie, or my gout,
> My five gray hairs, or ruin'd fortune flout . . .

> Call us what you will, wee'are made such by love;
>   Call her one, mee another flye,
> We'are Tapers too, and at our owne cost die,
>   And wee in us find the'Eagle and the dove.
>   The Phoenix ridle hath more wit
>   By us, we two being one, are'it.
> So to one neutrall thing both sexes fit.
>   Wee dye and rise the same, and prove
>   Mysterious by this love . . .[26]

Here the speaker first puts their love in the lowest, sexual terms—they are lecherous flies and self-destroying, phallic tapers (i.e., candles). Thus their love is admittedly sexual. These same terms of abuse have another aspect, however. Tapers are illuminating as well as self-destroying. The taper-fly, which was thought to burn itself to death because it was attracted to flames, implies suicidal lust. (It was thought that each orgasm took a day off one's life.) Hermetically, however, the taper-fly was considered hermaphroditic, like the alchemical hermaphrodite, and resurrectable,[27] like Christ. Thus the world's abuse of the lovers has a very different meaning to the hermetic reader. The insults of the world are shown to be false by the very words in which they are expressed.

"And wee in us find the'Eagle and the dove," the speaker continues, a line that makes little sense if taken literally. Newton used the eagle to symbolize the fixed volatile, which is the hermaphrodite, the Philosopher's Stone, etc. Donne seems to have preferred Paracelsus's symbolism, where the phoenix is the final product of the alchemist's labors. In this system, the eagle and the dove are both intermediate stages: "Death, or dissolution, is followed by regeneration, producing the eagle and the dove, both instrumental in the creation of the phoenix, which in turn symbolized the mystical union of the sexes."[28] Thus, the eagle and the dove, understood hermetically, lead us on to the phoenix. This mythical bird combined both sexes and burned itself to death when it grew old, but then rose again from the ashes; it is hermaphroditically reborn in fire just as the quicksilver is heated in the retort in order to hermaphrodically fix the volatile. The phoenix, then, is a resurrectable hermaphrodite, an immortal union of male and female principles.

In Christian terms, the phoenix represents Christ: "The Phoenix riddle hath more wit / By us, we two being one, are it." The perfect union

of true lovers, Donne says, can explain the riddle of the incarnation of
Christ, of the combination of the divine and human. Later, in his sermons, Donne expressed the union of body and soul, which in turn explains the Incarnation, in terms of marriage: "Death . . . is the Divorce
of body and soul, Resurection is the Re-union."[29] Thus Donne saw love
as an incarnation, a union of male and female, body and soul, so perfect
that two are truly one: "So to one neutrall thing both sexes fit." Like the
mystery of the Incarnation, the mystery of the tripartite nature of the
Trinity, or the mystery of the Resurrection—"Wee die and rise the
same, and prove / Mysterious by this love." Indeed, love is the
Phoenix—both the alchemist's Elixir and the incarnated and resurrected
Christ. Donne, thus, saw love as the perfect unity of both body and soul
and the lovers. It is love incarnate in two bodies that are one, "one neutrall thing," which is the hermaphrodite, the living gold, the Elixir.

Through both alchemical and Christian symbolism, Donne gives us a
pattern of love that unites body and soul as the lovers are united, that
denies the dominance of either while uniting both sexual and spiritual
love. This ideal love is expressed alchemically because the alchemists
believed in the necessity of the union of the two creative principles—
male and female, fixed and volatile, passive and active—to create the
hermaphrodite, the symbol of human perfection. Indeed, the riddle of
love has more wit by this alchemical explanation. Donne used alchemical imagery to express the spirituality of sexuality, the unity of
opposites—male and female, body and soul—to fix the volatile, to create human perfection, to find what we might call the Lover's Stone.

These two seventeenth-century alchemists illustrate the ways that alchemy was to go. The experimental aspect largely died out soon after
Newton's time, as the mechanistic world view came to dominate established Western culture. To the extent that alchemy had been a science, it
evolved into chemistry, and, through Newton's transmutation of its active principle into scientific force, into mechanics.[30] Donne's poetry had
little impact until it was rediscovered by Ezra Pound and T. S. Eliot
early in this century. Donne did, however, mark the way that alchemy
would follow in order to survive, the way of mysticism, poetry, and art.

During the Enlightenment of the eighteenth century, the strangest attempt to effect the alchemical transmutation took place. A Freemason
named Duchanteau decided that, since "the Low should be exalted on
High, and . . . the alchemical matter, the container, and the fire to heat
it should form part of the same object," that that alchemist would make

gold who drank his own urine, suitably purified by a forty-day fast. He died during his second attempt at fasting, his first having been thwarted by force feeding. The urine from his first attempt was venerated as a relic until it was destroyed during the French Revolution.[31]

The occult, mystical tradition of alchemy continued well into the nineteenth century, being especially popular among the Bohemian artists of Paris. As late as 1861 alchemical experiments were still being carried out by Alexander Branicki, (a friend of British poet Edward Bulwer-Lytton) and by a number of Parisians. By this time, however, the mystic, symbolic side of alchemy was of far more interest. Most alchemical artists preferred to leave the furnaces and retorts to the scientists.[32]

In 1836 the Austrian government granted a pension to Joseph Anton Rotli to make gold by the combination of various metals.[33] Thus, despite the repeated falsifications and scientific rejections, the profane side of alchemy survived the advent of chemistry—and probably will survive as long as greed and gullibility do.

The mystic aspect of alchemy is still with us today, albeit in a somewhat altered form: Peter Kolosimo, a student of UFOs, says that the Great Pyramid might have contained the Philosopher's Stone, left there by extraterrestrials.[34]

Was alchemy ever a science? The answer seems to depend on which definition of science you prefer.

According to Karl Popper, for a study to be classified as a science it must be disprovable. Could alchemy be refuted? Yes and no. Clearly many adepts must have failed. Some, including Newton, believed they had succeeded—although that seems unlikely to the modern mind. Individual alchemical recipes certainly could fail; many ingredients beside mercury and sulfur were tried. Newton spent years trying out different recipes, as did all practicing alchemists.

On the other hand, alchemy always had its spiritual aspect to fall back on: the adept was not pure enough to succeed. Or, of course, he might have misinterpreted the symbolic language of the recipe. These excuses seem to lead to a clear-cut Popperian verdict—alchemy was not a science.

As Lakatos pointed out, however, all sciences have a protective belt around their central core of theory. And, as Lakatos admitted, scientists are not readily convinced to abandon a theory. Alchemy lasted about two thousand years, which is a good deal longer than Newtonian physics lasted. Lakatos would object that it lasted so long precisely because it was not a science. Rather it was a mystical system that survived so long in the face of repeated disproof because its appeal was not to the reason.

As Kuhn has shown, however, science itself is not particularly reasonable. Scientists are well known to reject the falsifying experiments rather than reject their paradigm. This attitude is well illustrated by Paracelsus (1493–1541), one of the founders of modern medicine. He considered himself a practicing alchemist, although he was trying to find chemical cures for human ailments rather than trying to turn lead into gold. The differences between his system, called iatrochemistry, and the traditional alchemical system may indicate that alchemy was in a state of crisis at that time. Paracelsus, however, sounded very like a normal scientist when he said, "All the fault and cause of difficulty in alchemy is wholly lack of skill in the operator."[35] He seems, thus, to have felt that alchemy was a single, workable field—in Kuhnian terms, that it had a paradigm.

Newton, too, was convinced that all the major alchemists were doing the same work. Thus he was just as much engaged in normal science when doing his alchemical research as he was when doing his astronomical or optical research. His *Index chemicus,* the exhaustive list of alchemical symbols and processes, was not just personal jottings and reading notes; it was written to be read by fellow alchemists.[36] Various other alchemists published, or privately circulated, accounts of their researches, which were Newton's sources for the *Index*. All of this sounds very much like normal science carried on within a communally accepted paradigm. As Dobbs described the alchemy of Newton's time: "An alchemical paradigm was still widely accepted. . . . There were not very many who were ready totally to deny the possibility of transmutation at the beginning of the century . . .arguments did not yet turn very much on the question of whether metals really grew in the earth; rather men were more likely to argue whether art [alchemy] might assist nature in her movement towards perfection and whether those alchemists who claimed to have done so already were honest men, fools, or impostors."[37]

Earlier, Saint Thomas Aquinas, despite his Aristotelian, logical, nonmystical approach to religion, had accepted the possibility of the transmutation of metals. Another nonmystical group, jurists, also accepted the possibility and held that "the making and selling of alchemist's gold was a perfectly legal practice."[38] Thus one did not need to be a wild-eyed mystic, or a greedy fool, to believe in the basic theory of alchemy.

It had grown out of the same Neoplatonic background as the established faith, and it lasted as long as its Neoplatonic presuppositions were still accepted. It was the chemistry of the Neoplatonic world view.

But Plato was losing out to Aristotle and eventually to Newton. The commonsensical and the mystical are both aspects of the human mind, forever on a seesaw. As mechanics and chemistry rose, alchemy sank, becoming occult and rejected by established thought. This is its only real difference from established sciences. At first it was occult by choice. Only the worthy were allowed to learn its hallowed mysteries, just as only the Egyptian priests knew how to refine gold. Alchemy's relations with Christianity have always been confused. Alchemy was a heresy openly espoused by many devote Christians who used it "in Christ" to protect Christian mysticism from the onslaught of Aquinas's logic.[39] Alchemy was close enough to Christian Neoplatonic mysticism that the authorities could not easily challenge the one without challenging the other.

Thus alchemy survived until the materialists took over the Western world, a trend that started with the atoms of Democritus although it did not overcome religion until far more recent times. Even now alchemy lingers on, maintaining a weak, parasitic existence on the edges of the occult. What started out as the self-chosen exile of a moral elite, the secrecy of the early adepts, has thus increasingly become a forced exile at the hands of the materialists.

Nowadays we can afford to be charitable to alchemy's memory. Neoplatonism is as dead as a squirrel squashed by the ten-ton rig of modernism. As we have seen, however, earlier generations did not consider alchemy an interesting backwater of history. To Newton's eighteenth- and nineteenth-century admirers, his interest in alchemy was shocking and disgusting. Most modern readers would probably feel the same if it were reliably reported that Einstein had spent twenty or thirty years trying to prove true the beliefs of the Rosicrucians, alchemy's only surviving relative. The Master consorting with the Whore of Babylon!

Clearly this disgust is due to more than mere scientific falsity. Einstein largely disproved Newton, and much of Einstein's later work on unified field theory may be wrong, but these problems do not lessen our respect for Newton and Einstein. To what, then, is this disgust due? To alchemy's spirituality.

The real appeal of alchemy is spiritual—it purports to reveal a hidden truth that unites all of creation in a vast, spiritual web of growth and reproduction. Newton wrote, for example, that metals vegetate "after the same laws'' as vegetables; vegetation, he said, is the effect of a spirit that is ''the same in all things.''[40] Alchemy literally conjures up a God-filled universe where nothing is meaningless. If even a base metal such as lead can be transformed into the living gold of God, if the figure of Christ can appear in the alchemist's retort—then all life is meaningful, all creation is potentially divine. This beats the hell (quite literally) out of a meaningless, absurd universe composed solely of atoms and the void.

Except, of course, for those people who dislike an omnipresent diety. As Peter Cook put it, in the movie *Bedazzled,* ''You can't even change your pants without Him watching you!''[41] Materialists, who do not themselves feel the pull of the spiritual realm, dislike the very idea of its existence. It is so much less worrying, after all, to believe there is no hell, even if you thereby forfeit the hope of heaven. And even heaven can seem dull, ''an eternity of bliss in the company of the Dean of Studies,'' as Steven Daedalus puts it in James Joyce's *Portrait of the Artist as a Young Man.*[42]

These two points of view seem to be a basic part of human nature. To the religious person, the materialist is a terrible sinner. To the materialist, the religious person is at best a dupe and at worst an outright fraud. Alchemy tried to unite these extremes in order to perfect man. It was a spiritual science, taking an experimental approach to the soul, much as such current cults as Scientology still do.

This approach, however, terrifies the ardent materialist, whose freedom from the hellish tyranny of faith is threatened by a religious wolf in the clothing of the scientific lamb. Science freed us from superstition, gave us the freedom and dignity to control our lives and our environment, without the interference of any gods. To the materialist, then, science is familiar and useful, whereas religion holds all the terrors of the unknown. Therefore, a scientifically clad religion is outrageous, a sacrilegious parody of science, an evil to be uprooted and destroyed. Such drivel is ''not fit to be printed.'' It is ''the obvious production of a fool and a knave.''[43]

We will find that much of this emotional confusion is also true of astrology.

ASTROLOGY

Anyone who has seen the stars on a clear night, far away from the interference of city lights, cannot help being deeply impressed. The stars are a spectacular presence that rotate through the heavens, their orderly pattern of movement marred only by the occasional meteor or comet and by the wandering planets. It is no wonder that ancient man observed the sky, and it appears likely that the oldest records of systematic observation of nature are records of celestial events. Alexander Marshack has persuasively demonstrated that decorated bones from the Paleolithic, previously put in the archaeologist's catchall category of "ritual objects," are in fact records of the cycles of the moon.[44] Since prehistoric observers discovered that the cycles were regular, they were led to expect that nature is orderly.

Order can be found in the heavens in two ways, and the difference between them provides an important clue to the problem of pseudoscience. The first way is already evident in the Paleolithic bones: regularities in the movement of the moon, stars, and planets can be observed and recorded. Discovery of these regularities makes it possible to predict both celestial and earthly events, for the seasons correlate with changes in the heavens. Although such predictions would at first be no more than crude expectations, as more observations were made and regularities were precisely defined, the predictions would become increasingly exact.

Archaeologists' studies of ancient cultures have revealed that evidence of astronomical observation and prediction may be found almost anywhere in the world, from Stonehenge to the Americas. A whole subfield of archaeology called archaeo-astronomy has grown up around these findings. The ability to predict events in the heavens and on earth prospered because it was useful to both society and the observers. The society benefitted from more precise regulation of agricultural, gathering, and hunting activities. The observers and calculators benefitted because their abilities gave them importance and social power. That heavenly movements are regular made these benefits possible.

But there is a second way to perceive, and use, the heavenly order, a way that goes beyond prediction and control—dividing the stars into constellations. Even modern children learn to spot constellations, picking out Orion the Hunter and the Big Dipper. The constellations not only order the heavens for convenient reference, they also extend human meaning to the apparently meaningless night sky. This second response to the stars, this projection of human meaning onto the stars, onto their patterns and regular movements, led the ancients to tell stories about the regular cycles of the moon, planets, sun, and stars, and about eclipses.

Once the heavens acquired meaning as well as order, people began to explicate it, to divine its significance for human life, and to deduce from it the organization of the universe.

Thus, observers of the heavens could note regularities in their movements and use these observations to predict events and to regulate some of their activities. But they could also find meaning in star patterns and planetary movements, use this meaning to find meaning in celestial and earthly events, and, further, control earthly events by such predictions. The first of these enterprises we recognize as the science of astronomy; the second we recognize as the pseudoscience of astrology.

It is by no means apparent, however, that these enterprises are incompatible, and for a very long time astronomers and astrologers were the same people—although many histories of astronomy would prefer to forget about this blot on the escutcheon of their science. Both astronomy and astrology began in ancient Babylonia. The Babylonians kept accurate records of the movements of the stars and planets and developed mathematical systems for predicitng celestial events. At the same time, they looked to the stars for omens and clues to the future. The Babylonians already read animal entrails, particularly the liver, for signs and portents, and the system of divination based on liver reading was transferred to star reading.

The Babylonian diviner "somehow felt the blow of the sacrificial knife to link the victim with the whole universe in a sort of lightning-stroke which made the victim's organs reflect the structure of the whole at a given moment." Here is the beginning of the idea that earthly and cosmic events correspond—the "As above, so below" of the alchemists. It was natural, then, to begin to seek omens in the heavens, the home of the gods, and to believe that heavenly movement influenced earthly life. "Liver scrutiny and sky-observation merged," and the result was astrology.[45]

Predictions made by Babylonian astrologers were often precise and could therefore be proven wrong. Lindsay reports the following prophecy from the seventh century B.C.: "When on the first of month Nisan the rising sun appears red like a torch . . . then there will be a solar eclipse on the twenty-eighth or twenty-ninth day of the month, the king will die that very month, and his son will ascend the throne."[46] In this forecast astronomy and astrology are merged, for both an astronomical prediction (the eclipse) and an astrological prophecy (the king's death) are made.

Astronomy and astrology also appear in Egypt and Greece during the last eight centuries before Christ. It is unclear how much the development of these two studies was due to independent invention and how much to influences these cultures had on each other. In any event, the Greeks transformed both astronomy and astrology in significant ways and began to separate them conceptually if not in practice. It was also among the Greeks that attacks on astrology as a pseudoscience began.

Unlike the Babylonians or Mesopotamians, the Greeks after 500 B.C. developed a lively tradition of nonreligious philosophy and natural speculation. The Babylonian astronomers had been content to establish and use arithmetical regularities in the movements of the points of light in the night sky without trying to explain these motions. The Greek natural philosophers, on the other hand, wanted to construct a model of the universe and its workings; that is, they wished to know how there come to be eclipses, lunar cycles, tides, and so on. Out of this impulse came the pre-Copernican earth-centered universe described in Ptolemy's *Almagest*. Of course, this picture of the universe is wrong, but the Greeks did change the whole direction of astronomy from a calculational art aimed at improving the calendar into an explanatory science seeking to describe the world as it really is.

Early Greek philosophy down to Aristotle (d. 323 B.C.) took at least an ambiguous attitude toward astrology and other occult doctrines. The Atomists described a universe devoid of spirit, determined and mechanistic. In the *Timaeus*, Plato described the liver as the "seat of divination," but then said that "God has given the art of divination not to the wisdom, but to the foolishness of man." Plato at various times speaks of the stars as the houses of the gods, but in the *Republic* he denies that observing and studying the stars is necessarily uplifting.[47] A similar mixture of attitudes is found in the writings of Plato's pupil Aristotle.

In the Hellenistic period, following the deaths of Aristotle and Alexander the Great in the same year, astrology's popularity grew, and it was synthesized with magic and alchemy into the occult world view described earlier. The change began with the Stoic philosophers, whose conception of the universe justified divination, fortune-telling, and eventually even magic. It was the Stoics who stressed the microcosm-macrocosm concept with its system of correspondences between the two realms. They conceived of the universe as a divine, living being, rationally determined, in which all parts affect all other parts. Thus the movements of the planets could affect events on earth, and study of the heavens could predict earthly events. Magic finally worked its way into this system as people began to believe they could manipulate the network of universal causality and correspondences through talismans and spells. The Stoics similarly changed Greek cosmological speculations, reducing them to attempts to interpret the prophecies of astrology within a deterministic, causal model of the universe. The idea of causality through correspondence led to magic, but it also led toward scientific experimentation because of its implication that the world can be manipulated as well as observed.

During the broad period from 500 B.C. to the Renaissance, astrology acquired its modern form both practically and in finding a "scientific" justification. The first horoscopes began to be cast; astronomy and astrology separated as each found practical tasks to pursue. However, the same people were still astronomers and astrologers, although their social roles were different in each activity. As astronomers they sought to understand the motions of the heavens and to build precise models of the universe; as astrologers they used this knowledge to cast horoscopes for clients. This coexistence of astronomer and astrologer, of science and Neoplatonic occultism, continued until and through the Renaissance.

Claudius Ptolemy (A.D. 85–165) sums up the Hellenistic outlook. His *Almagest* was the great astronomical work of the classical period, and Ptolemy's world view was overthrown only with great difficulty more than a thousand years later. In addition, his *Tetrabiblos* was the great astrological treatise of the same period, although he did not believe in astrological magic.

Ptolemy distinguished astronomy and astrology as two separate but related fields. The first, self-sufficient and more effective, is astronomy, the study of celestial movements. The second, astrology, is less sure and depends on the first, but goes beyond it in "investigating the changes which [the heavenly movements] bring about in that which they surround."[48] By Ptolemy's time, attacks had been mounted against astrology, and Ptolemy's defense draws on the Stoic cosmography.

Ptolemy first defended the possibility of astrological predictions. He maintained that "a certain power" emanates from "the eternal ethereal substance"[49] and encompasses everything on the earth. He bolstered the plausibility of his argument by pointing out the obvious effects of the sun and moon on the earth, and extended this thinking to the other heavenly bodies. We can, by studying the motions of sun, moon, planets, and stars, predict many things about the growth of plants, the seasons, the winds, the tides, and so on, Ptolemy claimed. If this is possible, then we can "with respect to an individual man, perceive the general quality of his temperament from the ambient at the time of his birth . . . and predict occasional events by the use of the fact that such and such an ambient is attuned to such and such a temperament and is favorable to prosperity, while another . . . conduces to injury."[50]

Having established the model of the universe that informs astrology, Ptolemy next answered specific criticisms. Certainly astrologers have erred, but the practice of any complex activity is bound to produce mistakes. Nor should the adoption of astrology by self-seeking magicians who "deceive the vulgar" be any reason to reject its sincere scientific practitioners, for philosophy is not abolished upon discovery that it has "evident rascals" practicing it. Sounding rather Popperian, Ptolemy avers that astrology is like "every science" in being "conjectural and not absolutely to be confirmed."[51] He then constructs a protective belt of "accidental qualities" surrounding the hard core of astrological ideas. For example, astrological assessment of a man's temperament may be affected by his place of birth, which is nearly as influential as the time of his birth.

Having established the plausibility of astrology, Ptolemy shows that it is beneficial. As the Fowlers would say of their phrenology, Ptolemy says astrology can reveal a person's propensities and talents and can guide decisions about business and marriage. "What could be more conducive to well-being, pleasure, and in general satisfaction than this kind of forecast by which we gain a full view of things human and divine?" Moreover, even if it had no practical use in pursuing wealth and fame, it would still have some of the same improving virtues as philosophy. Prediction of events prepares us for them, calming the soul and preventing "excessive panic and delirious joy."[52] Such desire to avoid all strong emotions is characteristic of the Stoics.

Ptolemy also considers the problem of predestination, which had divided astrologers into two camps. An important difficulty with any system of prophecy is determinism or fatalism. If one's fate is set at birth, what is the point of living? Christians often denounced astrology for just this denial of free will. Some astrologers did indeed teach deterministic fatalism, but others backed away and taught that the stars only create tendencies to certain acts and outcomes but do not make them inescapable. We will find a similar division among phrenologists in the nineteenth century A.D.

Ptolemy upholds the second view, comparing astrology to medicine. If future events are unknown, or known but not acted upon, "all will follow the course of primary nature." If, however, remedies are applied, bad ends "do not occur at all or are rendered less severe."[53] Both the doctor, whom no one attacks for fatalism, and the astrologer predict what will happen unless one acts wisely, and they each offer practical wisdom. Ptolemy proceeds, in fact, to describe how the Egyptians combined astrology and medicine, thus supporting his view of astrology's professional and scientific nature.

Although Ptolemy does not himself advocate magic, by arguing that knowledge of the heavens can be used to affect earthly ends, he points toward astrological magic. And when magic appeared astrology began to slip into an egocentric world view in which immense cosmic forces could be known and manipulated solely for one's own selfish purposes. The cosmos became merely an extension of one's will; the disinterested search for knowledge disappeared.

Astrology changed little after Ptolemy's *Tetrabiblos*. As additional planets were discovered, new "influences" had to be added to horoscopes. Although Ptolemy was a Stoic, astrology fitted easily into the hierarchical universe described by Neoplatonism, and astrology's picture of the earth-centered cosmos surrounded by heavenly spheres gave Neoplatonism much of its plausibility.

Much of this plausibility was destroyed by the Copernican revolution. Despite attacks by orthodox Christians for its fatalism, and by various medieval scientists for its continued failings, astrology survived the Middle Ages and revived strongly during the Renaissance. But when Copernicus and his followers showed convincingly that the earth was not the center of the universe—thus negating an important belief of Roman Catholics and astrologers alike—the intellectual appeal of each lessened. The earth was not the central recipient of cosmic forces emitted by relatively close celestial bodies, but was instead a single small planet in one solar system near the edge of one galaxy in a vast universe. Trying to digest this new knowledge gave Christianity a bad case of indigestion, and a nearly fatal dose of botulism to astrology.

Newton's scientific additions to this mental menu provided a large serving of just deserts for egocentric mankind. Newton's mechanistic, materialistic understanding of the universe all but destroyed Neoplatonism, astrology, and even Christianity. Galileo, Descartes, and other scientists and philosophers from 1600 to 1800 constructed a new world view in which precisely measurable forces acted on material bodies in determinate ways. Newton himself described the mathematically precise celestial clockwork of planets and stars, and in the ensuing decades the mechanical conception of nature was extended to society and ultimately to mankind itself. Nowhere in this cosmos was there room for spiritual influences and occult powers. Magic, alchemy, and astrology were now denounced as superstitious frauds—and Newton's alchemical interests were a cause of shame to his biographers. But the scientific rejection of astrology did not result in its rejection by the people, although belief in astrology did for a time weaken. In France and Germany astrology almost completely vanished during the Enlightenment. In England, astrological books continued to sell throughout the nineteenth century, but these were mostly reprints of works from the Renaissance, which had produced England's last generation of practicing astrologers. English beliefs crossed the Atlantic to the American colonies and endured well past the American Revolution.[54]

In the nineteenth century, during the romantic period of rebellion against too much materialism and mechanism, astrology was rediscovered in England and spread to the rest of Europe and to America. Once again astrologers began to cast horoscopes and write books. Moreover, astrology achieved commercial success, taking its now familiar place among the newspaper columns and the ranks of bestsellers. Astrology now dominates the occult supermarket, purporting to give advice on love and sex, business, and friendship.[55]

Most popular works on astrology today do not even attempt to defend it but simply teach their readers how to use it. One book, however, *The Compleat Astrologer* by Derek and Julia Parker, does attempt to establish "scientific" astrology. Rejecting the Neoplatonic concept of the microcosm and macrocosm as pseudoscientific, the Parkers try to rehabilitate astrology by using impressive graphs and lengthy discussions of modern physics. After presenting the scientifically recognized physical forces that affect the universe, many of which were unknown even fifty years ago, the Parkers conclude that "it is quite logical to suppose that other emissions, unknown to us, are similarly affected. And can it be that these are the causes of astrological influences?"[56]

This is a rather lame defense for any "science," and ultimately the Parkers resort to astrology's past show that little has changed for the craft since Ptolemy's time. They picture the universe as consisting of "clearly woven harmonies" in which all things influence all things.

This view is pure Stoicism despite their use of C. G. Jung's concept of synchronicity, the noncausal connection between events—itself a fairly occult idea—to support it.

Such arguments have done little to protect astrology from established science. In 1975, aghast at astrology's revival among the populace and among students, 186 scientists, including 18 Nobel Prize winners, issued a manifesto denouncing astrology in *The Humanist* magazine. This manifesto was accompanied by several articles criticizing astrology.[57]

The scientists proclaimed astrology to have "no scientific foundation." The critical articles noted the vanishingly minute effects of planetary radiation and gravitation on the human body, astrology's dependence on the ancient magical principle of correspondences, statistical refutations of astrological predictions, and astrology's failure to describe a mechanism by which the stars and planets influence people.

The Humanist gave the astrologers room to reply in the next issue. Astrologers' reactions varied from the incoherent to the vituperative. The first letter called science "the New Superstition," a mere 170 years old, whose attack on the ancient science of astrology is "a move back to the time of the inquisitions." The president and vice-president of the Federation of Scientific Astrologers, in another article, detached "serious" astrology from worthless newspaper horoscopes. They claimed that a good horoscope "can give a fairly accurate description of individual potential and behavior traits" but denied that it could predict the future. A similar letter came from the director of the National Astrological Society, who also defended astrology as a pragmatically effective craft that is essentially descriptive and so needs to provide no explanation of its workings. Stoicism also surfaced in these letters. One wrote that a pattern "permeated the universe, but is simultaneous, not causative." Hence, "astrologers do not and cannot predict the future," but can give valuable advice to aid a client's search for self-actualization. The last letter appealed to synchronicity and correspondences to defend some predictive astrology. The author likened astrology to reading a railroad timetable. One can use the schedule to predict when trains will depart and arrive, but the schedule does not cause these events. Similarly, the stars, participating in the universal harmonies, foretell, but do not cause, human events. The writer also added the final defense of any practice: Even if "astrology weren't *factually* true, I think it is still valuable if it has a personal truth for the individual."[58]

One interesting trend is apparent in these letters, beyond their defenses of astrology. This is that, although a few still practice predictive astrology, most now have shifted their interest to what nineteenth-century German astrologers pioneered, the use of astrology to read and improve a person's character.[59] This trend makes modern astrology itself into something of an occult double of psychology. Like personality tests, astrology claims to give an "accurate description of individual potential and behavior traits" and to assist at self-actualization. We will see later that cults too offer these services.

Some psychologists have attempted to meet astrology's threat to their practice. Such refutations themselves possess a certain occult quality in that they have appeared, in most cases, in journals of low or marginal quality. Even a critical association with the occult can itself be rejected.

Most psychological studies demonstrate that there is no correlation between people's actual personality characteristics and those predicted for them by horoscopes. Other studies, however, have examined the belief in astrology itself. One found that, if people are given identical personality assessments and told that they derive either from psychological, graphological, or astrological methods, people are willing to believe them all about equally, with psychology not significantly ahead.[60]

Astrology is not dead, and it continues to resist its occult, "irrational" status. It has remained virtually unchanged since Ptolemy's time; it solves no new problems, it undergoes no progressive problem shift. But neither has it degenerated scientifically; it has simply fossilized. Its appeal today is neither to the protoastronomer, as in Babylonia or Egypt, nor to the religious and magically inclined as in Rome, the Middle Ages, or the Renaissance. Its appeal is like that of cults and popular psychology—it promises to put you in touch with "the real You," to tell alienated people how to touch others and how to make themselves happy. It is less pursuit of truth than a pursuit of happiness. The principles of casting horoscopes have not changed, but the social role of the astrologer has. Once an adviser to kings and farmers, the astrologer has now become a guidance counselor to the millions who want to believe something that gives the appearance of science with none of the threat. Believers in astrology want to look into their souls—but as "safely and sanely" as the Fourth of July without fireworks. Not for them the dark night of the soul, the assumption of responsibility for all aspects of one's being. They prefer an undemanding, comforting pseudoreligion that has been "sanitized for your protection," a religion that has as little threat, or depth, as a freshly cleaned, plastic-wrapped motel room.

Freud saw ineradicable evil in the human soul; astrologers see evil only in the stars, for whose influence we are not responsible. As we will see later, various cults offer this same irresponsible absolution within a more mystical setting. For those with only slight religious needs, the astrology column in your newspaper may well be as satisfying as lighting a candle to a saint or saying grace before eating. For those with a more religious nature, cults offer the same self-importance and absolution as astrology in a more religiously gratifying atmosphere.

Science, including experimental psychology, long ago reduced man to an insignificant machine living a short and meaningless life on a small and insignificant planet. To the astrologer, man is still at the center of the universe, beneficiary and victim of high cosmic influences that can be read and found meaningful. It is no wonder that so many people have long preferred the latter vision—one that will be found in many of psychology's other occult doubles.

PART TWO

Psychology's Occult Doubles

TOWARD THE END OF HIS LIFE, one of the great men of the nineteenth century, Alfred Russel Wallace, codiscoverer of evolution by natural selection, wrote an intellectual memoir called *The Wonderful Century*. As the title implies, he mainly praised the nineteenth century for "those great material and intellectual achievements [that distinguish it] from any and all of its predecessors." These wonders included the improvement of transport, labor-saving machinery, photography, and advances in all the natural sciences.

Against the successes, Wallace set a smaller list of of failures. Three no one would quarrel with were militarism, greed, and the plunder of the earth. The oddest so-called failure, to modern ears, was vaccination. Like a majority of the medical community, Wallace found vaccination a "delusion" at best, a "crime" at worst; politicians, not physicians, implemented vaccination. But heading Wallace's list of failures was the resistance of established science to three intellectual movements—phrenology, hypnotism, and psychical research.

Wallace was active in all these fields, and his enthusiasm made his mental stability suspect among some of his scientist friends. Nonetheless, Wallace thought highly of all three rejected fields. He believed that in the twentieth century phrenology would "prove itself to be the true science of mind," and its rejection would come to be regarded as "an example of almost incredible narrowness and prejudice" among men of science. Similarly, the phenomena of hypnotism and the manifestations of mediums would, with "absolute certainly," come to "be accepted as realities in the coming century."

Wallace was wrong in his forecasts. But he was far from alone in believing in phrenology, hypnotism (or animal magnetism), and psychical research. Belief in one generally accompanied belief in the others throughout the nineteenth century. We find a body of people who reject all these beliefs and a body of people who accept them, who are then also rejected by the first group. These ideas constituted an occult underground of common beliefs. These beliefs often shared only one quality: all were rejected by the established thought of the day. In the chapters that follow, we will examine each of these rejects of the Wonderful Century to illuminate the mechanisms of the creation of pseudosciences.

Three

Phrenology:
The Theory and Its Critics

The best known of all psychological pseudosciences is phrenology. It is remembered today exactly as its detractors would have wished: as a fraud perpetrated by half-educated charlatans reading the character of gullible marks from the bumps on their heads. In its time, however, phrenology, although the butt of some ridicule, was taken seriously by many leading men and women of the early Victorian period. Its influence on psychology and social reform has been lasting.

Phrenology must be considered in three aspects. First, it is a physiological doctrine claiming that the brain is the seat of the mind, and that the brain is a collection of specialized organs corresponding to the different departments of mental life. Second, it is a psychological doctrine claiming that the mind is divided into distinct faculties located in different parts of the brain. Finally, it became a social movement deeply involved with the progressive, sometimes radical, thought of its day.

BACKGROUND

The phrenologists were not the first to divide the mind into faculties or to attempt to locate these faculties in different parts of the brain. Aristotle had divided the soul into distinct faculties, such as imagination, memory, and intellect. Each was responsible for a different form of mental activity—e.g. recording experience, storing it, and extracting knowledge from it. Aristotle, however, thought the heart was the seat of the soul, and it was left to others to locate thought in the brain.

While numerous philosophers followed Aristotle in locating the soul in the heart, the physician Galen (A.D. 129–ca. 200) demonstrated experimentally that the brain is the center of the nervous system.[1] Later philosopher-physicians combined Galen's discovery with Aristotle's faculty psychology to pursue localization of brain function. During the early Middle Ages this work took place in Islamic countries.

One of the earliest writers on the topic was Costa ben Luca (or Qustá ibn Luqá) in the middle of the ninth century.[2] He attributed mental activity to the movement through the nerves of subtle "animal spirits" generated by the heart. The crudest spirits are associated with the senses; the most refined are associated with imagination, memory, and reason, which he placed in the brain.

Costa ben Luca even attempted a mechanistic explanation of how mental activity takes place in the brain. The brain was divided, he believed, into anterior and posterior ventricles connected by a small valve. When someone recalled something from memory this valve opened and spirits passed from the anterior to the posterior cavity. Anticipating an important theme of phrenology, Costa ben Luca explained individual differences in mental activity as due to different kinds of brains. Those who remembered quickly had rapidly opening valves. Those with the highest intellect had brains filled with the most subtle spirits.

Speculation of this nature continued throughout the Middle Ages in both Islam and Christendom.[3] The sixteenth century physician Berengario de Carpi deserves mention for anticipating phrenology's attempt to link skull shape to brain capacities, and hence to mental functioning. Carpi claimed that long-headed people possessed clearly distinct ventricles of the brain and so thought clearly, while round-headed people possessed confused ventricles and confused thoughts. Moreover, infants whose heads were deformed in accord with cultural patterns became intellectually confused.[4]

Understanding of brain and nervous functioning had advanced hardly at all by the time phrenology was founded toward the end of the eighteenth century; indeed one of phrenology's greatest credits is that it forced scientists to take seriously the idea that the mind is in the brain, and to work out the implications of this idea. Speculative philosophical psychology had become largely separated from speculation about brain function. By the eighteenth century, three philosophical systems dominated psychology—Cartesian rationalism, neo-Lockean sensationism, and faculty psychology.

French mathematician and philosopher René Descartes (1596–1650) maintained that the thinking soul is immaterial and separate from the body, although he did speculate about the physical basis of mentality. He believed animals were soulless automatons whose mental functions, like the lower mental functions of man, could be explained by his own speculative theory of nervous function. This theory was little more than a complex version of Costa ben Luca's views. In man, however, Descartes saw a further function: the soul interacted with the body through the pineal gland, whose reason-directed motions could regulate the flow of animal spirits in and out of the brain. The soul itself, Descartes argued, was simple, with no internal divisions or faculties, being purely a thinking, immaterial substance.[5]

Standing at the head of the British empiricist tradition, John Locke (1632–1704) had disposed of innate ideas, substituting the *tabula rasa,* the mind blank at birth, impressed by the outer world of experience and ideas. But Locke had not disposed of mental faculties, mental machinery that operated on experience and ideas. It was only the content of the mind that came from experience; separate and distinct faculties were God given.[6]

Although most British philosophers followed Locke's distinction between experience and innate faculties, some French empiricists did not. The most important and influential of the latter group was Etienne Bonnot de Condillac (1715–80), who "improved" on Locke by eliminating native faculties and claiming that the mind was entirely empty at birth. Condillac attempted to show that the entire mind, including the faculties, could be built up out of sensations. Memory, for example, would be created when two identical sensations were experienced at different times and associated by the mind.[7] This attempt was unsuccessful, for he had to assume an innate faculty of memory to retain the first sensation until the second came along. Nevertheless, Condillac's radical sensationism, which claimed that everything in the mind is either experience or its recollection, became quite influential in France, the intellectual birthplace of phrenology.

The third philosophical view of the mind was enormously popular in Great Britain and the United States and bears a superficial resemblance to phrenology. It was commonsense faculty psychology, originated by Thomas Reid (1710–96) and elaborated by his followers, especially by Dugald Stewart (1753–1828). Reid, a clergyman, was offended by the radical skepticism of David Hume. In Hume's philosophy both experience and reason, the only sources of knowledge, were considered fallible, which implied that no final truths could ever be attained. Such a conclusion violated the collective common sense of mankind and could not be allowed, Reid maintained.

Reid argued that the human mind is so constituted by God that its innate faculties lead persons to truth. These faculties are "a part of that furniture which Nature hath given to human understanding. They are the inspiration of the Allmighty." The faculties "serve to direct us in the common affairs of life, where our reasoning faculty would leave us in the dark . . . and all the discoveries of reason are grounded upon them. They make up what is called *the common sense of mankind.* " In a gibe at Hume, Reid concluded that anyone who gives up his common sense for philosophical absurdities has fallen into "metaphysical lunacy." [8]

Reid's philosophy, which grounded knowledge in God-given common sense, was turned into a widely popular psychology by his student Dugald Stewart. Stewart's *Elements of the Philosophy of the Human Mind*, published in 1792, became the basis for most psychology taught in Britain and America, both as a textbook itself and as a background for other textbooks.[9] Stewart divided the mind into many intuitively reasonable faculties such as sex, pity, veneration, and attention. (The whole list is given in figure 3.1, which compares the commonsense faculties to those of the phrenologists.) Each faculty was responsible for some department of human behavior. Unlike more austere systems, this one paid attention to feelings and desires as well as to ratiocination. It also had a practical aim in professing to lead students to self-knowledge and, hence, to self-improvement.

It was against this background that phrenology emerged. Nothing in it was entirely new, but it had something to offend everyone. Cartesians would resent its dividing up the mind; sensationists would resent its reintroduction of faculties; faculty psychologists would resent its new list of faculties; and all the Christian faithful would resent its reduction of the soul to the brain.

THE DEVELOPMENT OF PHRENOLOGY

Franz Joseph Gall and Craniology

> My purpose is to ascertain the functions of the brain in general, and those of its different parts in particular; to show that it is possible to

Fig. 3.1
COMPARATIVE TABLE OF FACULTIES

Thomas Reid, 1780	Dugald Stewart, 1827	Franz Joseph Gall, 1810	J. C. Spurzheim, 1834
Active Powers	*Acute Powers*	*Determinate Faculties*	*Mental Powers*
Self-Preservation			Desire to Live (no #)
Maintenance of Habits	Propensity to Action and Repose		
Hunger and Thirst	Hunger and Thirst		Alimentiveness (no #)
Lust	Sex	Instinct of Generation (1)	Amativeness (2)
	Acquired Appetite for Drugs		
	Desire of Society		
Instinct of Imitation	Instinct of Imitation	Mimicry, Imitation (25)	Imitation (21)
Language		Verbal Memory (14)	
Desire for Power	Ambition	Vanity, Ambition (9)	
Self-Esteem	Self-Love / Self Confidence	Pride, Self-Esteem (8)	Self-Esteem (12)
Desire of Knowledge	Desire of Knowledge	Educability (11)	
Conflilate Affection	Parental Affection / Filial Affection	Love of Offspring (24)	Philoprogenitiveness (3)
Gratitude	Gratitude		
Pity and Compassion	Pity		
	Sympathy		
	Universal Benevolence	Good Nature (24)	Benevolence (13)
Esteem of the Wise and Good	Desire of Esteem		Approbativeness (11)
	Veracity		
Friendship	Friendship	Friendship, Attachment (3)	Adhesiveness (11)
Sexual Affection	Sexual Affection		
Public Spirit	Patriotism		Inhabitiveness (5)
Emulation	Desire of Superiority		
Animal Resentment / Rational Resentment	Resentment	Courage, Self-Defence (4)	Combativeness (6)
Transcendent Good	Interest		Conscientiousness (16)
Duty	Sense of Duty		
Veneration	Veneration	Theosophy, Religion (26)	Reverence (14)
	Hope		Hope (17)
	Decency, Regard to Character	Firmness of Character (27)	Firmness (15)
Imagination (- - - invention)	Imagination	Poetry (23)	Ideality (19)
	Instinct for Construction	Mechanical Aptitude (19)	Constructiveness (9)
	Sense of Similarity and Contrast / Sense of the Ridiculous	Wit (22)	Mirth (20)
Beauty	Memory for Colors	Sense of Colors (10)	Coloring (26)
	Time		Time (31)
	Music	Music (17)	Tune (32)
		Wish to Destroy (5)	Destructiveness (1)
		Cunning (6)	Secretiveness (7)
		Sentiment of Property (7)	Acquisitiveness (8)
		Cautiousness (10)	Cautiousness (10)
		Mathematics (18)	Calculation (29)
Intellectual Powers	*Intellectual Powers*		
The Five Senses and Their Faculty of Perception	The Five Senses and Their Faculty of Perception		Individuality (22)
	Form	Memory for Persons (13)	Configuration (23)
Size and Novelty	Size / Novelty		Size (24)
			Weight (25)
	Locality	Local-Memory (12)	Locality (27)
	Language	Memory for Languages (15)	Language (33)
Memory	Memory		
Judgment and Reason	Judgment and Reasoning	Comparative Sagacity (20)	Causality (35)
Abstraction	Abstraction	Metaphysical Depth (21)	Comparison (34)
Conception	Conception		
	Attention		
Moral Taste	Moral Taste		Marvellousness (18)
	Association of Ideas		Order (20)
			Eventuality (30)

SOURCE: Howard Davis Spoerl, Faculties vs. Traits: Gall's Solution,
Character and Personality 4 (1935-36) 222.
Copyright 1935, Duke University Press. Durham, N.C.
Spurzheim's list of faculties added by the present authors. Gall and Spurzheim
numbered their faculties, and the numbers may be used to compare this table to the
ordered lists of Gall's and Spurzheim's localizations given in the text.

ascertain different dispositions and inclinations by the elevations
and depressions upon the head; and to present, in a clear light, the
most important consequences which result therefrom to medicine,
morality, education and legislation—in a word, to the science of
human nature.[10]

Thus wrote Franz Joseph Gall (1758–1828) in a letter to Baron Joseph
de Retzer that outlined Gall's new science of human nature. Gall's interest in the functions of the brain began in his youth, when he noticed that
schoolmates gifted with verbal memory had large, bulging eyes. Later,
as a medical student, Gall confirmed his adolescent observation and resolved to find its cause. He reasoned that human talents and dispositions
ought to be based on physiological organization just as the five senses
are based on the organs of sight, smell, touch, hearing, and tasting. Similarly, features of personality and intellect ought to spring from distinct
organs of the brain.[11] Gall's resolution defined a systematic research
program aiming to discover the fundamental constituents of the mind
and correlate them with underlying brain structures.

Gall's major work, *On the Functions of the Brain and Each of Its
Parts* (French ed. 1825; English trans. 1835),[12] was the fruit of the research program sketched in the letter to de Retzer. Gall summarized his
four basic principles:

1. the moral and intellectual dispositions are innate;
2. their manifestation depends on organization;
3. the brain is exclusively the organ of mind;
4. the brain is composed of as many particular and independent
   organs as there are fundamental powers of the mind;—these
   few incontestable principles form the basis of the whole physiology of the brain.[13]

Corollary to these principles was the inquiry, "how far the inspection
of the form of the head, or cranium, presents a means of ascertaining the
existence or absence, and the degree of development, of certain cerebral
parts; and consequently the presence or absence, the weakness or energy of certain function."[14] Implicit in this assertion is the assumption
that the more developed and consequently larger a brain organ is, the
more powerful is its corresponding mental ability.

With the exception of the corollary, the "doctrine of the skull," none
of this sounds particularly odd today, or out of keeping with our prevail-

ing views. Yet certain features of Gall's program set it off from its predecessors and rivals.

Against the Cartesians, Gall asserted the plurality of the powers of the mind. Whereas Descartes had insisted that the mind is a simple, thinking substance, Gall asserted that the mind is not simple but may be resolved into a set of "fundamental powers." Furthermore, the mind is not a separate dualistic substance that manipulates the body through the pineal gland (or brain). Instead, Gall said, the mind "depends on [the] organization of the brain," which is the "organ of the mind," just as the stomach is the organ of digestion. By making the mind depend on the brain, Gall seemed to support materialism, saying that there is no soul, and determinism, since to nineteenth-century minds, having no soul implied having no free will. Although Gall protested that he believed in the soul and free will, his protests were weak, and the fear of materialism and determinism was the motive force behind almost every attack on phrenology.

Against the sensationists, Gall asserted that human character and intellect are innate—a condition that would set limits on the perfectibility of man through education. Indeed, one of Gall's proposed innate dispositions was the tendency to murder, and although, Gall said, morality might control evil instincts in some people, in others there might be "an irresistible inclination to kill."[15] Gall maintained that the *tabula rasa* view of the empiricists and sensationists is false to nature. Different species of animals possess quite different abilities and propensities, which must be rooted in innate differences of their nervous systems. Within species, individuals differ in their talents: one person can draw while another cannot; one can remember faces while another cannot; one gets lost easily while another never does; one murders while another is meek. Gall believed these differences to be so deep, enduring, and early appearing as to defy environmental explanations.[16]

Against the Scottish philosopher-psychologists' lists of faculties, Gall asserted a new list of mental functions. His list is more than just an alternative set of faculties, however. It rests on an entirely new conception of the nature of psychology, a conception equally at variance with the Cartesians, empiricists, sensationists, and commonsense philosophers. Ever since the time of Plato, the aim of philosophical psychology had been epistemological—that is, to discover how the mind knows. In doing this, philosophers described only the general, normative mind acquiring the general, normative truth. The faculties they listed, such as imagination and memory, were intended to characterize a generalized concept of mind; they were not intended to explain the different characters and propensities of actual individuals. In other words, epistemologists describe only an abstract concept of mind contemplating truth, rather than concrete individuals acting in the real world.[17]

Gall attacked traditional lists of faculties as "mere abstractions":

> They are not applicable to the detailed study of a species, or an individual. Every man, except an idiot, enjoys all these faculties. Yet all men have not the same intellectual or moral character. *We need faculties, the different distribution of which shall determine the different species of animals, and the different proportions of which explain the differences in individuals.*[18]

Gall attempted to substitute a biological and behaviorist psychology for the traditional philosophical and mentalistic one. He wanted to discover those mental functions that actually operate in the day-to-day life of an individual of whatever species—functions that are rooted in the biological heritage of the organism. Gall shifted the emphasis in psychology from the mind's abstract contemplation of truth to the study of behavior adapted to the demands of the world and springing from the organic constitution. Gall's "most exciting conception,"[19] had it triumphed, would have rendered obsolete all the philosophical psychologies of his time.

Gall asserted, then, that there are certain innate mental abilities and dispositions possessed in differing degrees by different people. Each ability or disposition is rooted in its own organ of the brain, which is thus a collection of organs, not a simple organ. Individual differences in these faculties exist because different people's brains have developed differently, each having different large and small organs. A large organ implies a powerful ability or disposition; a small organ implies a weak ability or disposition. As the brain grows, the skull must accommodate to it; so Gall claimed that the shape of the skull parallels the shape of the brain. Large organs should produce elevations in the skull, while small organs would leave declivities. It then seemed possible to correlate behaviors with the shape of the skull, building up a picture of the brain's organs and the mind's faculties, which then might be used to read character. Gall did the former; his followers the latter.

Robert Young has schematized Gall's theory as follows:[20]

1		2		3		4
STRIKING BEHAVIOUR	implies / causes	FACULTY	implies / causes	CORTICAL ORGAN	implies / causes	CRANIAL PROMINENCE
(talent, propensity, mania)		(innate instinct)		(activity varies with size)		(size varies with under- lying organ)

Gall used a number of methods to implement and support his science. He listed seven of them in the letter to Baron de Retzer and expanded the list to nine in *The Functions of the Brain:*

1. Correlation of striking behavior with shape of the skull. Gall would seek out people well known for some marked ability or disposition and would feel the elevated parts of their skulls. He examined the heads of everyone from musicians to murderers.

2. Counterproof, obtained by seeking out people defective in certain qualities so as to feel their skulls.

3. Correlation of prominences with behaviors. Gall looked for people who had distinctive heads and then engaged them in conversation designed to ferret out their characters.

4. Collecting casts of the skulls of people with strong, well-known characteristics.

5. Collecting skulls of deceased people of striking character. Gall apparently made something of a pest of himself with his requests to the living for their skulls to be left to him after they died.

6. Anatomical demonstration of the correlation between brain organs and cranial prominences.

7. Comparative anatomy and physiology of the brains of different species. Examination of cases of animal brain damage with a view toward ascertaining the mental function affected.

8. Studies of cases of brain damage in human beings with the same end in view.

9. Study of the increase in number of organs from simple creatures to man and of their harmonious arrangement in the skull from the ''lower'' faculties, such as sexuality, at the base of the brain, to the ''higher'' ones, such as language, at the front of the brain.[21]

Anatomical studies are mentioned twice in this list. Beginning around 1800, Gall began a series of such studies that was nothing short of brilliant. Even his bitterest foe, Flourens, admitted that seeing Gall dissect the brain was like seeing the organ for the first time.[22] Gall's studies established numerous new facts about the brain, and his methods have stood the test of time.[23] However, the essentials of his system were already contained in the 1798 letter to de Retzer, and as critics in Paris noted, Gall's anatomical findings, however sound, were irrelevant to his system of craniology—inferring character from the shape of the brain. Gall himself would have acknowledged the justice of this claim, for he always insisted that the function of any organ cannot be determined from the anatomy of its structure. Dissecting a dead brain can tell us little of the life of its possessor. Therefore, we may pass over his anatomical researches and close by briefly describing Gall's characterology and organology, the systems shortly to form phrenology.

According to Gall, the organs common to people and animals are those responsible for the following tendencies and faculties:

1. Instinct of reproduction, including sexuality
2. Love of offspring
3. Affection and friendship
4. Instinct of self-preservation, courage, tendency to fight
5. Carnivorous instinct and tendency to murder
6. Guile and cleverness
7. Feeling of property, including hoarding, and the tendency to steal
8. Pride, arrogance, love of authority
9. Vanity, ambition, love of glory
10. Circumspection, forethought
11. Memory of things, facts; educability
12. Sense of places
13. Memory for people
14. Memory for words
15. Sense of language and speech
16. Sense of colors
17. Sense of sounds, music
18. Sense of connections between numbers
19. Sense of mechanics and construction

The uniquely human organs are those responsible for the following characteristics:

20. Comparative sagacity
21. Sense of metaphysics
22. Sense of satire and wit

23. Poetical talent
24. Kindness, benevolence, compassion
25. Tendency to imitate
27. Firmness of purpose, constancy[24]

Gall's System as a Research Program

Imre Lakatos has analyzed scientific research programs into two parts: the *hard core* of fundamental assumptions and the *protective belt* of specific empirical hypotheses.[25] During the life of a research program, the basic assumptions of the hard core are rarely, if ever, subjected to empirical test, and they may in fact be so abstract that they cannot be tested. Rather, the specific hypotheses of the protective belt are adjusted as incoming data indicate. Thus, faced with a problem, a researcher seeks a hypothesis compatible with both the data and the fundamental assumptions of the program. As a result, scientific progress is an interplay between data and assumptions, producing progressive "problemshifts" in the protective hypotheses and research concerning them.

The fundamental, hard core of Gall's research program was stated clearly in his "four incontestable principles"

1. Abilities and dispositions are innate.
2. Their manifestation depends on the organization of the brain.
3. The brain is the organ of the mind.
4. The brain consists of a plurality of organs.

It is important to observe that "the doctrine of the skull," essential to all later phrenology, is not among this list of Gall's "four incontestable principles." The doctrine of the skull embodies the assumptions that the larger a brain organ is the stronger it is, and that the larger an organ is the larger is the cranial prominence above the organ. Since Gall did not list these assumptions as essential, he presumably considered them provisional only, subject to confirmation, or disconfirmation. The doctrine of the skull is not, therefore, part of the hard core of Gall's program; instead, it was just a working hypothesis that could be discarded, if warranted by the facts, without upsetting the tenets of the hard core. The failure of the doctrine of the skull would make it harder to pursue the aims as stated in the letter to de Retzer but would not make the program impossible.

Gall's specific hypotheses about the enumeration of mental faculties and the localization of their underlying organs belong even more clearly to the protective belt. Gall could easily have admitted error in his analysis of a particular organ without abandoning his four fundamental principles. Such a mistake would not even threaten the doctrine of the skull. Indeed, a progressive "problemshift" in the research emphases of craniology would have meant the successive proposing of specific localizations followed by their replacement as more precise and accurate data became available, producing an ever more reliable and valid map of brain functioning. No brain scientist of today would challenge Gall's "incontestable principles," for they have been found to be incontestable.

Unfortunately, both Gall and his followers, as we shall see, tended to treat the doctrine of the skull, and to a lesser extent Gall's specific localizations, as truths on a par with Gall's fundamental four. They sometimes modified, but never overhauled, Gall's specific organology, and they treated the doctrine of the skull as central to phrenology. Thus the research program changed. Indeed, it changed because it ceased to be a research program, becoming instead a program in applied science. Gall himself perceived the potential social utility in his new science; his followers saw nothing else and turned his fledgling science into a reform movement. These changes turned phrenology into an occult double of orthodox psychology. Instead of a science, phrenology became a social movement that could be rejected on purely social grounds. This change was begun by Gall's longtime collaborator, J. C. Spurzheim, and fulfilled by Spurzheim's adherent, George Combe.

JOHANN CASPAR SPURZHEIM AND PHRENOLOGY

Gall lectured extensively on his new system of the mind, and one of his converts was a young medical student, Johann Caspar Spurzheim (1776–1832), who began to assist at Gall's lectures in 1800. In 1804, after finishing his medical studies, Spurzheim began to collaborate with Gall on anatomical research, which culminated in 1813 with their massive work on the anatomy and physiology of the brain. After that they went their separate ways.[26] By 1833 Spurzheim admitted that his and Gall's views on the nature of man were "very different."[27]

Gall continued his craniological work, but Spurzheim criticized Gall's approach as "merely physiognomical"[28] and as "an empirical method only."[29] In contrast, Spurzheim's "proceeding was philosophical, founded on principles."[30] Spurzheim took Gall's nascent functional psychology, which had been rooted in a distinct concept of the brain, and transformed it into a mental philosophy rivaling, and in his view surpassing, previous systems from Plato's and Aristotle's to the Scots' and Kant's. Brain functions became mental powers that happen to be located in the brain. By systematizing Gall into a philosophy, Spurzheim made phrenology attractive to those looking for guidance in life.

The change is marked in Spurzheim's new name for the discipline, phrenology. Gall had never consistently adopted a name for what he did, but it was generally known as Gall's doctrine of brain and skull, or, in German, *Galls Hirn-und-Schedellehre*. Spurzheim, however, in turning a biological science into a mental philosophy, "found it necessary to change the name" to phrenology. It "is derived from two Greek words: [*phrein*] mind, and [*logos*] discourse," and meant the "doctrine of the special phenomena of the mind" and the relations between mind and body, especially brain.[31]

In his *Outlines of Phrenology*,[32] Spurzheim enunciated his four basic principles of phrenology:

1. The brain is the organ of the mind.
2. The mind is a plurality of faculties, each springing from a distinct brain organ.
3. In the same person, larger organs show more energy, smaller organs show less.
4. The size and form of the skull are determined by the brain.

Two of Gall's principles, that mental dispositions are innate and that their manifestation depends on brain organization, are no longer explicit, although Spurzheim clearly accepted them. More significantly, the doctrine of the skull is no longer a corollary to the principles of phrenology. Instead, it has become explicitly fundamental in Spurzheim's third and fourth principles. While elsewhere Spurzheim blames Gall's methods as the reason why phrenology was ridiculed as "bumpology,"[33] it was really Spurzheim himself who made the doctrine of the skull central to the movement.

Spurzheim introduced a number of changes to Gall's list of functions, increasing them in number from twenty-seven to thirty-five (see table 3.1). He also adjusted several of Gall's localizations, moving them slightly and subdividing them to make room for his eight new faculties (see figure 3.2). The tendency to keep adding faculties, which critics of phrenology saw as a defect, was strong; as early as 1840 an author of a self-styled "perfected phrenology" laid out forty-six faculties.[34]

The most important changes Spurzheim introduced, however, appear the most trivial: the renaming and classifying of the faculties. Gall, having rejected the philosophers' faculties, "observed man in action, and named the organs accordingly."[35] Thus his nomenclature indicated "actions rather than powers."[36] Taking a biological view, Gall had named the brain organs after specific behaviors. Consequently, he was a true functional psychologist, studying the actions of men and animals in the world. Spurzheim, on the other hand, found Gall's methodology and consequent nomenclature "very defective." Spurzheim argued that behaviors are usually the result of joint action by more than one mental power. Consequently, "no organ should be named after any action [behavior], and certainly not after the abuse of its function,"[37] as in Gall's organs of theft and murder. Instead, "in my nomenclature, the powers themselves are designated without referring to any good or bad purpose."[38]

Spurzheim's faculty names refer to the inferred faculties or powers of the mind that produce actions; they do not refer to actions themselves. Spurzheim thus turned phrenology into a faculty psychology that differs from that of Stewart or others only in the specific faculties admitted. The brain organs have become unnecessary, for Spurzheim speaks of faculties of the mind that express themselves through the brain. Cutting phrenology off from development as a biology of brain and behavioral functions, Spurzheim turned it into the latest faculty psychology. Thus his competitors are not rival views of the brain, but are instead rival views of the mind. Spurzheim's phrenology, then, decisively turned away from biological science and toward personal and social philosophy.

An interesting consequence of Spurzheim's "philosophical proceeding" is that, although he listed the doctrine of the skull among the fundamental principles of phrenology, which Gall had not done, his methodology gave it up altogether. Gall's doctrine of the skull was primarily methodological, not substantive. He wanted to correlate brain organ with behavior, and lacking medical techniques for studying the brain he had to assume the conformation of skull to brain and the direct ratio of organ size to strength. This assumption guided his research program: look for prominent bumps and distinctive behaviors, then try to correlate the two. As Spurzheim said, it is an empirical (i.e., scientific) method.

But in shifting the doctrine of the skull into the basic principles of phrenology, Spurzheim made of it a substantive, not methodological, thesis; it became part of the irrefutable hard core of the program. Consequently, Spurzheim needed new methodological assumptions on the basis of which to continue the researches of phrenology. He listed seven (or eight) criteria by which to establish a faculty as fundamental and for which "*a particular organ must be pointed out.*"[39] A faculty was seen as fundamental:

1. Which exists in one kind of animal and not in another
2. Which varies in the sexes of the same species
3. Which is not proportional to the other faculties of the same individual
4. Which develops at different rates in an individual
5. Which may act or repose singly
6. Which is individually propagated in a distinct means from parents to children; and
7. Which singly may preserve its proper state of health, or be affected by disease.[40]

None of Spurzheim's criteria referred to the doctrine of the skull or to brain anatomy and physiology. Now psychological and philosophical considerations defined a faculty, and anatomy and physiology were adjusted to fit it. Phrenology thus became a mental philosophy rather than a biological science. As Spurzheim said, "Gall did not determine any of the organs in conformity with theses views . . . following an empirical method only. . . . But . . . my proceeding is philosophical, founded on principles."[41]

Spurzheim's philosophical approach led him to classify his faculties in the traditional way. Gall had not classified his functions except by locations in the brain beginning, "at the base of the head and ending at the top."[42] But, as Spurzheim said, "I on the contrary . . . conceive it possible to divide, and to classify them according to their primitive functions. I arrange the mental powers into two orders: a division admitted from the remotest antiquity, and known under the names soul and spirit. . . ."[43] Spurzheim's preferred headings were affective and intellectual faculties, which were then further subdivided into classes, as shown in figure 3.2.[44]

Spurzheim thus created a systematic philosophy of the mind by building on—and distorting—Gall's biologically inspired gropings for a physiology of the brain and a functional psychology. Spurzheim's system was a worthy rival to traditional faculty psychologies, and it gained

Fig. 3.2. Spurzheim's Localization
of the Phrenological Faculties
Source: Frontispiece to *Phrenology* (Philadelpia: J. B. Lippincott, 1908).

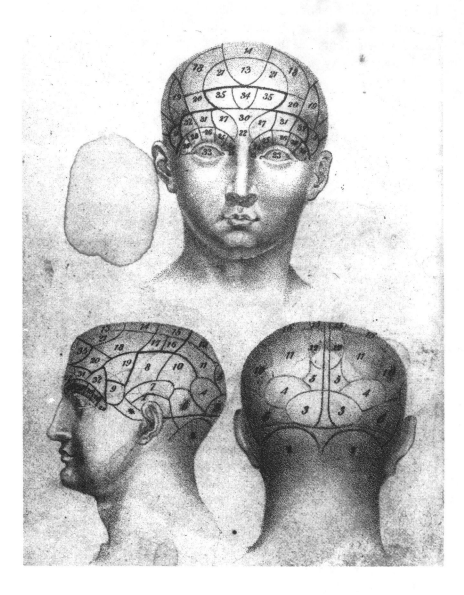

(Fig. 3.2. continued.)

POWERS AND ORGANS OF THE MIND,

MARKED ON THE FRONTISPIECE.

AFFECTIVE.

I.—PROPENSITIES.

† Desire to live.

* Alimentiveness.

No. 1. Destructiveness.

2. Amativeness.

3. Philoprogenitiveness.

4. Adhesiveness.

5. Inhabitiveness.

6. Combativeness.

7. Secretiveness.

8. Acquisitiveness.

9. Constructiveness.

II.—SENTIMENTS.

10. Cautiousness.

11. Approbativeness.

12. Self-esteem.

13. Benevolence.

14. Reverence.

15. Firmness.

16. Conscientiousness.

17. Hope.

18. Marvellousness.

19. Ideality.

20. Mirthfulness.

21. Imitation.

INTELLECTUAL.

I.—PERCEPTIVE.

No. 22. Individuality.

23. Configuration.

24. Size.

25. Weight and Resistance

26. Coloring.

27. Locality.

28. Order.

29. Calculation.

30. Eventuality.

31. Time.

32. Tune.

33. Language.

II.—REFLECTIVE.

34. Comparison.

35. Causality.

61

strength from the fact that it could claim a greater scientific basis than the others. Spurzheim and his followers could always claim that phrenology sprang from the empirical researches of Gall and the anatomical work of Gall and Spurzheim. Phrenology gained its cachet precisely from its claims to be a science founded on fact, rather than just another speculative system. Spurzheim tidied up phrenology philosophically and moved it in a new direction, but it still thought itself a science.

George Combe and The Constitution of Man

According to George Combe (1788–1858), who had endured a stormy and doubt-filled youth, "phrenology conferred on me the first internal peace of mind that I experienced."[45] For Combe, phrenology functioned as a substitute religion, a scientific world view to replace the traditional Christian one, which for him had lost its credibility. It was Combe's mission to popularize and institutionalize phrenology and to use it as a vehicle for social reform. He added nothing to it as a science or as a philosophy of the mind.

Initially a skeptic, Combe was converted to phrenology by Spurzheim himself, which constituted a sort of phrenological laying on of hands. Combe became the main defender of phrenology in Britain and also lectured on the subject in the United States, finishing a tour begun by Spurzheim some years earlier but interrupted by his death. He founded the most important phrenological society, that of Edinburgh, where the most important controversies over phrenology took place. Combe wrote several works on phrenology,[46] but his most important and popular work was *The Constitution of Man.*[47] It appeared in 1835 and sold two thousand copies in ten days; the cheaper "people's edition" sold seventeen thousand copies in 1836.[48] Harriet Martineau considered it as popular as the *Bible, Pilgrim's Progress,* and *Robinson Crusoe.*[49] Its full title is *The Constitution of Man Considered in Relation to External Objects,* which announces that here we will find a natural, not supernatural, treatment of human nature. Combe's object was to work out for the first time the relation between the laws of nature "and the constitution of Man; which must, nevertheless, be done, before our knowledge can be beneficially applied." "My purpose is practical," with "a view to the improvement of education and the regulation of individual and national conduct." Phrenology finds a place in Combe's system as the "clearest, most complete and best supported system of human nature," although the practical value of the *Constitution* does not "depend entirely on phrenology."[50]

In common with many pre-Darwinian writers who accepted a God-guided theory of evolution, Combe presented a naturalistic and evolutionary picture of the development of Earth from a "fluid mass" to its present state.[51] He left no doubt that evolution was progressive, claiming that through geological change "the physical world is gradually improved and prepared for man."[52] Indeed, the whole world is arranged in all its departments on the principle of gradual and progressive improvement," exhibiting "successive orders of living beings, rising higher and higher until man appeared."[53]

Man in this scheme of things was an animal with God-given "moral sentiments and reflecting faculties," which set him over and apart from the other animals.[54] The modern study of the functions of the brain was the first to provide man with scientific instead of speculative self-knowledge. This self-knowledge, when complete and accepted, would usher in a "new era" in which man assumed his proper "station as a rational creature."[55] While man might not be eternally saved by scientific knowledge of his world and of himself, nevertheless, "To enjoy this world, I humbly maintain, that man must discover and obey the natural laws."[56] Part of these laws, of course, were the laws of the mind and brain revealed by phrenology, as summarized by Spurzheim.[57]

After reviewing the laws of nature—physical, organic, and moral—Combe went on to argue that misery stemmed from ignorance and violation of these natural laws, while happiness sprang from their acceptance and use. He advised each reader how to cultivate one's body and mind and so improve oneself. Everyone ought to devote several hours each day to physical exercise and improvement, to "sedulous employment of the knowing and reflecting faculties," and to the "cultivation and gratification of our moral and religious sentiments."[58] God had given us our thirty-five faculties, and happiness consisted in the development of each faculty as fully as possible.

Combe took phrenology another step away from the functional brain physiology of Gall. Spurzheim transformed Gall's physiology into a systematic philosophy of the mind. Combe took both the philosophy and physiology for granted and set out to reform individuals and society. Gall's approach was empirical; Spurzheim's was philosophical; Combe's was practical. Elsewhere Combe said that phrenological societies ought not preoccupy themselves with reading heads, for the constant replication of Gall's and Spurzheim's findings was "uninteresting."[59] Rather, "every Phrenological Society, to be permanently successful, must engage in practical objects,"[60] becoming agents of "physiological, moral and intellectual reform."[61]

To Gall's physiology Spurzheim wedded philosophy and Combe wedded reform. It only remained for Americans to wed this *ménage à trois* to business.

The Phrenological Fowlers and the Business of Phrenology

In 1836 Combe's periodical, the Edinburgh *Phrenological Journal,* denounced "Phrenological Quacks." "The most prevailing evil . . . is the practice of examining heads; not of well-chosen cases, where examination may be of use to the science, but indiscriminately." Worse, "there are individuals who make it their business to . . . receive pay . . . at so much per head! . . .It turns a dignified science into . . . *legerdemain.*"[62]

The most enterprising and successful of the phrenological "quacks" or conjurors were the American brothers Orson Squire Fowler (1809–87) and Lorenzo Niles Fowler (1811–96), as well as assorted relatives and associates. Their sound business principles kept phrenology going in America long after it was dead in Britain. Their *American Phrenological Journal* endured boom and bust, war and peace, from 1838 to 1911, all the while adapting itself to the demands of the American public. Far from an evil, head reading was "practical phrenology" to the Fowlers, and Orson Squire Fowler defended it as "the Alpha and the Omega of the entire science," its "only bulwark and anchor," quite unlike "theoretical phrenology," which "like speculative metaphysics is valueless." Like Houdini, the famous magician, the Fowlers conducted blindfolded tests of their skills, and, like Houdini, they boasted that "we never fail."[63] Combe pointedly avoided the Fowlers on his trip to America.

For Combe, phrenology was a systematic philosophy of conceivable practical application. For the Fowlers, phrenology was its application. The Edinburgh phrenologists continued with Gall to read only exceptional heads, but the Fowlers read any heads "in all their various degrees of development," and they did a thriving business advising employers about employees, fiancés about fiancées, and everyone about himself.[64]

The Fowlers wrote endlessly about phrenology and its applications, especially to sexuality and marriage,[65] child care,[66] and self-improvement.[67] In their earliest works they stayed close to the system of Spurzheim and Combe,[68] but they gradually added such faculties as Human Nature (ability to detect sound or poor character in others), Agreeableness, Conjugality (mating for life), Spirituality (believing in the unseen), and Bibativeness (propensity to drink).[69] Despite these small additions, they contributed nothing substantive to phrenology; rather, they made it American.

"To Americanize whatever in science and the arts, is capable of improving or adorning the mind, or of otherwise benefitting mankind, is no less the duty, than it would prove the glory, of every American citizen."[70] The Fowlers responded to the "one predominant characteristic of our age and nation, namely a desire for FACTS," by aiming "to render phrenology highly *practical,* and adapted to the *million,*" whom they addressed "in a plain, clear, direct, condensed, and common style," recognizing Americans "to be thoroughly practical. They do not require deep, profound, labored, learned, or lengthy essays. . . ."[71] They saw that in America phrenology would have to respond to America's evangelical religion. In the first number of their journal, the Fowlers announced that the feature of phrenology to which they attached "the highest importance" was "its religious character." "We say our journal shall be 'evangelical'; it shall be in harmony with divine revelation."[72]

Nevertheless, they followed Combe in presenting a naturalistic view of man-in-nature. Like him, they traced the evolution of the earth from a semifluid state "progressing upward, link by link" to "the monkey race—that connecting link between man and brute." They proclaimed, "Behold the grand system of *progression,* as characterizing all nature! Behold man, the last, the greatest work of God!"[73] Like Combe's, their naturalism was optimistic as well as progressive. Nature supplied man "his every *constitutional* demand," protecting him, for example, against the "appalling" consequences of overpopulation, since "man was *made* to multiply."[74] Phrenology they held to be divine: "the highest evidence . . . that Phrenology is true, is this: Whatever is true bears indisputable evidence of its divine origin. . . ."[75]

But above all, the Fowlers agreed with Combe that "society *must* be reformed, and this science, under God, is destined to become the pioneer in this great and good work."[76] Phrenology "unfolds the *original* condition of man. That condition was . . . as perfect even as its divine author could render it. And in pointing out the original constitution of humanity, Phrenology shows who departs therefrom, and wherein. . . . It teaches one and all . . . how far they conform to, and depart from, this perfect human type, and thereby becomes the great reformer.'' Phrenology ''settles all questions in morals, in ethics . . . in every phase and aspect of life, down to the minutest details and requisitions, thereby becoming the great lawgiver of humanity.''[77] Phrenology here is truly ''evangelical,'' replacing Christianity with God-given science in the search for perfect living. And, like evangelical Christianity, reforming phrenologists wanted to connect each individual to truth rather than tamper with the larger institutions of society.

John Shertzer Hittell and Open Phrenology

In his *Biographical History of Philosophy,* George Henry Lewes reproached phrenologists for having abandoned the physiological program of Gall for mere skull reading,[78] a shift that we saw begin with Spurzheim, intensify with Combe, and find its fullest expression in the work of the Fowlers. Undoubtedly, one reason for this change was that phrenology, just as its opponents claimed, did indeed tend toward atheism, materialism, and determinism. Most phrenologists, however, found these beliefs as appalling as did their critics. They strove mightily, therefore, to meet these charges, inevitably neglecting the physiology of the brain as a result. But there was one remarkable phrenological writer who not only accepted these tendencies but gloried in them, and who therefore tried to incorporate the findings of physiologists into his phrenology.

John Shertzer Hittell (1825-1901) remains an obscure figure, little known even among the brigade of modern scholars studying phrenology. He is best known to historians as a local historian, journalist, and statistics collector in California. Judging from some of his books, such as *The Evidence against Christianity,* he must have been an aggressive freethinker. He wrote one work on phrenology, *A New System of Phrenology,* which shows a path not taken by phrenologists.[79]

Hittell was not really a phrenologist, for he neither read heads nor lectured on the subject.[80] He was, however, familiar with the works of Gall and Spurzheim, which he found to be ''in the main correct,'' but ''very defective in some points.''[81] He had a low opinion of the Fowlers, considering their work to be ''beneath comment.''[82]

Hittell's attitude was even more naturalistic than the Fowlers' or Combe's. In his presentation of evolution, which was progressive like Combe's, he made no mention of a creator, referring everything instead merely to nature. He rejected any appeal to vital forces in living creatures and treated the body as a collection of factories interlinked by the brain and the nervous system: the liver was an acid factory; the eye a daguerrotyping establishment; the brain a galvanic battery; and the nerves telegraph lines.[83] People had "minds differing in power, but not substantially in kind,"[84] from the animals'. The relation was so close, Hittell believed, that fruitful human-animal matings had occurred![85] Contrary to Combe, Hittell argued that man's general superiority to the animals does not derive primarily from reason but rather by such peripheral gifts as the hand, erect posture, and a tongue and thorax adapted for speech, attributes which made possible man's unique possession, educability. He considered the human infant to be less intelligent than an ape, the difference between the adults of the two species coming from education.[86]

Hittell listed ten "General principles of phrenology," most of which are familiar from Gall and Spurzheim. Hittell, however, presented them in a way that indicates his own materialism and incipient behaviorism. He believed that

1. the brain is the organ of the mind;

2. mind is a function of brain—"organs are material, functions are immaterial"—and there is no soul;

3. the mind is composed of separate faculties, "all of which are active in nature and impel the animal to action";

4. each faculty has its own brain organ;

5. the larger the organ, the more powerful the faculty;

6. every thought or sensation is accompanied by a physical change in the brain";

7. Gall's localizations are mostly correct;

8. character may be inferred from the shape of the skull;

9. There is no faculty of Memory, for each organ remembers its own impressions;

10. There is no organ of Will, for Will is "only a vicissitude of the supremacy of the different faculties."[87]

In his system of faculties and organs, Hittell was original. Alone among Gall's successors, he cut back the number of organs, from Gall's twenty-seven or Spurzheim's and Combe's thirty-five, to only twenty-two. He also returned to Gall's original notion of naming each organ after some action, or function, rather than after a mental power. He rejected Spurzheim's terms as linguistically barbarous, and, more important, because they conveyed at best an improper idea of the organ's function. "The proper name for each organ would be an English word made by prefixing the main characteristic of the faculty to the world 'impulse.' "[88] For example, Amativeness, if it existed, should be called the lust-impulse. Hittell provided such new names for most of the faculties.

Hittell's willingness to revise phrenology can be seen in his treatment of Amativeness, or the lust-impulse. Gall and Spurzheim had located it in the cerebellum, but physiological experiments quickly showed the cerebellum to be responsible for equilibrium and the coordination of action. Most phrenologists responded by sticking with Spurzheim and the "facts" of head reading. Hittell, however, simply threw Amativeness out of the cerebellum, and put a new faculty in its place, the "motor-impulse," the "combination of the actions of the muscles in harmonious motion," as well as balance and equilibrium.[89] That the lust-impulse exists is undeniable, but Hittell treated it as generalized, unlocated sensuality.[90]

Other faculties were treated in an interesting and unique manner. Destructiveness became the "discontent-impulse," which was the great civilizer, for it created wants and hence human enterprises.[91] Veneration, to which Hittell gave no new name, no longer was used to establish any particular kind of religious belief. Hittell considered it only an impulse to "piety" and "reverence of a sacred principle of whatever sect."[92] Sociobiologists have recently come to very similar conclusions (see chapter 4).

Hittell rejected Adhesiveness or Friendship because people live in society for mutual advantage.[93] As a radical socialist, he found Acquisitiveness unacceptable. The "hoard-impulse" resulted simply from material gratification and Cautiousness, while theft was just weak Conscientiousness.[94] Color was rejected, for it was invented to account for color blindness, which might be better explained by a defect in the optic nerves.[95] As for the belief of Combe and the Fowlers that one could exercise "an organ and hope to see it grow—that is fudge."[96]

Hittell thus agreed with Gall that character is fixed and innate, beyond our control. Neither can we control our environment or circumstances, and therefore our actions are determined. Moral responsibility is a meaningless notion: "Man is the slave of motives"; "the purpose of all action is self-gratification." A person is only a "blind link in an endless chain" of cause and effect.[97]

Unlike his contemporaries, Hittell was willing to draw out and set down the implications of materialism and determinism present in phrenology from the beginning.

Finally, unlike his contemporaries, Hittell did not regard phrenology as a complete and finished system, for he devoted a whole chapter to "Problems not solved by phrenology," including the lack of anatomical divisions between the cerebral organs, the mysterious source of nervous electricity, the problem of how thoughts are remembered, and the mystery of split personality.[98]

Hittell's new system shows us a phrenology that on the one hand returned to Gall's vision of a physiologically based theory of brain functions and on the other hand was flexible enough to admit new data and new conceptions. His work could have made phrenology the basis of the sensorimotor conception of brain localization that was only a few decades away. Hittell emphasized that action was the final outcome of the organs, and he considered the organs to be sources of impulses, the most basic being the motor-impulse. These views are quite consonant with later theories that consider the brain to be a collection of sites where sensory input links to motor output. It also takes phrenology away from Spurzheim's dated philosophical conception of mental "powers." But as far as we can tell, Hittell's new system had no effect on anyone. It truly represents the path not taken by Gall's successors, the path of the physiology of the brain.

CRITICAL RESPONSES TO PHRENOLOGY

From the sales of Combe's *Constitution of Man* and the long success of the phrenological Fowlers, we can see that phrenology was widely popular. Yet it also attracted critical comment ranging from sober consideration and rejection to sarcasm and vituperative denunciation. The critical response came largely from the establishment, scientific and political, and a long war was waged between phrenologists and their critics. Phrenology ultimately lost this war and so became an occult double of established psychology.

The critics were many, but their criticisms fall into a few main categories. We will summarize the four most important critical articles and consider the attitude of the press, especially that most prestigious of newspapers, the *Times* of London. We will also summarize some of the lesser critics and then consider the phrenologists' responses.

The Big Four

The first major public critique of phrenology appeared anonymously in the *Edinburgh Review*[99] in 1803, only five years after Gall's letter to de Retzer. It was titled "Of Dr. Gall, and his skulls, who has not heard," and it set off a lively debate. After first assuring his readers that Gall's tendency towards materialism was nothing to fear, the reviewer considered the arguments for phrenology and then adduced several against it.

To begin with, "our experience is completely against the assertion" that the strength of mental powers depend on the size of the brain. There are fools with big heads, geniuses with small ones. Arguments from comparative anatomy prove nothing in this connection, for experiments have shown that different functions of the cerebellum exist in different species.[100] Gall had argued that the mind and brain are collections of faculties; his evidence was the refreshment gained in turning from one intellectual task to another. One organ was fatigued; the new one was not. The Edinburgh reviewer asserted that this phenomenon might be explained by the change of subject matter alone. The eye, for example, felt fatigue after staring at one color and was refreshed by a new one; the organ remained the same.[101] It was conceded to Gall that madness, disease, and injury of the brain partially affected mental functions, but it was pointed out that only rarely was one function completely lost while the others remained intact, which would support phrenology. Usually there was partial loss of one faculty—which supported no one and remained mysterious.[102] The indubitable existence of individual mental differences provided no special support for the existence of phrenological organs, the reviewer pointed out. The mathematician with no poetic taste, for example, could be said to have applied his mind to mathematics and not to poetry. Learning can explain such differences without a need to postulate innately differently powerful organs of Calculation and Language.[103] Similarly, dreaming need not mean that some phrenological organs are active while others are dormant. Dreams might result instead when the "unknown cause of sleep" differently affected the motor and sensory powers.[104]

Turning to positive arguments against phrenology, the reviewer argued that cases of brain damage and disease ''are sufficient to show, that there is not a single part of the encephalon, which has not been impaired, or destroyed, without any apparent change of the intellectual or moral faculties.''[105] There is thus no strong localization of mental powers, for if there were, damage to the same part of the brain should always have the same effect, which was not the case. Gall asserted that the organs were double, one in each cerebral hemisphere. But then a person could both believe something (with one organ) and disbelieve it (with the other organ), which was absurd and never happened.[106]

Furthermore, the reviewer argued, the correspondence between organ size and skull prominence was doubtful on two grounds. First, the skull only very generally paralleled the brain, while phrenology required great precision in locating twenty-seven organs. In any event, some organs must lie under others and therefore could not be reflected on the skull. Second, Gall failed to consider quality of brain matter. A coarse, low-quality brain might be large yet its mind remain weak, while a small, high-quality brain might boast a fine mind. Next Gall's argument of differential fatigue of the organs was cleverly turned back on him. Fatigue, the reviewer pointed out, did not diminish the size of the organ and must work by somehow affecting the quality of its operation. Therefore size alone could not be the measure of brain power. In the same connection, the reviewer objected to the theory of innate fixity of the organs, for it rendered moral education useless. Sensing phrenology's determinism, the reviewer said we would become helpless to prevent the corruption of an innocent young man should his harmful faculties be strong.[107]

The reviewer concluded with an excellent example of a paradigm clash. Spurzheim, Combe, the Fowlers (and even Hittell) had taught phrenology secure in the belief that once their students had mastered the system they would confirm the truth of phrenology for themselves. And, as they had followers for many years, many of whom testified to their conversion by facts, this belief was indeed confirmed. Yet the reviewer wrote: ''It is unfortunate for Gall's theory, that he has entered into the detail of it with minute exactness, as it enables every one too easily to compare its predictions with the skulls of those around him. . . . But how can Gall expect his disciples to be numerous, when they cannot put their hand to their head, without being upbraided, at every unlucky depression, for the want of some taste, or power, or virtue'' they had always thought they possessed.[108] The phrenologist expected to find, and did find, easy confirmation of phrenology; the skeptic expected to find, and did find, its falsification.

The second major attack on phrenology was delivered in an article in the 1818 supplement to the fourth, fifth, and sixth editions of the *Encyclopaedia Britannica* by the physician Peter Mark Roget, better known for his thesaurus.[109] Roget was no hasty or vituperative critic. He took phrenology seriously and directed the bulk of his article to a complete summary of the work of Gall and Spurzheim and to a survey of the phrenological lists of faculties. He even carefully refuted common but poor criticism; for example, he said that phrenology was no more conducive to materialism than any other physiology. He offered only carefully considered, though harsh, reproaches, intending to expose phrenology's "sandy foundations" and "flimsy" construction.[110]

He began by reiterating the argument that all the organs of the brain had been destroyed in different patients without "any apparent change in the sensitive, intellectual, or moral faculties."[111] Roget argued further that far too much of phrenology rested on analogy rather than on direct proof. Most important, the organs of the brain were held to be analogous to the liver, pancreas, kidneys, etc., with a one-to-one relation between organ and function. Yet analogy cut both ways. The stomach digested many foods; there were not separate stomachs for meat, fish, vegetables, and fluids. So why must there be special organs of Tune, Calculation, and so on, rather than one organ doing several things?[112] Roget asserted that anatomy would not serve phrenology's purpose. The anatomy of the brain was "so complex, and so void of apparent adaptation to any purpose we can understand, that it would suit any physiological system nearly equally well. Moreover, anatomy of brain and skull flatly ruled out any simple inference of organ size from shape of skull.[113]

Having shown how "hollow are the foundations of this theory," Roget moved on to the superstructure, "still more frail and unsound. The whole fabric rests upon the validity of a single proposition, which in itself is extremely questionable, namely that the size of an organ is . . . a criterion of the energy with which its function is performed." Should this assumption prove false, "the fantastical edifice" had no prop to arrest its fall. The only real argument in its favor was analogy again, to the size and strength of muscles. Yet, as the Edinburgh reviewer had pointed out, surely quality may play a more important role than size.[114]

Even if such a questionable assumption were true, the supposed "facts" of phrenology provided no reason to accept the assumption. Anticipating Kuhn, Roget pointed out how dispositions, motives and interests shaped experience "to very different results" depending on the "sagacity and good faith" of the observer. If you tend to accept a theory, you naturally see many confirmations and are blind to falsifications. "How willingly we repel the evidence that opposes, and how eagerly we catch at whatever corroborates our previous notions. . . ."[115] And he found "strong indications of bias" in the phrenologists. He poked fun at the "numerous stories, each more ridiculous than the preceding" of irresistible tendencies to murder, steal, wander, etc., and the "metaphysical labyrinth" of Spurzheim's mental philosophy."[116] He concluded his original article, in the 1818 *Britannica* supplement, with an attack on the "frivolous arguments" of the phrenologists and how they could squirm out of any contrary evidence. For example, a person with a large lobe of Destructiveness might be found meek and mild because education had made him so, or because other strong faculties overpowered the Destructiveness. "With such a convenient logic, and accommodating principles of philosophizing, it would be easy to prove anything. We suspect, however, that on that very account, they will be rejected as having proved nothing."[117]

Perhaps the most widely read attack on phrenology was *Phrenology Examined* by the eminent French physiologist, and bitter opponent of Gall, Pierre Flourens (1794–1867).[118] Generally, Flourens repeated most of Roget's arguments, but two things set off Flourens as a critic of phrenology. The first was that he was the greatest physiologist of his day and furthermore conducted experiments designed to refute Gall. He cut away (ablated) an animal's brain piece by piece and found that intellect gradually weakened as brain was cut away, but did remain until very little brain was left. "When one faculty disappears, all the faculties disappear. . . . The understanding is, therefore, a unit."[119] As a physiologist, however, he appreciated Gall's greatness as an anatomist, for Gall "recalled the true method of dissecting the brain."[120] And Gall's "by no means slender merit consists in his having understood" that the brain is the seat of understanding, and "in having devoted himself to its demonstration."[121]

The other unique feature of Flourens' criticism was his complete dedication to Cartesian philosophy, which has as its central conception the idea that mind is a unit. Flourens dedicated his book to Descartes and opposed Gall's bad philosophy to recall Descartes's sound one. The book abounds with sarcastic statements such as, "Descartes goes to die in Sweden, and Gall comes to reign in France."[122]

Flourens stated that "Gall's philosophy consists wholly in the substitution of multiplicity for unity," or, more flippantly, Gall "makes half souls." According to Descartes, "we are incapable of conceiving of half a soul."[123] Our consciousness," against which we can prove nothing,"[124] tells us our soul is a single point. Therefore, Gall must be wrong in his doctrine of plural faculties and organs. According to Flourens, Gall had vainly attempted to deny our feeling of *me*, Descartes's *cogito ergo sum*. Having eliminated the *me*, Gall had eliminated the soul, and thus fell into materialism.[125]

Just as Flourens was attached to Cartesian dualism, he was also attached to the free will of the soul. Gall, followed by most phrenologists, denied that Will was a free power. Rather, our actions are always determined by motives, among which the strongest prevails. Free will is then a result of contests between our inherent motives, not an independent power. Flourens found this offensive to the "facts of conscious sense." "Freewill is either a power, a force, or it is merely a result. Gall therefore abolishes the freewill."[126] Flourens could stand determinism no more than materialism.

Descartes proved the existence of God from his own existence as a thinking thing. Yet Gall, according to Flourens, reduced proof of God to the material operations of the organ of Veneration, which must have an object. But Gall had said that a person with poor Veneration will have "no God." To which Flourens responded, "What! If I happen not to possess a little peculiar organ . . . can I not feel that God exists! And how can I be an intelligence, knowing myself, and yet not knowing what God is? I do not more strongly feel that I am, than that God is."[127] Flourens could stand atheism no more than materialism or determinism.

All of this added up for Flourens to the undermining of morals. He quoted Diderot to the effect that denying liberty "overthrows all order and all government, confounds vice and virtue together, sanctions every monstrous infamy, extinguishes all shame and remorse, and degrades and deforms without recovery the whole human race."[128] He then accused the phrenologists of doing just that. The final Cartesian touch came when Flourens, the eminent scientist, approved of Descartes shutting himself up in a stove (unlit and quiet) to meditate on human nature, while Gall talked to people about their interests. "According to Gall, there is no necessity for one's shutting himself up in a stove."[129]

Since Flourens's experiments "proved"—falsely, we now know—that the understanding is a unity, we can see that the real basis of his rejection of phrenology was his Cartesianism, not the contradiction of scientific facts. Roget's skepticism about the "facts" of phrenology had its counterpart in Flourens's adherence to Cartesian philosophy. Gall and Flourens stood on opposite sides of a paradigmatic chasm.

The last extended criticism of phrenology was Alexander Bain's (1818–1903) *On the Study of Character*,[130] which appeared in 1861, well after the peak of interest in phrenology had passed in Britain. Bain had already published his masterpieces of associative psychology, *The Senses and the Intellect* and *The Emotions and the Will*. He was phrenology's most sympathetic and sober critic, admiring it for awakening an interest in the study of character, and lamenting the decline of that interest with the decline of interest in phrenology. Phrenology, he acknowledged, had "done good service" by showing that human beings are widely different in their mental tastes and attitudes" and by providing "the only System of Character hitherto elaborated."[131] Nevertheless, he found phrenology sadly deficient.

Bain was unique in the kinds of criticism he offered. Aside from arguing that quality of brain tissue may be as important as quantity, he repeated none of the other objections leveled by other writers. He treated phrenology essentially as a philosophy of character, and while he adduced problems with the phrenological localizations, these did not loom large. Instead, his criticisms sprang from introspection, the traditional method of both philosophical and scientific psychology, to each of which Bain contributed a great deal. He reviewed Spurzheim's criteria for establishing a faculty as primitive, but immediately substituted his own: "namely, our own consciousness of agreement or disagreement of character among our several feelings or mental states."[132] Bain used this introspective approach, within the framework of his own associationism, as the entire basis of his critique of phrenology.

Bain proceeded exhaustively through Spurzheim's faculties and showed that, in the light of introspection, most could be seen to be, not separate powers of mind, but the results of other mental activity. Self-Esteem, for example, was simply admiring in ourselves what we admire in others.[133] Comparison—the supposed ability to see similarities, make metaphors, draw analogies, and the like—Bain reduced to the association of ideas by similarity.[134] Bain also claimed that phrenology omitted important faculties evident to introspection. The phrenologists said nothing, for example, about Sympathy, "a great fact of human nature, and a point in which individuals differ widely." Similarly neglected were Love of Truth, Fine Art, and Memory. With the exception of sight, phrenology failed to recognize the role the senses played in shaping personality. Finally, phrenology wholly ignored the force of education and the environment, that is of learning, on the adult character, leaving phrenology at best "only a *part* of the science of character," the part concerning "original or innate tendencies."[135]

Since Bain then went on to offer his own science of character, it is clear, as he hinted in the preface, that he was using phrenology as a vehicle for reawakening interest in the study of personality. Its familiarity to the public made it perfect for his purposes. But by his time the heat had died away from phrenological controversies, so he could afford to be sympathetic. He was, however, eager to replace it with what he saw as the psychology of the future, associationism.

While the learned doctors of Edinburgh and Paris were offering their critiques of phrenology, the organs of literate middle class opinion, on both sides of the Atlantic, were offering mixed reviews of the new science.

The *Times* of London, otherwise a liberal and reform-minded paper, was uncompromisingly hostile, and it enjoyed poking fun at phrenological pretensions. The *Times* first noticed phrenology in January, 1824, commenting that it "is not likely to be long in fashion" and telling how a farmer sent some phrenologists a cast of a large turnip as a Polish professor's head and received "analyses" remarking on the "professor's" wisdom and intelligence.[136] The next month the *Times* ridiculed phrenologists as "bumpologists" practicing "mechanised quackery."[137] In March, the *Times* admitted that the doctrine would be useful if it were true but said "the whole practice is humbug." If fake, it was noted, practical application was dangerous—if, for instance, a bank fired an honest teller who had marked Secretiveness. The early systems of Gall and Spurzheim were admitted by the *Times* to be clear and open to disproof, but phrenologists in general were taxed with protecting their theory with "mystification after mystification" until it said no more than common sense and committed itself to nothing definite. The *Times* attributed character to education and circumstance rather than to innate propensities. The article concluded by calling phrenology a search for the philosopher's stone.[138]

The *Times* reviewed Spurzheim's lectures in 1825, and seemed amazed that "the doctor gave us to believe that the cerebral substance was to be considered as the seat of thought."[139] After that, the *Time*'s attacks were less frequent but more sarcastic. A poem derided the reading of bumps,[140] commenting that "there are gaping simpletons who swallow these crudities and call them science."[141] The last notice came in August, 1837; it told of a phrenologist who read the head of a man renowned for his piety, found Veneration to be small, and who concluded, "I have no faith in that fellow's religion."[142]

The *Foreign Quarterly Review* gave phrenology a more balanced hearing. Noting that phrenology had been best welcomed in Great Britain, "the freest of nations," and her colonies, the *Review* in 1828 gave a full treatment of the careers and discoveries of Gall and Spurzheim and reviewed the arguments for and against phrenology. On the whole, the critics got the worse of it and phrenology won through. Indeed, the anonymous author (R. Chevenix) later wrote a book on phrenology approved by Spurzheim. Toward the end of the article, Chevenix enlisted the aid of phrenology in the cause of British imperialism: "We will tell the men of every country their faults and their vices, their virtues and their talents and hold them up, as clearly as size and form [of skull] can be held up, to the notice of mankind. . . . The day will come when they [African, Indians, etc.] shall advance [only] by us. . . . We shall instruct the rulers how to govern, and subjects how to submit."[143]

George Henry Lewes, in *Blackwood's Magazine* for 1857, offered another careful analysis of phrenology. Writing about its reception in France, Lewes found it little noticed there because there was no French "thinking public." In England and America, philosophers and physiologists denounced phrenology, while the thinking public embraced it. Nevertheless, Lewes brought to public notice the work of Louis Peisse, who, of all the phrenological critics, met "the phrenologists on their own ground," by his own skull readings. There was, for example, the French idiot savant, Mangiamele, who had astounding calculational abilities but a cranial depression over Number. Lewes showed how the phrenologists tried to squirm out of this counter-instance by arguing that the boy "effected his calculations by other faculties." As Lewes pointed out, this argument destroyed the whole groundwork of phrenology because it implicitly abandoned localization of function. Lewes presented other such cases, the most notorious being Spurzheim's dismissal of Descartes as an overrated thinker! Nevertheless, Lewes did not reject phrenology as an "exploded error," although he considered it badly constructed.[144] In his history of philosophy (1866), Lewes admired Gall, whose name "will always live in the history of Science," but reiterated his criticism that phrenology fell into error and absurdity when it turned from cerebral physiology to head reading.[145] By 1879, however, Lewes's little text on psychology ignored phrenology altogether and ridiculed Comte's brain physiology, which had been based on Gall's.[146]

In America, opinion was also mixed, with most of it negative. One of the earliest notices of phrenology appeared in the *North American Review*, which in 1833 reviewed five phrenological works, three by Spurzheim himself. Although the *Review* cited a variety of criticisms, it is clear that phrenology's kinship to the radical enlightenment of the French Revolution is what really offended the *Review*. Phrenology "differs little" from the philosophy of Voltaire and the "skeptical school of the last century." Phrenology was incompatible with Christianity and was a dangerous doctrine, recalling the "furious mob" of the French Revolution. The core of the *Review*'s argument against phrenology was that it tended "to diminish the horror of guilt" and encouraged too much charity for the malefactor. It did the former by, for example, opposing incest not on moral grounds but because it led to degenerate offspring. It did the latter by dismissing, for example, infanticide as no "more [an] unnatural crime than any other murder because the natural love of offspring is very weak in some women.' " The popularity of phrenology was attributed to European gullibility. There, "in the dense and motley population of Europe . . . it matters little whether a man promises to discover character by the bumps on the head, or the lines on the hand, to fly over a church steeple, or get into a quart bottle; so long as he asserts his position manfully, he will always find believers." By implication, this would not happen in America;[147] the Fowlers proved otherwise.

In the same year, the *Knickerbocker* savaged Combe's *Constitution of Man*. The reviewer stated that Combe had elevated phrenology into a complete metaphysics and admitted that his reasoning, illustrations, and applications were "irresistible and conclusive." The problem, to this critic, was, rather, that the premises from which Combe worked were but "a creation of the fancy." Combe had simply taken the ideas of eighteenth-century English and Scots philosophers and adapted them to phrenology. The reviewer was eagerly awaiting "the master hand that would topple phrenology for good."[148]

The *Knickerbocker,* however, also carried articles favorable to phrenology. One such was a refutation of the attack in the *North American Review.* This *Knickerbocker* writer maintained that phrenology supported religion as an "innate and integral" part of human nature and accused the *Review* of being "antediluvian" and blind to the immense popularity of phrenology in America.[149]

The "Editor's Table" of *Harper's Magazine* echoed the *North American Review* in blaming "the increase of crime" on phrenology:

> Wrong habits of thought and wrong actions in the masses may ultimately be traced to a false philosophy in the few, [whose abstractions] infect healthy common sense. . . . Thus phrenology has infected language with its miserable cant, and socialism is evidently aiming to produce the same effect. . . . Its aim is wholly to unspiritualize . . . sin or crime—in other words to get crime out of the soul into something . . . external of our spiritual humanity. . . Phrenology begins the work, by getting all sin out of the soul properly into its next neighbor, the brain. [Sin loses its] intolerable hideous, [and crime should] be soothed . . . instead of being scared [with whips, imprisonment, and the gallows].[150]

One bad implication of phrenology was that society must now share the burden of human guilt, while conscience may be abandoned. Hence the increase in crime. Criminals may not read the works of phrenologists and socialists, but they soak up their spirit and blame society, not themselves, for their criminous state.

Harper's views are a pale and more reasonable version of an earlier depiction of phrenology as completely evil, espousing "gross and unmitigated atheism:"

> Infidelity personified could desire no more willing votary [than the phrenologist Amariah Bingham on whose soul] the evil genius of Phrenology, like a mighty incubus, sits enthroned.[151]

Phrenology did find enthusiasts in popular literature. Edgar Allen Poe was a convert,[152] and while editor of the *Southern Literary Messenger* he opened its pages to phrenology. In 1835 Poe wrote: "Phrenology is no longer to be laughed at. It is no longer laughed at by men of common understanding. It has assumed the majesty of a science and as a science ranks among the most important.'' In 1839 the *Southern Literary Messenger* ran seven articles reprinting Combe's American lectures on phrenology.[153] Elsewhere, in a rather different vein, an anonymous writer used phrenology as a basis for establishing the rights of man and the proper shape of government.[154]

The critical responses to phrenology may be gathered together under five main heads.

1. The rarest were those who used phrenological evidence to disprove the science. The only clear case was Peisse of France, as described by Lewes.

2. There were those, most notably Roget and Flourens, who argued from physiological evidence that Gall's idea of brain function was misconceived.

3. Almost all critics commented on the tendency of phrenologists to explain or otherwise wriggle around contrary data rather than modify their beliefs. Although philosophy of science was not yet a formal discipline, such criticisms resemble Popper's reproaches of psychoanalysis.

4. Rival philosophical systems sometimes served as the basis for criticism, as when Bain used associationism to furnish an alternative explanation of mental phenomena, or when Flourens asserted the validity of Cartesian philosophy over phrenology. Both Flourens and Bain also appealed to introspection as a method superior to head reading.

5. Finally, many critics, especially in the popular journals, found phrenology morally repugnant in its tendencies toward atheism, materialism, and determinism. These fears often seemed to motivate writers to offer the other lines of criticism and are perhaps the crux upon which acceptance or rejection of phrenology turned.[155]

Of course the phrenologists sought to refute the various criticisms directed at their science. But to attempt a point-by-point reconstruction of the phrenologists' replies would be to connive at criminal boredom. Some feeling of their answers can be achieved by considering one of the best-documented public exchanges between critic and phrenologists, and by sketching the general lines of phrenological response to the five categories of criticism.

Roget's antiphrenological article in the 1818 supplement to the *Encyclopaedia Britannica* drew a quick letter of protest from Combe, followed by published replies. We will consider the reply issued in the *Phrenological Journal* by Andrew Combe, George Combe's brother, who was a physician as well as a phrenologist.[156] Roget responded to the phrenologists in an appendix to the 1842 reprint of his original article.

Andrew Combe admitted that Roget's was widely regarded as "the most formidable attack phrenology ever had to sustain" and welcomed the "opportunity of undeceiving the public" about the supposed special virtue of physicians' opinions. Combe laid down the two findings that might truly refute phrenology—finding that a brain organ served a function other than the one claimed by phrenology, or finding that the phrenological function was inconsistent with anatomical structure. Roget failed to do this when he admitted that the brain's functions are "incomprehensible" and its known structure suited to any physiological system. Moreover, this argument removed any special authority Roget might have had to speak on the physiology of the brain.

Roget's supposedly "most important" objection was that clinical cases showed that every part of the brain had individually been destroyed without loss of function. Combe referred his readers to standard phrenological treatment of these cases. Fundamentally, the difficulty was that reports of such cases were prepared by surgeons who were ignorant of phrenology and had no interest in testing it. Their reports were extremely vague and did not refer to the retention or loss of specific functions but only to the patient's general mental state. Additionally, since the phrenological organs were double, damage to one would not altogether eliminate the corresponding function. Most important, perhaps, phrenologists pointed out that anyone who believed the brain to be the organ of the mind (i.e., doctors, physiologists) must find absurd the assertion that brain damage resulted in no behavioral change, whatever their views on phrenological organology.[157]

Combe then turned to Roget's animadversions on phrenology's use of analogical reasoning, alerting us to the "inconsistency into which a man unavoidably falls when writing on a subject with which he is unacquainted." Gall and Spurzheim did not reason from analogy alone, as is shown by their anatomical researches and by Gall's inductive examination of skulls and behavior. But Roget did not oppose any positive evidence to Gall's and Spurzheim's, for he found the brain functions "incomprehensible" and suited to any system. Roget's arguments, then, were founded, not upon data, but upon analogy and were consequently weaker than phrenology's. For example, Roget argued that the stomach digests a variety of foods but we do not postulate a separate organ for each food. By analogy, the brain too may perform various tasks as a single organ. Combe replied, "very true; but the function is the same in all, the subject only is different." Similarly, no phrenologists argue that different organs of the brain compose loud music, soft music, warlike music, etc.; all are produced by Tune.

Combe dismissed Roget's complaint that variations in skull thickness obscure supposed differences in brain-organ size by pointing out that phrenological organology was based on the study of extreme cases of brain development that exceeded the relatively slight irregularities to which Roget had alluded. Roget attempted to refute the principle that organ size indicated faculty strength by claiming that it was based on analogy and might be vitiated by differences in tissue quality. Combe claimed that Gall and Spurzheim discovered the size-strength ratio and reported it. Thus it was based, not on analogy, but on positive evidence. Combe also asserted that "physiologists and pathologists are agreed that while too small a brain is constantly attended by idiocy," a healthy, larger one "is uniformly accompanied with a greater degree of mental power, as the result of its greater size." Then, too, phrenologists had themselves long been aware that organ size did not always indicate faculty strength; qualitative differences might be overriding, as, for example, when a brain organ was enlarged by disease.

These were Roget's only objections to phrenology. Combe did accuse Roget of misrepresenting the doctines of phrenology, but he did not list these errors, for he felt they sprang from ignorance alone. Combe's general point was that Roget's objections were not directed against any fundamental phrenological doctrine, but only against difficulties of application of which phrenologists had long been aware.

The replies of the Combe brothers left Roget unmoved. He had *Britannica* simply reprint his original article in later editions, appending to it his answers to the Combes' objections.[158] In reply to Andrew Combe's charge that he was guiltier of arguing from analogy than were the phrenologists, Roget appeared to assert, in a vague passage, that his arguments from analogy were not designed to refute phrenology, but rather to show that all such arguments are "completely illusory," capable of supporting any position, and so not to be relied on.[159]

Roget cleared up his remark that the physiology of the brain was "incomprehensible" and suited to nearly any physiological system. What he found incomprehensible, he now said, was the connection of mind and body: "All the notions we can form of the nature of mental operations are so completely and essentially different from any of the affections of which we can conceive matter to be capable, that it is utterly impossible for us to understand'' how they are connected, ''or to imagine any physical structure whatsoever, which shall, in the remotest manner, correspond with the metaphysical constitution of the soul.'' Having said this, Roget asserted that phrenology offered the physiological system least consistent with brain anatomy, for its organs had no ''visible lines of demarcation'' between them.

Roget reasserted his claim that phrenologists persisted in paying attention to facts ''confirming of phrenology'' but ''shut their eyes to those which oppose it.'' He claimed that an ''enlarged inquiry'' would reveal at least as many contradictory as confirming facts and that his own skepticism about phrenology was based on such falsifying facts in his own experience. Roget referred to a collection of casts of heads of the insane made by the French asylum director Esquirol which was entirely inconsistent with phrenological localizations. Nevertheless, argued Roget, the phrenologists attempted to squirm around such contrary data. Roget quoted another article by Andrew Combe in which Combe attacked the competence of Esquirol to judge phrenological developments but failed to directly address the data. ''This happy talent'' of the phrenologists, ''of shaping their course either one way or the opposite'' as it suited them, enabled them ''at one time to proclaim, that the evidences of their science are palpable and demonstrative . . . [and] open to all inquirers,'' but at another time, confronted by contrary evidence, they accused the observer of being ''doubtless incompetent to the task he has attempted; and that his testimony, being of no value, ought to be wholly set aside.''

Roget followed up this argument with a lengthy example of how the phrenologists could always find a way out of an embarrassing situation if they only looked for it. For example, a person might have Combativeness large, yet be shy. A contradiction? No, the subject might have Cautiousness or Conscientiousness large, overriding his Combativeness. On the other hand, a person with small Combativeness might be pugnacious. Here we might appeal to Firmness (he sticks to decisions and fights for them), Destructiveness (he fights to destroy), Concentrativeness (he screws his courage to the sticking place), Imitation (of combative individuals), or Approbation (fighting to gain admiration). Surely one of these would be large enough to explain the recalcitrant instance. The phrenologist could always achieve ''the exact resultant which corresponds with the actual fact to be explained.''

Roget concluded by speculating on the causes of phrenology's popularity. "Numerous classes of persons find in it a source of agreeable occupation, giving exercise to their ingenuity in discovering striking coincidences, and gratifying their self-complacency by inspiring them with the fancy that they are penetrating far into the mystic regions of psychology." They had been swayed by "popular writers and lecturers without number" who expounded phrenology to "wondering and admiring audiences." Yet, "had it been a real science," phrenology, with its wide popularity, "could not have failed by this time, of being generally recognized as true." It had not, however, "gained the universal assent."

Despite some acid attacks by the Combes, which added nothing to the debate, this was Roget's last word on phrenology.[160]

The exchanges between Roget and the Combes may be taken as a fair specimen of many debates between phrenologists and their critics—the exchanges formed an inconclusive intellectual tennis match that each side thought it had won. Who really won is a most difficult question that we will not try to answer until the next chapter, following a brief survey of phrenological replies to various classes of criticism.

It is unfortunately true that phrenologists responded to such evidence as Peisse's with arguments much like Roget's example. Given a skull that was inconsistent with a person's behavior, phrenologists went to any length to explain away the discrepancies, and they had many avenues of escape open to them. The easiest and most obvious method, as Roget pointed out, was to appeal to the interaction of organs, playing one off against another until the desired behavior was explained. The final "out" was to accuse the subject of fakery, as in the case of the phrenologist who doubted the piety of a famously religious man with small Veneration. Gall himself was less guilty of this than his followers. He left areas of the brain unlocalized, writing, "I do not yet know the functions of all the cerebral parts."[161] Spurzheim filled in the gaps, thereby forcing phrenologists to explain away all evidence contrary to his complete philosophical system.

Besides being horrified at physiological experiments on living animals,[162] phrenologists were able justly to reply to experimental physiologists that they did not "understand the nature of phrenological inquiry" and that such experiments were "incapable of leading to scientific truth."[163] The ablation method was too crude to test phrenological localizations, since "the physiologists do not pretend that they can cut out particular organs from the brain without impairing the functions of other organs."[164] This method was also too crude to use as a discovery procedure for exploring the functions of the brain. George Combe asked his readers to imagine "an instrument capable of emitting an unknown number of sounds by means of an unknown mechanism."[165] This instrument would than be smashed [ablated] a few pieces at a time, and, assuming that it still worked at all, we listen for the sounds the machine does not produce! We cannot "discover unknown faculties, by destroying at random convolutions whose functions are unknown!" One must know all the behaviors of which the instrument (or an animal) is capable before cutting out parts of the machinery (or the brain) to see what does not happen.[166] Moreover, in the case of animals there was too little control over their behavior: We "cannot make the animal . . . manifest all [the] propensities, sentiments and intellectual powers" it might still possess after ablation. We cannot make it love its young, fight, conceal, fear, build, etc., so if we cut out a part of the brain we will find the animal not doing many things, and other animals will not do the same things, when other parts of their brains are removed. In short, this "method is fundamentally defective . . . when relied on for discovering the primitive faculties connected with particular parts of the brain."[167]

In dealing with the question of the disprovability of phrenological ideas, as argued by Roget, we must carefully distinguish between the hard core of the phrenological program and its protective belt. The hard core of Gall's program asserted only that the brain is the organ of the mind, that the organs are plural and correspond to mental faculties, and that the faculties and organs are fixed innately. Only a few arguments could be directed at this hard core. To some, the link between mind and matter was "inconceivable," but this is a very weak argument, easily refuted by appeal to the effects of alcohol, fatigue, and poisons on the mind. Others, such as Flourens, asserted the unity of mind and consequently of brain action. But the unity of consciousness is apparent only to Cartesian introspection; the theory breaks down when confronted by such abnormal phenomena as multiple personality, fugue states, or hypnosis. The unity of brain action was supported by experiments that we have seen to be poor, experiments that are not accepted today. To what extent the faculties are fixed at birth was debated not only by phrenologists and their critics, but within phrenology itself. In whatever form, it is an issue that is wholly unresolved today. The assumption of innate traits was, in any event, not inherently unreasonable.

We see, then, that as far as Gall's program was concerned, there was no good reason for absolutely rejecting any part of the hard core; and each assumption not only predicts certain correlations, but also excludes others, as Popperians would demand.

In the protective belt, we find Gall's "empirical proceeding" of correlating distinctive heads and outstanding behaviors, and the particular organology that resulted from it. Gall's program was vulnerable here— exactly where it should be, in the protective belt. As we have seen, Gall was open-minded about the ultimate nature of all the organs to be discovered. Had he had more followers devoted to physiology, the method and commitments to specific organs, could have been given up without abandoning the hard core, and phrenology could have progressed.

But Gall had no such followers save the isolated Hittell. Spurzheim shifted the doctrine of the skull to the hard core where Combe left it, being bored with phrenological research. Only the specific organology remained in the protective belt. Any progress with this restructured theory would have been difficult, for every refutation of the organ-locations, as offered by Peisse for instance, would inevitably have reflected badly on the doctrine of the skull. As matters went, no such reflections were allowed; counter-instances were explained away, and phrenology remained static. Such a static philosophy well served the general world view of the *Constitution of Man,* by providing an apparently scientific certainty to replace lost religious certainty. Or, as the Fowlers put it, phrenology rendered the study of mind "tangible, certain, absolute KNOWLEDGE. . . . We can, I mean, KNOW FOR CERTAIN— that our results embody NATURE's institutes and ordinances concerning mind."[168] Science, however, is not certain, and it is not complete. Spurzheim's "philosophical proceding" and his shift of the doctrine of the skull to the hard core made phrenology a science that could not progress. Combe and the Fowlers, using phrenology as a new world view and agent of reform, made it instead a social doctrine that would not progress.

Those who accused phrenologists of worming their way out of any difficulties were partially correct. As phrenology moved from science to reform movement, it lost the capacity to respond to new information and ideas.

Arguments against phrenology based on rival philosophical systems were necessarily weak, as they presupposed acceptance of that other system. Quoting Descartes against Gall, as Flourens did, proves nothing, no matter how much Flourens praised the former and ridiculed the latter. Arguments against the Cartesian unity of the soul could always be supported by reference to split personality, for example.[169] Bain's associationistic reanalysis of some phrenological concepts seems to have been published too late to draw a reply from phrenologists.

Certain among these philosophical considerations carry over into our most important class of phrenological criticism, moral objections to phrenology.

Phrenology was accused of supporting atheism, materialism, and determinism, which in their turn would undermine society and increase crime. In responding to these charges, phrenologists split into a large group of moderates and a smaller group of radicals.

The moderates, led by Gall, Spurzheim, Combe, and the Fowlers, denied that the charges were true or admitted them only partly. As to atheism, the moderates frequently referred to a Creator in their works, and they even argued that phrenology supports belief in God, for Veneration must have an object to venerate. The harmony of the faculties also supported the argument from design—an ordered universe implied the existence of an Orderer.[170] Against the charges of materialism they argued that the brain was simply the organ through which the soul manifested itself, as a violinist plays the violin. Phrenology did not need to argue that matter was the only reality. Against the charges of determinism, they maintained that free will was not the freedom to determine against all motives, as Flourens maintained, but was instead the freedom of "choosing" the strongest of conflicting motives. In their view, this did not undermine moral responsibility, for no faculty was inherently evil. Gall indeed had posited the faculties of Theft and Murder, and so he did remove the onus of moral guilt from thieves and murderers. But Spurzheim changed these faculties into Acquisitiveness and Destructiveness, maintaining that they were not inherently evil but were subject to abuse. Large Destructiveness could equally be found in a war hero or a murderer; the former morally channeled his destructive propensities via Conscientiousness and Benevolence, while the latter let his impulses run riot. The "guilty individual has no right thus to indulge the passion and thereby enlarge the organ . . . this indulgence is the clearest, the *strongest possible* proof of the subject's guilt."[171] You are not responsible for the organs you have, said the moderate phrenologists, but you are responsible for what you do with them.

All these replies were evasive and at best showed that a phrenologist need not embrace atheism, materialism, and determinism. These tendencies are indeed present in phrenology, however, and a few radicals, such as Hittell, embraced them. Hittell was not alone in his impatience with the shilly-shallying of his fellow phrenologists. The London branch of the movement, in its journal *The Zoist,* exclaimed sarcastically, "Cerebral Physiologists not necessitarians!" (i.e., determinists). Simply by calling themselves scientists, phrenologists assumed "that the thoughts, actions, and feelings of men, can be made a subject of scientific investigation," which presupposed that they "aver that there is a constant and unchanging series of effects resulting from recognized and specific causes. What more is required to prove that we are assisting to promulgate the doctrine of necessity?"[172]

On dualism, *The Zoist* said:

> Let us not imagine an unexpected phenomenon to be the result of a species of effervescence between an essence and cerebral matter—in the language of Mr. Combe: the result "of the compound existence of mind and body, which act constantly together"—let us not rush for relief to the doctrine of free-will . . . but let us recognize the existence of unascertained causes."[173]

Faith in Combe's "existing dogmas" led to a "parade of unintelligible theories" and to "the languid state of our science." Moderate phrenologists remained so committed to "a mysterious and non-describable constituent in man's nature" and to "the presumed freedom of man's thoughts and actions" that through apathy little progress has been made in cerebral physiology; indeed "cerebral analysis has yet to be commenced" beyond the broad cerebral geography accomplished by Gall.[174]

Nor were radical doctrines dangerous and antisocial, according to *The Zoist.* On the contrary, "When the cause of every thought and every action is sought for in man's cerebral organism . . . then will man be convinced that he has the power to promote and carry out changes in the civilization of his race." "Onward! is the cry of our race . . . and universal inculcation of the truths of Cerebral Physiology is one of the means to hasten" progress.[175] Increase in crime is not to be attributed to phrenologists but rather to the traditional beliefs in freedom and the soul, and to the corresponding punitive "remedy [which] has been tried and found wanting." Prisons and torture "appeal to man's weak fears, instead of his reason," but "Vengeance can destroy the being but never reform him; it can destroy the vitality of cerebral matter, but it will never prevent certain actions resulting from certain combinations." "Cast a glance around and about; behold the misery, the destitution, the crime; shudder at the pestilence of your own creating; for you have neglected the truths which science has freely developed to you."[176]

The radical phrenologists embraced the radical tendencies of Gall's science and were not afraid to proclaim them. Yet they, no less than the moderates, aimed to use phrenology as a means to moral uplift, to individual and social improvement. This aim leads to our next topic, the simultaneous popularity and denunciation of phrenology. Having examined the rational arguments both for and against phrenology, we will next look at the causal social context in which phrenology was born, grew up, and died.

Four

Phrenology:
Success and Failure

Phrenology failed as a science when Gall's followers took his cranios-copy and turned it first into a philosophy and then into a social reform movement. As a reform movement it had considerable appeal for Brit-ons and Americans in the first half of the nineteenth century. Ulti-mately, however, phrenology's scientific failure caught up with its pro-gressive offspring, and phrenology disappeared from the intellectual and social currents of the late Victorian age. In this chapter we will ana-lyze the social and intellectual reasons for phrenology's immense popu-larity and its inevitable decline.

THE APPEAL OF PHRENOLOGY

Combe's *Constitution of Man,* said English statesman and economist Richard Cobden, read "like a transcript of [my] own familiar thoughts." Phrenology was appealing because it could be made to har-monize with the major tendencies of nineteenth-century ideology. This harmony made it difficult for those who shared many of its intellectual components to completely reject it, even if they were not fully con-vinced of its truth or utility. Unitarian leader William Ellery Channing, for example, saw Combe's book as "excellent in spite of its phrenol-ogy."[1] Similarly, Phrenology could be easily added to the intellectual baggage of many people who had not thought much about it. It fit the nineteenth-century world view comfortably. As R. J. Cooter has put it,

91

"the quintessence of phrenology's appeal was . . . in its ability to shelter and legitimize existing beliefs in a scientific mold."[2]

Figure 4.1 sketches the major appeals of phrenology and the interconnections among them. The currents of nineteenth-century thought that are shown could readily assimilate phrenology, and its popularity was assured as a result. This figure stands against a backdrop that says IMPROVE. The central feature of early Victorian society was change and improvement—improvement in self, society, and nature: "Onward! is the cry of our race. Progressive improvement and happiness should be the sum total of our aspirations."[3]

Thus the central idea of figure 4.1 is reform, and the period of phrenology's widest popularity was also the richest in movements for political and social reform in British and American history.[4] From the time of Gall on, phrenologists were actively involved in a variety of reform movements and also inspired other reformers through their writing and lecturing. Phrenologists were active in penal reform, educational reform, and psychiatric reform, as well as in many other liberal movements. As Orson Fowler wrote, "Society *must* be reformed, and this science, under God, is destined to become the pioneer in this great and good work." In Britain, after his cry of "Onward," "L.E.G.E.," writing in *The Zoist,* continued, "and the universal inculcation of the truths of Cerebral Physiology is one of the means to hasten" progress.[5]

But there have always been two approaches to the reformation of society—reforming the individual and reforming the social institutions. The traditional Christian, and especially Puritan, way has been to seek the salvation of individuals, who will then create a necessarily reformed community of saints. Structural changes in society are seen as futile, working as they must on unregenerate humanity. Phrenology stands squarely in this camp. If character is determined by a complex set of biologically determined faculties, then reform will best be accomplished by changing these faculties themselves. Thus individuals, through study, exercise, and efforts of will, can first determine and then improve their characters. Such a practical outcome was the goal of all the Fowlers' writings. They exhorted their readers to know themselves through knowing their skulls, and then to follow exercises to strengthen or weaken their various faculties.[6] The human race was to be improved by a sort of phrenological eugenics. In both America and England, readers of phrenological literature were urged to use phrenology in the choice of mates, which would ensure sound offspring and the gradual improvement of humanity.[7]

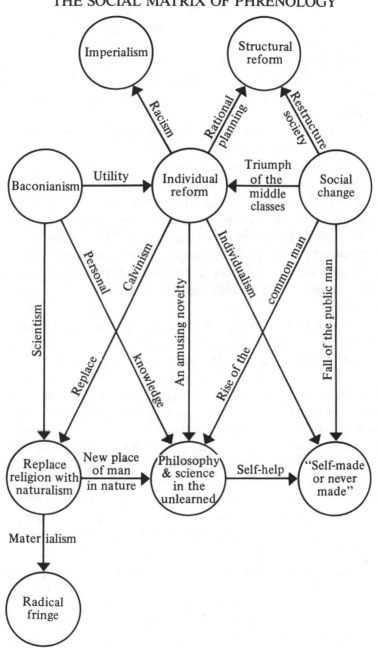

Fig. 4.1
THE SOCIAL MATRIX OF PHRENOLOGY

93

Phrenology's place as a neo-Puritan cult was noticed in 1852 by the *Westminster Review,* which lumped it with vegetarianism, homeopathy, teetotalism, and related movements, all embraced by the Fowlers: our age "is pre-eminently the age of physiological reformers. A new sort of Puritanism has arisen . . . the Puritanism of the body," the common purpose of which "is the healing, cleansing, and restoration of the animal man." As "L.E.G.E." had proclaimed, phrenology "is to regenerate humanity."[8]

The other approach to reform, which tries to reshape society's structure so as to reform individuals, was also active in the nineteenth century. Indeed, the structural reformers are today better known than the moral reformers and were ultimately the more successful. Examples are the political reformers—Charitists, unionists, factory reformers, Owenite socialists, etc. Structural reformers such as Robert Owen (1771–1858) generally assumed that human character is shaped by the environment, by society, Their way to improve individuals therefore is to improve society, not the other way around. Owen and his followers therefore founded Utopian socialist communities that would rework human nature.

While the phrenologists were generally apolitical, relations between Owenites and phrenologists were often close. George Combe's brother, Abram, founded a large and unsuccessful Owenite community. While phrenology and Owenism are linked by their belief that rational scientifically based reform is possible, George Combe was less impressed than Abram by Owen's New Lanarck and his environmentalist philosophy. George Combe believed that Owen's theories neglected innate human nature, especially its evil side, and that no community could be built on such a naive basis.[9] Later as the Owenite communities failed and the movement faded, some Owenites hoped to save Owenism by an infusion of phrenology and its recognition of stubborn human nature.[10]

In other ways, too, phrenology was at odds with some aspects of liberal political reform. Since they believed human character traits and intelligence to be innate, phrenologists tended to find ineradicable native differences between the races and the sexes. In so doing, they supported traditional racist and sexist views that the liberal structural reformers often struggled against. In his appendix to Samuel Morton's *Crania Americana,* George Combe denied that the human mind is everywhere and at all times the same and shaped into different molds by the environment, as reformers such as Owen maintained. Instead, only among Europeans did Combe find "a strong tendency towards moral and intellectual improvement," while "the people of Asia early arrived at a point comparatively low in the scale of improvement, beyond which they have never passed," and the African races "exhibit one unbroken scene of moral and intellectual desolation." He considered American Indians to be even more hopeless since despite being surrounded by "European knowledge, enterprise and energy" since 1620, they remained "miserable, wandering, houseless and lawless savages . . . destined to flee at the approach of civilized man . . . and disappear forever."[11] All this followed from the principles of phrenology and the evidence of native skulls such as those collected by Morton. "Permanent subjection" was the fate of "an inferior aggregate development of brain."[12]

Just as the heads of savages confirmed their savagery, so the heads of women confirmed their place as "the lesser Man."[13] Phrenologists maintained that there was "less vigor in the female intellect."[14] Lorenzo Fowler spelled out the differences between the sexes in detail. Males were noted for "Amativeness, Combativeness, Destructiveness, Self-Esteem, Firmness, Acquisitiveness, Constructiveness, Causality and Comparison," while females possessed "Benevolence, Veneration, Approbativeness, Conscientiousness, Adhesiveness, Secretiveness, Ideality, Individuality and Philoprogenitiveness."[15] Woman's place was thus in the home, where she shaped society through her children.[16] Political movements toward female equality were at odds with such opinions, although the Fowlers did support female suffrage.

The impulses that moved the phrenologists and the reform movements in which they took part were those that aimed at the regeneration of the individual, the fitting of the individual into his or her proper place in society, and the improvement of society through the improvement of its children. Phrenology's reforms, aiming as they did at the individual, presented no very deep threat to the established order, except insofar as some of the movement's partisans espoused materialism. As schemes for reform were widespread, it harmonized with the tenor of the age and found favor with others working for reform through physiology. But since phrenology was unconcerned with political reform and serious structural change, it ignored the lasting movements of the nineteenth century and faded as they reshaped the intellectual climate of Victorian Europe and America.

The change or reform of society was made necessary by the Industrial Revolution, effects and tensions of which were becoming clear in the early nineteenth century. The period saw the triumph of the middle classes, as they imposed their Calvinistic values on both the workers and the aristocracy. The aristocrats had to be convinced of the virtues of the middle class so that they would assimilate the newly prosperous into the ruling circles of government and society. The workers had to be persuaded to practice the regular work habits, diligence, and self-discipline necessary to the new industrial order, and to expect the rewards of ''that 'good time coming' which was just around the corner.''[17]

Phrenology was well suited to spread middle class values to all strata of society through the ''whip of the word.''[18] Lectures reached workingmen's associations, among whom phrenology was extraordinarily popular, and publications addressed the more affluent strata of society. Home, family, and marriage were the central bourgeois values, and phrenologists in both America and England applied their science to support these ideals among all classes. Thus, an address to a workers' institute by Alexander Smart, ''On the application of phrenology in the formation of marriages,'' also reached the readers of the *Edinburgh Phrenological Journal.*

The ideal of marriage preached by Smart was bourgeois: while ''the impulse to the connubial union'' is Amativeness, or the sexual feeling,'' which in itself ''leads to libertinism and conjugal infidelity,'' when ''under the guidance of the moral and reflective faculties, it excites to mutual kindness, and the exercise of all the milder amenities between the sexes.'' Indeed, the higher faculties are needed to control all the domestic affections—Amativeness, Love of Offspring, and Adhesiveness—''for their gratification is pregnant with evil.'' One must therefore choose one's partner carefully, not being carried away by blind emotion, or ''bitter days of repentance must follow.'' Correct choice is ''guided by intellect to an object pleasing to itself and the moral faculties . . . doubling the delights afforded by the domestic affections, and rendering the enjoyment lasting.''[19]

Smart first amuses his audience with the courtship practices of ''the natives of New Holland,'' where the male clubs unconscious the female of his choice and drags her off ''to some secret spot,'' insensitive to her injuries. Smart then turns to ''the nobility of our own country,'' who do not fare much better in his view, their courtship being ''nearly as much an affair of the animal faculties as is the marriage of the New Hollanders.'' The nobility sell their daughters through arranged marriages, completely ignoring the desires of the women. ''And what is the result?

Mutual loathing and disgust quickly ensue—libertinism becomes the pastime of the peer; too often the infidelity of his consort ensues; and the progeny of this unhappy marriage inherit the powerful animal, and weak moral and reflecting faculties of the parents.''[20] Smart sadly admits that marriage based on property has become the frequent vice of the middle classes, too.

The vice of the working people, or "the operative classes," is the reverse of the nobility's vice: "A mere boy and girl, under the blind impulse of the sexual feeling alone, *rush* into marriage, destitute alike of the means necessary to enable them to sit down with comfort in their own house, of the judgment to retrieve a past error . . . and of the physical strengths which might enable them to emerge from poverty." The ensuing marriage will suffer from "quarrels . . . feelings of remorse . . . consciousness of inferiority . . . immorality of the offspring . . . excessive labor, and irregular habits." Marriages "contracted for the direct gratification of the domestic faculties, without reference to the moral and intellectual powers, prove . . . pregnant with evil to both parties."[21]

In contrast to the unhappy marriages contracted by the traditional habits of the different classes, Smart goes on to extol happy marriage based on the new scientific principles of phrenology, for "man, as an organized being, is subject to organic law"—law we should understand and apply to marriage. He tells his hearers to examine the temperaments and phrenological developments of themselves and their potential mates, choosing as spouses those who complement one's own development. Thought should also be given to the qualities desirable in one's offspring. The animal breeder is careful in "the rearing of his stock," for it is acknowledged that animals are subject to organic laws; so are men and "if they desire to improve their own race, they have only to obey them."[22]

But the bulk of Smart's advice was bourgeois platitudes unrelated to phrenology. To women: Acquire "orderly, cleanly, and industrious habits"; be "habitually agreeable"; "act with great caution"; do not be fooled by "the honeyed accents of a lover" until you prove his moral and intellectual worth, and if he fails to measure up, "shun him as you would a pestilence." To men: Know "the physical and moral sciences, to fit you for . . . the duties of active life"; "know yourself" (through phrenology); know and obey the "laws of the Creator," for only through them will you succeed; do not despise your inferiors, but "improve those who are behind you''; cultivate your own judgment of scientific truth. Then, the "joyful husband" will find "by delightful experience" that:

> It is to lovely woman given
> To sooth our griefs, our woes allay,
> To heal the heart by misery riven,
> Change earth into an embryo heaven,
> And drive life's fiercest cares away.[23]

Through phrenology one aspires to reach the very pinnacle of Victorian domestic happiness.

Thus, phrenology, especially as adapted by Spurzheim and sold by Combe and the Fowlers, was a perfect tool by which the middle class could domesticate its social, moral, and economic inferiors. But phrenology appealed to the reformers not only because its content could be harmonized with middle class morality, but also because it presented itself as a useful science in the Baconian mold—inductive, hardheaded, commonsensical, and free of fantastical metaphysics. It offered itself as a scientific tool of reform and was so used.

Since the triumph of Newtonian physics, the kind of Baconian science Newton preached had become the norm for all sciences, especially in Britain and America. According to English philosopher Francis Bacon, science should avoid theories and hypotheses, sticking instead to the facts. Facts should be collected in large number, from which cautious generalizations—ever subject to the challenge of new facts—should be drawn. Finally, science could not be justified unless it was socially useful through technological innovation or moral improvement. Although even Newton did not actually practice what Bacon had preached,[24] Baconianism became science's fetish.

That phrenology, at least in the hands of its British and American adherents, molded itself in the image of Baconian science has been noted by almost every modern writer on the subject.[25] The inductive scientific ideal was loudly proclaimed by the phrenologists themselves. Richard Chevenix observed that, according to the phrenologists, Gall "adhered to his mode of amassing knowledge as closely as if Lord Bacon had rocked him in his cradle," and added that we must "commend the Baconian spirit with which [phrenological] researches are conducted." In America, Orson Squire Fowler said phrenology was "truly Baconian" and that "theoretical phrenology like speculative metaphysics, is useless'' without practical demonstration. Phrenology thus fit into the "one predominant characteristic of our age and nation, namely a desire for FACTS.'' As to application, "phrenology is pre-eminently a *moral* and *philanthropic* science,''[26] and, as we have mentioned, phrenology was applied to a wide range of moral and social problems.[27]

The nineteenth-century successor to Baconianism was Auguste Comte's positivism, and we find that Comte himself believed phrenology to be the only acceptable psychology, for it reduced the illusory metaphysics of mentalistic psychology, with its unobservable entities such as memory and imagination, to observable brain organs and their manifestations on the skull. Although he found phrenological science to be imperfect, Comte argued that "all the signs of the progressive success of a happy philosophical revolution are present in this case,'' and that the "illustrious Gall'' has "exposed the powerlessness of metaphysical methods'' in psychology.[28] Positivism was a very influential movement, attracting many of the leading progressive thinkers of the day, including G. H. Lewes and Harriet Martineau. Although they could be critical of phrenology, these thinkers still acknowledged its appeal and the soundness of its antimetaphysics.

A major influence on the nineteenth century was the final collapse of the traditional Christian-medieval world view, which had been undermined by the scientific revolution. The Christian world view had begun to totter and disintegrate during the Enlightenment, and it finally crashed during the Industrial Revolution. Its passing left a spiritual and intellectual vacuum still felt today. To fill this vacuum arose both religious and secular movements. The first half of the nineteenth century was marked by individualistic revival movements and widespread religious change in both England and America, which produced prophets whose movements were as short-lived as Joanna Southcott's or as durable as Joseph Smith's Mormonism.[29] Other movements, such as Owenism, were secular, although they frequently had ties to the evangelical sects.[30]

Phrenology too was a secular movement of an evangelical cast. It was at bottom the study of brain function, but nevertheless, the *American Phrenological Journal* proclaimed its own "religious character'' and promised to be "evangelical'' and in harmony with divine revelation.''[31] In its emphasis on saving the individual first and society second, phrenology was compatible with the evangelical movements of its day.

What gave phrenology its special character was its appeal to the growing scientism of the nineteenth century.[32] The rule of reason over religious superstition had been the message of the Enlightenment, and the achievement of Newtonian physicists and Baconian technologists was more concrete than the other worldly promises of the Church. All the universe was to be understood in natural scientific terms; the resulting technology would improve the human lot. The study of human nature could not be excluded from this process of naturalizing the supernatural, and the resulting psychology was expected to improve the condition of men and women.

Phrenology, of course, pretended to be just that new psychology: "The true SCIENCE OF MIND is as dubious as ever. . . . But the true star of MENTAL SCIENCE has at length dawned upon man. That star points out the immutable relations of *mind to organization.*" Phrenology rendered the study of mind *"tangible, certain, absolute,* KNOWLEDGE," like mathematics and astronomy. "Behold, then, the true SCIENCE OF MIND! Behold the study of this godlike department of our nature reduced to DEMONSTRABLE CERTAINTY!"[33] So effused the *American Phrenological Journal* in 1846. The followers of Gall hitched their star to science, and they based their appeal on the claim of science to replace old doubt with new truth.

Thus science was moving to fill the vacuum left by the erosion of the old religious view, and phrenology was one of its most popular vehicles. The message of the phrenologists was Enlightenment naturalism. Newton had showed that the physical universe could be understood naturally, without regard to supernatural influences, as subject to a few physical laws of motion. Many philosophers of the eighteenth century were self-styled "Newtons of the mind," who strove to show that mankind too was subject to scientifically knowable, organic and mental laws. Phrenology was the most popular of the new scientific psychologies, demonstrating that character, personality, and intellect could be understood by studying the functions of the brain. The whole burden of Combe's *Constitution of Man,* the most popular phrenological vehicle, was to show that mankind was subject to organic laws, explicated in part by phrenology, and that human happiness lay in knowing and obeying these laws while misery resulted from flouting them. Phrenology, then, along with the rest of science, was a popular candidate for replacing religion in the industrial age, and it appealed to those who felt religion's absence.

Although phrenology might replace religion, it rarely attacked religion or the religious impulse as such. Phrenologists recognized the organ of Veneration and accepted the need for faith in the supernatural as an inherent part of human nature. The Fowlers remained the closest to traditional Christianity. Like most Enlightenment philosophers, Gall, Spurzheim, and Combe inclined toward a Deistical natural religion, encompassing the "best" of existing religions.

From the earliest time, there have been radical thinkers who set scientific knowledge against all religion, and naturally some phrenologists shared this radical view. We have already seen that most phrenologists believed in God and the soul. Others, especially those associated with the London Phrenological Society and *The Zoist*, advocated complete materialism and determinism. While such advocacy repelled many, some of those interested in phrenology found it grounds for belief. Ralph Waldo Emerson, usually a critic of phrenology, nevertheless wrote that "the value of phrenology and mesmerism is not as a science but as criticism of the Church & [sic] Schools of the day; for they show what men want in religion & [sic] philosophy which has not been hitherto furnished." More outspokenly, one English radical, Richard Carlile, approved phrenology for being "centered in Materialism, and a philosophy that annihilates . . . all ideas of spirit or human soul," therefore striking "at the very source of religion" while furnishing "invincible proof" of Atheism.[35] The radical fringe of Victorian thought thus found in aggressively scientific, that is materialistic, phrenology, an ally and valuable tool.

In Protestant England, to some extent, and especially in America, the religious void being filled by phrenology was left by the decline of Puritanism and Calvinism, and we find in reform works generally, and particularly in phrenology, Calvinism without God. Victorians generally feared excessive pleasure and strove to avoid it. The means physicians prescribed hoping to achieve the goal of sexual purity are mindboggling. One suggested cure for masturbation was to make the patient sleep in a wet sheet. Straitjackets were another item in the bizarre sleepwear of purity. The masturbator could also have his hands chained to the bedposts or wear a device on his genitals that would stab him whenever he got an erection. These "purity" prescriptions were supposed to retain the great strength of the sperm, which would then be reabsorbed by the brain and increase the patient's mental powers. Such treatments would also forestall the lethargy, insanity, and eventual death that were supposed to be the fate of the masturbator, or even of the overly amorous husband.[36]

Another side of this insistence on purity is seen in "free love," which did not teach the joys of sex. The uses of abstinence instead were its concern; its motto, "Progress not pleasure is our aim." With much hand holding and soulful gazing, the advocates of "free love" sought to regard their companions as "moral & [sic] intellectual beings merely," who maintained "pure & elevated & dignified" relationships— preferable, even in marriage, without sex.[37] Orson Fowler wrote, "only lust creates semen; pure love never does."[38]

Phrenologists, in company with many others, preached the virtues and rewards of abstinence, prudence, caution, and restraint, as we have seen in Alexander Smart's advice to the young. In America, the Fowlers offered similar advice at much greater length. Jessie Fowler, last of the phrenological Fowlers, dedicated a copy of her work on child care to Miss Farmer of Eliot, Maine, with whom she felt "one in [our] belief that the body is subservient to the Mind and Spirit." She continued, "Both are conscious [of the need to morally train the young] and the important call for setting one's life in holier channels than for the gratification of selfish ends. . . . By crowding in the good, we may leave no room for evil thoughts."[39]

As Merle Curti has pointed out, "What the more esoteric mental philosophies were supposed to do for the college-bred man, phrenology claimed to do for any man."[40] Phrenology was especially appealing as a philosophy and science for the unlearned man. Nineteenth-century workers, persuaded of the value of middle class literacy and the need to improve, were touchingly respectful of knowledge and of the word that embodied it. Workingmen would band together and build a small collection of books to be read and regularly discussed;[41] the *Constitution of Man* was commonly one of these books. As such circles of self-education prospered, they could become formal mechanics' institutes that hired speakers to give improving lectures; phrenology was one of the most popular topics.

Phrenology appealed to such groups in a number of ways. As reworked by Spruzheim and Combe, it offered a complete scientific system of mind. It enumerated the mental faculties, showed their interrelationships, and left no embarrassing questions unanswered. It was a complete system, capable of giving guidance in any area of life.

Another important reason for its popularity was that the phrenological system could be rendered "highly *practical*, and adapted to the *million*," as Orson Fowler put it. He knew that "the mass of American minds . . . do not require deep, profound, labored, learned essays, but something short, plain, in point, and that they can understand at a glance."[42] Phrenology put psychology into a form that the newly educated could understand and use.

The reigning Baconian ideology also contributed to phrenology's popularity with the unlearned. In opposing metaphysics, Bacon saw science as commonsensical knowledge of the real world that every person should explore firsthand. Rather than relying on the words of academic philosophers, everyone should know the world through his or her senses and test every idea against personal experience. This opinion had become commonplace by the nineteenth century. The self-educated Timothy Claxton said, "Be assured, brother mechanic, there's nothing like observing, and thinking, and doing things for oneself."[43]

Phrenology was no abstruse psychology built on the philosophy of Aristotle or the introspective meditations of Descartes. Students of phrenology had their own heads readily available and were exhorted to "*examine [phrenology's] truthfulness for yourself. Put its claims to the ordeal of personal experiment*. . . . If it will not stand this test, expose its fallacies. If it will, embrace its glorious doctrines." Nor is this ordeal difficult. "This volume will make it easy . . . communicating precisely that *matter-of-fact* knowledge which amateurs and the community so much require, and so eagerly seek. In short we shall show our readers how to *examine heads for themselves*. . . ."[44] The eager reader need therefore rely on no one else's word, even the phrenologists'.

The Baconian appeal to personal knowledge made phrenology especially attractive to the unlearned common man and woman, for it meant that they could effectively challenge elitist snobs, "the advocates of antiquated measures."[45] Steven Shapin believes that perhaps the greatest appeal of phrenology was to cultural outsiders who could use it to "wave a red flag in the faces of the academic mental philosophers." The phrenologists liked to attack their opponents as conservative advocates of the status quo, which in psychology meant introspective psychology. They attacked introspection as a "mystification" designed to prevent the participation of the public in philosophy and science.[46] Phrenology could thus appeal to upwardly mobile workers, who were challenging the political elite, by giving them a psychology with which to challenge the academic establishment.

One should not underestimate the appeal of phrenology as an amusing novelty by which the message of reform could be spread. The mechanics' institutes wanted Entertaining knowledge as well as Useful and Scientific knowledge. Phrenology was all three. A journalistic observer of phrenology confessed "considerable sympathy" with phrenology "for the very reason that will prejudice some others against it, namely its NOVELTY." He dreaded "the STAND STILL system" and wanted to keep society "agitated." "I would rather witness a THUNDERSTORM OF REFORM, occasionally, than the sickly stagnation which so generally prevails."[47] Phrenology's content was novel, and its practice amusing. The Fowlers decked phrenology out in the trappings of vaudeville, challenging at demonstrations all comers to have their heads read by a blindfolded phrenologist. Among the more serious phrenologists, George Combe was an accomplished public speaker who commanded very high fees.

"Self-made or never made" was the motto of the Fowlers, appealing to the urge towards self-improvement and betterment that was most strongly felt in the Victorian era. Phrenology was always concerned principally with the individual, seeking to reform society by improving men and women. It exhorted the individual to find out the truth of phrenology firsthand. Above all, it instructed its followers in the phrenological arts of self-help. Happiness could be had by obeying the organic laws of nature as expounded by phrenology. Self-knowledge could be had by feeling one's skull. Harmonious marriage could be had by feeling the skulls of prospective mates. Sound employees could be had by reading their skulls. One could improve oneself by cultivating one's weak organs and restraining the more developed ones. This pitch to self-improvement was perfectly suited to the early Victorian period when the idea of self-help got started. Samuel Smiles's book *Self-Help* (1844) was one of the best-sellers of its day, and self-help advice abounded everywhere.[48] Phrenology preached the same ideology as the other advocates of self-help—thrift, hard work, perseverance, purity—supporting this advice with the scientific findings of Gall's brain physiology and adding to it the enjoyable personal knowledge of skull reading. Phrenology offered the way to be "self-made" in an era that praised hard work and saw no other way to happiness.

Richard Sennett has argued that the Industrial Revolution and the rise of capitalism brought about "the fall of public man." In the busy metropolises of strangers in the eighteenth century, men had adopted public roles whose presentation was under conscious control. In coffee houses, an eighteenth-century variety of public club where all sorts of men gathered to discuss the latest news, rumors, and styles, all men—playing their roles as public men—talked and jested as equals, although their clothing made it evident who was rich and powerful and who was not. They were all acting as informed gentlemen whose news and comments were of equal interest; attention was paid to wit rather than to class. Such role playing gave the politicians, writers, and landowners a free and gracious way of communicating with their social inferiors. This easy communication provides the governing classes with a sample of the opinion of the governed, while also letting the governed feel that their attitudes and needs were being attended to.

By the nineteenth century, however, such camaraderie was extinct. An eminent Victorian had no comparable chance to talk sensibly with a stable groom, a small shopkeeper, or an enlisted soldier, for example. The rise of industrial capitalism had fixed everyone in his or her social role. On the other hand this period placed great emphasis on individuals and the need to know their "real" and "sincere" beliefs. People did not value skillful portrayal of a public role but rejected role playing as insincere deception. In fact, they did not believe behavior could be completely self-controlled: they scrutinized it for clues to underlying real character, for "involuntary disclosure of emotions." The effacing of the boundary between the public and the private, or intimate, "showed itself most clearly in the flourishing practice of phrenology."[49]

Gall himself exploited the notion of the involuntary disclosure of character to collect evidence in support of phrenology: "Do you wish to spy out the character of a person, without the fear of being misled as to your conclusions, even though he might be on his guard?" Discuss that person's childhood or games or conduct toward relatives and friends. "Few persons think it necessary to dissemble upon these points." Consequently they will reveal their character, and "the whole man stands unveiled before me."[50]

As the Industrial Revolution progressed, Gall's followers taught the new ideology of a world without impersonal public behavior. If mentality were not manifested, wrote the *American Phrenological Journal,* "every human being would be completely isolated from all others," an "incalculably great" evil, cutting us off from discovering "the beauties of their characters." Language (the public mode of expression par excellence) "can be too easily perverted" to dissembling. We want and need to know our fellow man:

> To this requisition—*imperious demand*—for knowing our fellow
> men, Nature has kindly adapted the *expression* of those mental
> qualities of the one hand, and our recognition of them on the other.
> Nature has ordained that we do not hide the light of our souls under
> the bushels of impenetrability but that we should set them on the
> hill of conspicuosity, so that all that are within sight may observe
> them. She even *compels* such expression. She has rendered the
> suppression of our mentality *absolutely impossible.* She has ren-
> dered such expression *spontaneous and irresistible,* by having in-
> stituted the NATURAL LANGUAGE of emotion and character . . .
> which compels us to tell each other all about ourselves.

The journal noticed the problem of the anonymity of strangers in the
city, which created the public man: "Must we then be excluded from all
possible means of ascertaining the mentality of those thus casually
met?" Of course not, for by sound physiognomy and phrenology "we
can read the very thoughts, and feelings, and motives, of our fellow
men, in spite of all attempts at concealment or deception." The ability
to "know human character is among the strongest aspirations of our nature. Who would not give *all he is worth* to be able to look completely
through the characters of all he meets?" Through the natural language
of character we can tell the rogue from the honest man, the vulgar from
the pure-minded, the religious man from the atheist, the talented from
the untalented.

Such knowledge is not only compulsive, it is complete: "It is desirable for us to know *all . . . all* the existing emotions of mankind *are
legible. They come to the surface.*" The natural language of character
penetrates the public man, it " 'speaks louder than words' " and requires "only to be *known* in order to become a mirror to the *inner man*
of all whom we meet."[51] In the *Journal's* view all privacy vanishes, replaced by the joys of intimately knowing the character of the least stran-
ger. As Sennet argues, the distinction between public and private is
abolished.

Finally, two quite different, and even opposing, factors conditioned
phrenology's acceptance, although they do not fit neatly into the scheme
of figure 4.1. One was a daring book, *Vestiges of the Natural History of
Creation* (1845) by Robert Chambers, which is widely regarded as a
precursor to Darwin's *Origin of Species.* It was published anonymously
for fear of a religious reaction, but it was enormously popular. It
presents a thoroughly naturalistic view of the world slowly evolving out

of primordial chaos into its present form. When he came to the mentality of animals, Chambers adopted phrenology as the "only [system of mind] founded upon nature."[52] He used phrenology to establish continuity between even the lowest animals and mankind (e.g., ants and beavers display Constructiveness), and to show that man is subject to natural laws. In Chambers's work, phrenology is uncompromisingly used in the interest of naturalism, and the *Vestiges,* with its phrenology, helped prepare the public's mind for the greater shock of the theory of natural selection.

On the other hand, another subject that helped prepare the way for phrenology was magic. Like Spiritualism, phrenology can be viewed as a reemergence of ancient occult beliefs during the nineteenth century despite Enlightenment naturalism. Phrenology taught its initiates how to divine character from cranial signs, much as the astrologer divines character from zodiacal signs. It offered participation in a "mystery" and allowed its followers to feel superior to the uninitiated. The possession of paths to special truths denied others is one of the appeals of the occult, and this claim was a factor in the popularity of phrenology.

THE DECAY OF PHRENOLOGY

Obviously all the factors that led some to accept phrenology could lead others to reject it, or at least to remain indifferent to it. Proponents of structural reform could view phrenology as counterproductive meism; antiimperialists and feminists might well dislike its racism and sexism; opponents of all reform might condemn its liberalism; religions might resent its attempt to replace them.

We believe that the most important social reason for the rejection of phrenology was its tendency toward materialism, which attracted a few but revolted many more. L.E.G.E. wrote:

> If we had the power of combining the elements which form cerebral molecules, and then the power of arranging these materials so as to form brain, and of subjecting this portion of brain to the regular stimulus of blood, & c., we believe a manifestation of cerebration would be the inevitable result.[53]

Here, in cold prose, is Dr. Frankenstein, creator of the thinking but soulless machine that radical naturalism saw as Everyman. Frankenstein and his monster still shock and thrill us—the power of science to make life while we doubt (and fear) that it is life, and that there are no more sacred mysteries. Phrenology was the first psychology to do more than speculate that man is a machine.

T. M. Parssinen has suggested four reasons for the gradual decay of phrenology.[54] Externally, phrenology was harmed by its very popularity and by its association with quacks, and by a new conception of brain function. Both the *American Phrenological Journal* and the *Edinburgh Phrenological Journal* regularly complained about poorly educated quacks who set up as phrenologists and did bad head readings for a fee. The sincere phrenologists correctly saw that the quacks made an easy target for ridicule by important voices of public opinion such as the *Times* of London. And phrenology's several appeals to the vulgar masses of the unlearned hurt it in the estimation of those who wanted a more exclusive and refined mental science.

Among scientists, Flourens's erroneous conception of the brain as a single unspecialized organ held sway for many years and only began to unravel when Pierre-Paul Broca, under some influence of phrenology, discovered a cerebral area regularly associated, when damaged, with language impairment. Broca's discovery was a victory, not only for the concept of localization, but also for Gall's preference for natural clinical evidence over artificial mutilations. As neuroscience progressed, a picture of the brain as a collection of functional localizations began to emerge. But these localized centers were not the autonomous mental powers of Gall, despite the fact that physiologists now spoke of the "new phrenology." Rather, the brain was seen as a reflex device that linked sensory input to motor output, and the localized areas were just places where specific sensorimotor connections were made. This is the conception that dominates brain science today.[55]

Internal reasons for the decline of phrenology adduced by Parssinen are its disruption by controversies over materialism, and the drift of many of its adherents into mesmerism and phreno-magnetism, another suspicious fringe science. We have seen that most phrenologists, including Gall, Spruzheim, and Combe, did not let their phrenology lead them to complete materialism. But more radical phrenologists did, and the movement divided over this issue. Moreover, even among the more conservative phrenologists, Combe's advocacy of a free will that was no more than determinism by motives alienated orthodox believers in free will. These controversies, and the inevitable personal incompatabilities, drove phrenologists apart exactly when they needed a unified movement to survive criticism.[56]

Socially, phrenology succeeded and failed because it was at once ahead of its time and too much of its time. It became popular because of its novel familiarity. Its broad content harmonized with everything the Victorians were coming to believe, and it expressed the deepest attitudes of the emerging middle classes. No wonder then that Richard Cobden felt that reading phrenology was like reading his own thoughts. And to this familiarity phrenology added the trick—parlor game, even—of head reading. One could discover one's own character, undoubtedly confirming one's own good opinion of oneself, and one could read the minds of strangers, rogues and suitors, salesmen and servants. And it was certified by the new authority of Science, being founded on the best inductive principles. Those who found head reading silly, as many did, could indeed conclude that phrenologists talked sense despite their phrenology.

But precisely because phrenology was of its time, it could not last. As values changed, as people became less earnest, as structural reform progressed, phrenology, rejected by the best scientists, became at best a bore and at worst an object of ridicule. Even Combe abandoned phrenology for more general political causes such as monetary reform.

On the other hand, phrenology was also rejected for being ahead of its time. Despite the intentions of its leading authors, phrenology did tend towards materialism and determinism, commonplaces in scientific psychology today but offensive in the nineteenth century. One of the ironies of the pseudosciences is that, while phrenology was rejected for its materialism, parapsychology is rejected for its spiritualistic affront to materialist science.

ESTIMATE OF PHRENOLOGY: WAS IT A PSEUDOSCIENCE?

The most obvious answer to the question, Why did phrenology disappear? is, It was wrong. Yet, by the most conservative criterion of scientific status, Popper's demand for falisfiability, phrenology's very wrongness demonstrates its status as a science. Phrenology proposed a specific set of brain locations; these were in error, and were shown to be in error; phrenology stood refuted. If wrong, it could still claim to be scientific.

This answer, however, is too simple, reflecting much more on the demand for falsifiability than on phrenology. Theories are complex entities that evolve over time, and it would be absurd to suppose that a theory should be able to explain everything presented to it. Typically, great scientists propose a complex theory that is right in certain features, wrong in others, and capable of explaining only a limited range of data. At their outset, scientific research programs are inconsistent with much that is already believed or known and should therefore fail miserably—if scientists adhered to strict falsification.

Newton, besides being involved with alchemy, consciously fudged many of the astronomical data he offered in support of his theory. Darwin was wrong about evolution in many respects, including his belief in the inheritance of acquired characteristics.[57] Yet neither Newton nor Darwin is regarded as a notorious pseudoscientist or a fraud. Each outlined a particular picture of nature, a paradigm, and left puzzles for his followers to solve. In solving these puzzles, Newtonians and Darwinists had to alter features of the founder's scheme, but they did so without abandoning Newtonianism or Darwinism, instead regarding each change, and the puzzle solutions each gained, as triumphs, not as falsifications.

Gall was the founder of phrenology, and he spelled out his essential ideas in four propositions: (1) that the moral, affective, and intellectual faculties of man and animals are innate; (2) that they depend on the organization of the brain; (3) that the brain is the organ of the mind; and (4) that the brain contains as many organs as there are faculties of the mind. Related to this hard core of phrenology were the propositions relating to the doctrine of the skull: (1) that organ size was a measure of power; and (2) that size was accurately reflected by the shape of the skull. Finally there were Gall's specific claims about the localization of specific organs.

Surveying Gall's ideas, we find, as in the ideas of any scientific founder, some of lasting worth and others of no value. In its specific details, Gall's theory, like Darwin's, fares the worst. Gall was right about only one of his localizations, that of language. Darwin's account of the mechanics of heredity has proved to be incredibly wrong and has been replaced by Mendelian genetics, just as the New Phrenology of modern neurophysiology has replaced the old.

Similarly, the doctrine of the skull was wrong, just as Darwin was wrong about the inheritance of acquired characteristics. But even the doctrine of the skull was not entirely wrong. The brain does leave its mark on the skull—on the inside of the skull, where paleoneurologists look for evidence of the mental powers of fossil humans.[58]

Gall's central propositions are hardly unscientific, and three of them are unexceptionable to modern scientists. No one any longer doubts that the brain is the organ of mind, that the brain is a collection of specialized centers, and that there must be a correspondence between these centers and mental abilities. Gall's first premise, that animals' affective, intellectual, and moral powers are innate, is arguable. It finds its champions today among the sociobiologists who, like Gall, are often accused of immorality and pseudoscience.

Various sociobiologists and ethologists tell us: aggression is innate (cf. Destructiveness); altruism is innate (cf. Benevolence); religion is innate (cf. Veneration); language is innate (cf. Language); sex roles are innate (cf. Amativeness and Philoprogenitiveness).[59] Should the sociobiologists prove correct, Gall's premise will have been upheld, although we will be forced to conclude that he looked in the wrong place for mental dispositions. If the brain is, as modern physiologists contend, merely a connector of input and output, then the material bases of psychological dispositions such as optimism or altruism will have to be sought elsewhere; sociobiologists seek them in the genes.

Examined carefully, then, Gall's thought offered the same mixture of truth and falsity, shrewd guess and hopeless mistake, that any basic scientific innovation has offered. Like Newton and Darwin, Gall set out a clear picture of some part of nature together with some of its details. Why then is Gall not respected by neurophysiologists as Newton is by physicists and Darwin by biologists?

There can be no doubt that Gall's ideas could have led to a progressive research program ultimately culminating in the modern view of the brain as a collection of localized centers of activity. Along the way, Gall's detailed organology and the doctrine of the skull would have been discarded, but his central contentions could have been maintained. In "Recent advances in phrenology," neurophysiologist John McFie argues that "much of phrenological theory is in fact acceptable today." He reviews evidence supporting the localization of cortical function and concludes by outlining the remaining problems that Gall himself saw: Experimental brain study alone can reveal little about mental functions. Furthermore, McFie echoes George Combe's critique of Fourens by pointing out that mutilations of the brain are as useless to understanding its function as would be "machine-gunning a computer to see what goes wrong."[60] Joining McFie, Macdonald Critchley praises Gall as "the

all-important empiricist in phrenology,'' reviews his anatomical discoveries, and even found virtue in the doctrine of the skull, for it led to
craniometry and stereotaxic surgery.[61]

Why then is Gall not more generally honored? Why is phrenology
considered a pseudoscience? The answer is that scientific theories are
not static entities outside human social and intellectual activity. Gall's
concepts could have led to a progressive scientific research program,
but in fact they did not. The establishment in neurophysiology—led by
Flourens and Charles Bell and supported by widely read doctors such as
Roget—found Gall's ideas deeply offensive, and brain physiology took
a long and roundabout route away from Gall's localizations into the
Cartesian fantasies of the unified soul and brain, and finally back to the
localizations of the New Phrenology. Gall's own followers abandoned
his empirical method for Spurzheim's philosophical approach and the
reforming of Combe and the Fowlers. Phrenology, in replacing religion, abandoned the path of scientific research.

What phrenology teaches us about pseudoscience is that no specific
theory can really be judged scientific or pseudoscientific. The ideas of
scientists will sometimes be right and sometimes wrong, but error and
pseudoscience are not synonymous. How a scientist's ideas are received
is conditioned by factors that have little or nothing to do with the supposed canons of philosophy of science but depend instead on the social
and intellectual currents in which thinkers must swim and to which theories must adapt or die. As David Hull has suggested, Gall and his followers were not ''sufficiently adept at finagling''[62] and so drowned.

It is not surprising, then, that estimates of Gall's achievement and
phrenology's importance have varied greatly. In the later nineteenth
and early twentieth centuries, most neuroscientists tried to sever any
connection between themselves and phrenology, maintaining that phrenology was ''obsolete'' and ''mystic'':[63]

> The old phrenology was wrong in its theory, wrong in its facts,
> wrong in its interpretation of mental processes and never led to the
> slightest practical result. The new phrenology is scientific in its
> methods, in its observations, and in its analysis, and is convincing
> in its conclusions. And who can now set a limit to the benefit it has
> brought to mankind by its practical application to the saving of hu-
> man lives.[64]

The old phrenology was sometimes accorded grudging status as a forerunner: ''Still, it must be acknowledged that the pseudophrenology in a

certain sense paved the way for the cautious researches of the true science of a possibly distant future."[65]

Phrenology retained its status as a crank science through the 1950s, enshrined as such in Martin Gardner's *Fads and Fallacies in the Name of Science,* even though the dean of American historians of psychology, E. G. Boring, had written favorably of phrenology's role in the founding of scientific psychology.[66]

The recovery of phrenology as a serious attempt at a science of brain and mind began in 1947 with Owsei Temkin's "Gall and the phrenological movement" and received further impetus from *Franz Joseph Gall, Inventor of Phrenology and his Collection* by Erwin Ackernecht and Henri Vallois, both of which works gave favorable impressions of Gall, if not of other phrenologists.[67] But it was only in the 1960s and 1970s, following the breakdown of logical positivism and the rise of historically attuned studies of science sensitive to large social and intellectual currents, that studies of phrenology exploded in number. Gall won new respect as a brilliant if erratic scientist, and phrenology came to be seen as an important and revealing part of nineteenth-century intellectual life.[68]

Franz Joseph Gall was an Austrian physician forced to abandon Vienna, who traveled to Paris hoping to convince supposedly open-minded French scientists of the truth of his ideas. He found instead establishment rejection, and popular support. In this he repeated the path of Franz Anton Mesmer, whose mesmerism was linked to phrenology by the London phrenologists. Mesmerism, also, is second only to phrenology as a science whose neglect was one of the failures of Alfred Russel Wallace's Wonderful Century.

Five

Mesmerism

In both theory and fact, mesmerism is the opposite of phrenology. In phrenology, Gall proposed a fundamentally correct theory of the mind-brain relationship and cortical localization of function, but this theory was supported by the illusory doctrine of the skull and its supposed "facts." In mesmerism, the basic facts—the trance state and the induction of nervous crises—are sound, but the theory adduced by Mesmer to explain them, animal magnetism, was incorrect and contentious.

In its development as a movement, mesmerism resembles phrenology, although ultimately it proved to be at once more scientifically successful and more outré. Like phrenology, mesmerism pointed in two directions from the outset, one scientific, the other occult and political. Mesmer had his Spurzheim in Nicolas Bergasse, who used mesmerism as a cudgel with which to attack the aristocrats of the *ancien régime* but did not develop it as a scientific theory. Mesmer's posthumous reputation fared better than Gall's when the phenomena of mesmerism became the object of scientific interest. After a period of controversy, mesmerism was transformed into hypnosis and made acceptable to physicians. Despite their differences, phrenology and mesmerism were sufficiently similar to be directly linked in the brief movement known as phreno-magnetism, in which an entranced subject's phrenological organs were manipulated by touch and suggestion.

The most important difference between the two, however, is mesmerism's early and enduring links to the genuinely occult: to communication with the dead, to table rapping, to the spirit world, to clairvoyance and extrasensory perception. With mesmerism we will plunge deeply into the bizarre caverns of the occult underground.

ANIMAL MAGNETISM

The Advent of Mesmerism

The house which Mesmer inhabited was delightfully situated; its rooms spacious and sumptuously furnished; stained glass and colored blinds shed a dim, religious light; mirrors gleamed at intervals along the walls; a mysterious silence was preserved, delicate perfumes floated in the air, and occasionally the melodious sounds of the harmonica or the voice came to lend their aid to his magnetic powers. His *salons* became the daily resort of all that was brilliant and *spirituel* in the Parisian fashionable world. Ladies of rank whom indolence, voluptuous indulgence, or satiety of pleasures, had filled with vapors or nervous affections; men of luxurious habits, enervated by enjoyment, who had drained sensuality of all that it could offer, and gained in return a shattered constitution and premature old age, came in crowds to seek after the delightful emotion and novel sensations which this mighty magician was said to dispense. They approached with imaginations heated by curiosity and desire; they believed because they were ignorant, and this belief was all that was required for the action of the magnetic charm. The women, always the more ardent in enthusiasm, first experienced yawnings, stretchings, then slight nervous spasms, and, finally, cries of excitation, according as the assistant magnetizers . . . multiplied and prolonged the soft passes, or *attouchements*, by which the magnetic influence was supposed to be communicated. The emotions once begun were soon transmitted to the rest, as we know one hysterical female if affected will induce an attack in all others similarly predisposed in the same apartment. In the midst of this strange scene, entered Mesmer, clothed in a long flowing robe of lilac-colored silk, richly embroidered with golden flowers, and holding in his hand a long white wand. Advancing with an air of authority and magic gravity, he seemed to govern the life and movements of the individuals in crises. Women panting were threatened with suffocation,—they must be unlaced; others tore the walls, or rolled themselves on the ground, with strong spasms in the throat, and occasionally uttering loud shrieks,—the violence of the crises must be moderated. He approached, traced over their bodies certain lines with his wand; they became instantly calm, acknowledged his power, and felt streams of cold or burning vapors through their entire frames according to the directions in which he waved his hand.[1]

Such was the scene at the house of Dr. Franz Anton Mesmer (1743–1815) in Paris, only a few years before the French Revolution. Like Gall, Mesmer was a Viennese physician of unorthodox ideas who left the authoritarian atmosphere of his home for the headier airs of the capital of the Enlightenment. A more outlandish and disagreeable character than Gall, Mesmer was known for flamboyance and occult airs that damaged the prospects of his beloved offspring, the theory of animal magnetism.

Son of a gamekeeper, Mesmer first studied law and then turned to science, specifically medicine, receiving a sound medical education at the University of Vienna beginning in 1760. His occult leanings first emerged in his dissertation, *A Physico-medical Inquiry Concerning the Influence of the Planets.* He believed that the most widespread and deeply held beliefs, however absurd on the surface, must contain a germ of truth. Astrology was such a belief, and Mesmer was "induced to seek, among the ruins of that science, brought so low by ignorance, what it might have contained that was useful and true."[2]

Mesmer's account, however, is not at all mystical. Newton and other physicists had demonstrated the mutual influence of celestial bodies on one another, the most obvious earthly manifestation being the tides. Mesmer attributed the influence of gravitation to a universal fluid whose intensification and remission caused the ebbing and flowing of the seas. But the forces of the planets and the influence of the universal fluid were not, in Mesmer's view, limited to inanimate matter. Living bodies are physical, and they too are subject to the ebbing and flowing of the fluid, which acts especially on the nerves, causing "tides" to run through the nervous system. Mesmer called this influence "animal gravitation," and believed it to be involved in health and disease.[3]

Mesmer thus interpreted the "ruins" of astrology in materialistic terms, for which treatise he received his doctorate in 1767. He did not pursue his fluidic ideas for some years, maintaining a conventional and successful medical practice until 1773, when a case presented itself that recalled his old ideas. He was presented with a twenty-nine-year-old woman named Francisca Oesterlin who displayed a wide range of symptoms that would today be called largely psychosomatic: earaches and toothaches, delirium, rage, vomiting, and swooning. As her symptoms seemed naturally to ebb and flow, Mesmer saw the case as "a highly favorable occasion for observing accurately that type of ebb and flow" he had years earlier called animal gravitation. Mesmer knew that magnets attract and repel at a distance and that they had been used elsewhere to treat stomach and tooth pain. So Mesmer conceived of manipulating the universal fluid with magnets in order to effect a cure of his patient, and he had an astronomer friend, Father Hell, provide the magnets.

On July 28, 1774, Mesmer applied his magnets. The patient reported feeling within her "painful currents of a subtle material," followed by easing of her symptoms. Repeated attacks were cured by repeated application of the magnets. However, the first of what Mesmer saw as a series of betrayals took place when Father Hell claimed for himself the credit for the discovery of magnetic therapy. This prompted Mesmer to publish, on January 5, 1775, a pamphlet providing his first account of his ideas, in which he used the phrase "animal magnetism" for the first time.

> I set forth the nature and action of ANIMAL MAGNETISM and the analogy between its properties and those of the magnet and electricity. I added "that all bodies were, like the magnet capable of communicating this magnetic principle; that this fluid penetrated everything and could be stored up and concentrated like the electric fluid; that it acted at a distance; that animate bodies were divided into two classes, one being susceptible to the magnetism and the other to an opposite quality that suppresses its action." Finally, I accounted for the various sensations and based these assertions on experiments which enabled me to put them forward.[4]

In addition to alleviating her symptoms, Mesmer found that his patient could be thrown into a "fainting fit" in which she was unconscious yet sensible, almost certainly a hypnotic trance. In this state Miss Oesterlin exhibited those extraordinary powers of perception that would later be called "the higher phenomena of mesmerism," which greatly resemble spiritualistic and psychical phenomena. To a skeptical visiting physician, Mr. Ingenhouze, Mesmer offered six china cups of water and "magnetized" the water in the cup of Ingenhouze's choice by touching it. Mesmer then touched the cups to the unconscious woman's and, and when touched with the cup of "magnetized" water, Miss Oesterlin's "hand made a movement and gave signs of pain." The experiment was successfully repeated by Ingenhouze himself.[5]

According to Mesmer, these and other experiments seemed to convert Ingenhouze, but two days later Mesmer was again betrayed when Ingenhouze reversed himself and publicly proclaimed the demonstration to be "a ridiculous prearranged fraud." These "odious insinuations" spread, aided by Hell and other physicians. Mesmer sought to have the university establish a commission of inquiry into his ideas and practice but met only "indifference, coldness, and reserve." He undertook further cures and circulated his pamphlet among the learned societies of Europe.

However only the Berlin Academy took any notice of him, and its members confused mineral with animal magnetism, attributing the cure to the action of the magnets. But by now Mesmer was convinced that the magnets were merely conductors of the animal magnetic fluid, for he could get the same effects with a variety of materials. He conceived himself to be a repository of animal magnetism with the ability to create in a patient artificial ebbs and flows of the fluid, or to infuse it and draw it off through various hand passes around the body and by touch. In 1776, in order to completely separate animal from mineral magnetism, Mesmer forever abandoned magnets as the conductor of the fluid.

Despite further clinical successes, Mesmer could win no acceptance for animal magnetism in Vienna. Being "wearied by my labours and still more so by the continual animosities of my adversaries. . . . I felt I had done my duty by my fellow citizens."[6] Mesmer, like Gall, left Vienna for Paris, where he hoped, in the center of the Enlightenment, to win acceptance of his theories and credit for his discovery of animal magnetism.

Mesmer's theory and practice were by no means novel. A trance or ecstatic state in which extrasensory knowledge becomes possible is known from religions around the world, including Christianity, which considered it one of the main routes to sainthood (see chapter 6). Healing by personal power, whether called miracle or exorcism, was also familiar in the Western world. For example, in the seventeenth century Valentine Greatraks became known as "The Stroker" for his ability to cure scrofula by merely touching a patient. Scrofula had long been called "The King's Evil" because the king was supposed to be able to cure it by his touch, an idea that lived on at least into the eighteenth century—Dr. Samuel Johnson, the great lexicographer, had been taken as a child to be royally touched, with no known result. Greatraks, however, was a mere squire.

In explaining Greatraks's talent, his scientific contemporaries resorted to a theory not unlike Mesmer's theory of the animal magnetic fluid. After the mid-sixteenth century, the idea that objects, plants, and animals give off potentially unhealthful or curative effluvia had grown in popularity. These supposed effluvia could be used to explain apparently magical influences, as when Robert Boyle, a founder of modern physics, explained the curative powers of amulets by postulating that their effluvia treated disease. A physician, Henry Stubbe, used Boyle's theory to explain Greatraks's success. As he observed in a letter to Boyle:

> God had bestowed upon Mr. Greatraks a peculiar temperament, or composed his body of some particular ferments, the effluvia whereof being introduced sometimes by a light, sometimes by a violent friction, should restore the temperament of the debilitated parts, reinvigorate the blood, and dissipate all the heterogenous ferments out of the bodies of the diseased, by the eye, nose, mouth, hands and feet.[7]

Other physicians and scientists such as van Helmont, Fludd, and Maxwell also believed that fluids were involved in sickness and health.

Despite having such scientific proponents, all these theories still had something magical about them, as is seen in their use to explain the power of amulets. Moreover, the fluids were generally thought of as in some sense divine—descended from the alchemical *pneuma,* the breath of the universe that joins body and soul, the quintessence, the spirit of the universe that could be used, in retorts or amulets, to overcome age, illness, and decay—even death itself (see chapter 2). In a similarly unscientific vein, Stubbe referred to Greatraks's skill as God given.

During the seventeenth and eighteenth centuries, then, personal healing through the influence of invisible fluids, or effluvia, was familiar, although it was more magico-religious than scientific. Mesmer strove to bring both personal healing and invisible fluids within the circle of eighteenth-century naturalism.

This difference between the religious and the scientific interpretation of personal healing is well illustrated in Mesmer's reaction to Father Johann Joseph Gassner (1727–79), the most famous faith healer of Mesmer's time. Gassner thought of himself as an exorcist, curing diseases by casting out demons. He effected his cures by suggestion, touches, and passes, which produced trances and convulsions. The Elector of Bavaria called on Mesmer to help investigate Gassner, which Messmer did in November, 1775. Mesmer described Gassner as a "man of good faith but of excessive zeal" whose cures of "various disorders of a nervous nature . . . appeared to be supernatural" to the populace, but to be "imposture and fraud" to Viennese skeptics. Mesmer, however, argued that both views were wrong and, in good Enlightenment fashion, concluded that "the man in question was nothing but a tool of Nature." Mesmer supported his conclusion by demonstrating some of his own mesmeric phenomena for the elector.[8]

Thus neither Mesmer's practice nor his ideas were new. His innovation lay in trying to reconcile science with traditional mystic, magical ideas and practices. Such attempts can be found in many of psychology's occult doubles, from alchemy to Spiritualism and parapsychology. Mesmer's attempted union of science and religion was eminently of the Enlightenment. He saw in Gassner and himself neither miracles nor magic but only the operation of nature through material, if invisible, means. Nevertheless, he was defeated by the aura of magic that clung to personal healing, by his own outré practice, and by his habitual secretiveness, which always hinted at occult mysteries still to be revealed.

The Paris that Mesmer entered in February 1778 was well prepared to receive the magnetic mysteries. Robert Darnton has masterfully described the lush and fertile intellectual swamp that was prerevolutionary France.[9] Journals of the time reflected the feverish growth of science, metaphysics, and the occult. "Physics, chemistry, natural history have become a craze," observed one; "Never have so many systems, so many theories of the universe, appeared as during the last few years," said another; a third noted the times' plethora of "hermetic, cabalistic, and theosophic philosphers"; and a fourth stated that "secret remedies of all kinds are distributed daily, despite the rigor of the prohibitions." It was a time and place in search of marvels, whether stories of fantastic creatures or the first balloon flights. The public seized on "any invisible fluid, any scientific-sounding hypothesis, that promised to explain the wonders of nature." Mesmer supplied both: the wonderful cures at his séances, and his theory of animal magnetic fluid.

The difficulty was that Mesmer craved recognition as a scientist by scientists, not fame as a wonder-worker. Mesmer tried first to interest the French Academy of Sciences in his theory. He attempted to do this through reason alone and without referring to his medical successes. Mesmer was well aware that medical evidence can be quite weak, for patients often recover naturally whether a physician intervenes or not, and that consequently a parade of cures would present only equivocal support. Mesmer, however, was trapped by his reputation as a miracle curer. The academy found his theory incomprehensible and demanded a demonstration of magnetism's curative powers. Mesmer resisted, members of the academy became uncivil, and most left before Mesmer finally and reluctantly agreed to a demonstration. With an unfamiliar patient Mesmer achieved very limited success, and the head of the academy pronounced Mesmer's effort a failure.[10]

Mesmer cured still more people and "I had reason to flatter myself that recognition would follow"[11] from the Royal Society of Medicine, to whom he addressed his less-preferred evidence based on medical cures.[11] Despite many testimonials from patients he had restored to health, however, Mesmer could not win the recognition he craved. This is not to say that Mesmer won no converts at all. He did attract a loyal circle of mesmerians, a few physicians but mostly otherwise, but he never attained the scientific status that was his real goal.

Giving up on the learned societies, Mesmer went directly to the public by publishing in 1779 his *Mémoire sur la Découverte du Magnétisme Animal.* In it, he recounted his trials and tribulations as the discoverer of animal magnetism and set out his scientific theory in twenty-seven "Propositions Asserted":

    1. There exists a mutual influence between the heavenly Bodies, the Earth and Animate Bodies.

    2. A universally distributed and continuous fluid, which is quite without vacuum and of an incomparably rarified nature, and which by its nature is capable of receiving, propagating and communicating all the impressions of movement, is the means of this influence.

    3. This reciprocal action is subordinated to mechanical laws that are hitherto unknown.

    4. This action results in alternate effects which may be regarded as an Ebb and Flow.

    5. This ebb and flow is more or less general, more or less composite according to the nature of the causes determining it.

    6. It is by this operation (the most universal of those presented

by Nature) that the activity ratios are set up between the heavenly bodies, the earth, and its component parts.

7. The properties of Matter and the Organic Body depend on this operation.

8. The animal body sustains the alternate effects of this agent, which by insinuating itself into the substance of the nerves, affects them at once.

9. It is particularly manifest in the human body that the agent has properties similar to those of the magnet; different and opposite poles may likewise be distinguished, which can be changed, communicated, destroyed and strengthened; even the phenomenon of dipping is observed.

10. This property of the animal body which brings it under the influence of the heavenly bodies and the reciprocal action of those surrounding it, as shown by its analogy with the magnet, induced me to term it ANIMAL MAGNETISM.

11. The action and properties of Animal Magnetism, thus defined, may be communicated to other animate and inanimate bodies. Both are more or less susceptible to it.

12. This action and properties may be strengthened and propagated by the same bodies.

13. Experiments show the passage of a substance whose rarified nature enables it to penetrate all bodies without appreciable loss of activity.

14. Its action is exerted at a distance, without the aid of an intermediate body.

15. It is intensified and reflected by mirrors, just like light.

16. It is communicated, propogated and intensified by sound.

17. This magnetic property may be stored up, concentrated and transported.

18. I have said that all animate bodies are not equally susceptible; there are some, although very few, whose properties are so opposed that their very presence destroys all the effects of magnetism in other bodies.

19. This opposing property also penetrates all bodies; it may likewise be communicated, propagated, stored, concentrated and transported, reflected by mirrors and propagated by sound; this constitutes not merely the absence of magnetism, but a positive opposing property.

20. The Magnet, both natural and artificial, together with other substances, is susceptible to Animal Magnetism, and even to the

opposing property, without its effect on iron and the needle undergoing any alteration in either case; this proves that the principle of
Animal Magnetism differs essentially from that of mineral magnetism.

21. This system will furnish fresh explanations as to the nature
of Fire and Light, as well as the theory of attraction, ebb and flow,
the magnet and electricity.

22. It will make known that the magnet and artificial electricity
only have, as regards illnesses, properties which they share with
several other agents provided by Nature, and that if useful effects
have been derived from the use of the latter, they are due to ANI-
MAL MAGNETISM.

23. It will be seen from the facts, in accordance with the practical rules I shall draw up, that this principle can cure nervous disorders directly and other disorders indirectly.

24. With its help, the physician is guided in the use of medica-
ments; he perfects their action, brings about and controls the beneficial crises in such a way as to master them.

25. By making known my method, I shall show by a new theory
of illnesses the universal utility of the principle I bring to bear on
them.

26. With this knowledge, the physician will determine reliably
the origin, nature and progress of illnesses, even the most complicated; he will prevent them from gaining ground and will succeed
in curing them without ever exposing the patient to dangerous effects or unfortunate consequences, whatever his age, temperament
and sex. Women, even in pregnancy and childbirth, will enjoy the
same advantage.

27. In conclusion, this doctrine will enable the physician to determine the state of each individual's health and safeguard him
from the maladies to which he might otherwise be subject. The art
of healing will thus reach its final stage of perfection.[12]

The twenty-seven propositions can be reduced to four classes. The
first seven propositions postulate the existence of a universal fluid and
expound its nature, operations, and scope—claiming nothing beyond
what Mesmer set forth in his doctoral dissertation. Propositions 8–19
define animal magnetism more narrowly, describe its nature and effects, and note that some bodies oppose its effects. The third set of propositions, 20–21, relates animal magnetism to physics. The fourth set,
22–27, describes the involvement of animal magnetism in disease and
outlines how it may be used by the physician.

In the *Memoire* Mesmer said, ''I quite realize that compared with old-established principles and knowledge my system may appear to contain as much illusion as truth.'' Nevertheless, he appealed to physicians, ''the repositories of public trust for everything connected with the preservation and happiness of mankind,'' to listen to him, for only they had the knowledge to ''judge of the importance'' of mesmerism, to ''realize its implications. In a word, they alone are qualified to put it into practice.''[13]

This appeal to the professions failed, and Mesmer had to settle for a very different audience.

The Royal Commission of 1784

Mesmerism was all the rage of Paris. It was the subject of numerous books and pamphlets, poetic lampoons, and even two successful satirical plays attacking the mesmerists as quacks. It had become too popular to be ignored, and King Louis XVI appointed a scientific commission to look into animal magnetism. The president of the commission was no less than Benjamin Franklin, one of the renowned men of the age; other eminent members were Antoine Lavoisier, codiscoverer of oxygen and founder of modern chemistry, Jean Bailly, France's leading astronomer, and physician Joseph Guillotin, whose invention would soon become the instrument of the Reign of Terror.

The committee was formed to investigate the mesmeric practices not of Mesmer himself but of his follower, Charles Deslon. Deslon was a well-connected French physician, doctor to many aristocrats, and had been Mesmer's most important supporter until mid-1782. Mesmer, like Freud, always wound up quarreling with his best disciples; Deslon was too prominent and independent to be kept on Mesmer's short leash, and after a series of disagreements he set himself up in practice closely following (despite Mesmer's disavowals) Mesmer's own techniques. It was Deslon who invited the formation of the commission, and, over Mesmer's objections, it was Deslon they investigated.[14] The commission was appointed on March 12, 1784, and filed its report, apparently written by Lavoisier, on August 11, 1784.[15]

First, the commission visited Deslon's clinic. Its description of his techniques and cures is parallel to the lurid description of Mesmer's practice quoted earlier but stated rather more objectively. Nevertheless, the scene clearly impressed the commission: ''Nothing can be more astonishing than the sight of [mesmeric] convulsions; he that has not had it can have no idea of it. . . . It is impossible not to recognize in these regular effects an extra-ordinary influence, acting upon the patients, making itself matter of them, and which he who superintends the process, appears to be the depository.'' Like Mesmer, Deslon explained his effects as the manipulation of a fluid.

Having witnessed Deslon's public practice, the commissioners ''were speedily of the opinion'' that it ''could not be made the scene of their experiments'' for reasons both of science and of social tact. In the public group practice there were too many events taking place to see any one well, and investigations might annoy Deslon's largely aristocratic clientele. So the commissioners decided to merely drop into the clinic from time to time.

They chose instead to focus the investigation on proving or disproving the existence of the animal fluid, for ''animal magnetism may exist without being useful, but it cannot be useful if it does not exist.'' The problem arose as to the criteria for accepting the fluid's existence. Even the proponents of animal magnetism insisted that the fluid ''is after all perfectly invisible,'' so indirect effects would have to serve as inferential evidence for the fluid. Deslon and the commission differed over what effects were the most appropriate indicators of the fluid. Deslon said the criterion should be the fluid's curative powers. But the commissioners sided with Mesmer in rejecting the cure of disease as establishing anything: they approvingly quoted him, saying, ''It is a mistake to imagine that this kind of proof is unanswerable. It cannot be demonstrated that either the physician or the medicine causes the recovery of the patient.'' Consequently, the commission confined itself ''to argument purely physical, that is, to the instantaneous effects of the fluid upon the animal frame, excluding from these effects all the illusions which might mix with them.'' They determined to experiment on ''single subjects . . . capable of giving an exact and faithful account of their sensations.''

The commission members began by submitting themselves to Deslon's magnetism, but they felt nothing ''which ought to be ascribed to the action of the magnetism.'' They were struck with the difference between the private and public séances: ''All was calm and silence in one, all restlessness and agitation in the other.'' Although they did not say so, it was undoubtedly at this point that the commission members ceased to believe in the fluid and began to see the mesmeric phenomena as products of social and psychological, not physical, forces.

Next came several experiments on individual sick people, including a group of lower-class patients, a group of upper-class patients, and a few commission members, including Franklin himself despite his advanced age and ill health. Of fourteen sick people, nine felt nothing after Deslon's efforts, and two felt minor effects that the commission decided were not due to mesmerism. Three cases of magnetic effects remained, all of them from the lower-class group. The effects of class puzzled the commission, for "those of more elevated rank, of more enlightened understandings" felt nothing.

The commission offered a social explanation of the effects on the lower-class subjects, invoking what today would be called the demand characteristics of the experiment. The subject is lower class, ignorant, and ill. He is brought into an eminent company of scientists who want to cure him, and who expect, he thinks, "prodigious effects." Moreover, he is paid, and wants to please his interested audience. Therefore, the subject reports what he thinks is wanted: the action of animal magnetism. The commission concluded that "magnetism has seemed to have no existence for those subjects, who have submitted to it with any degree of incredulity" and argued that the sensations of magnetism, "supposing their reality, were the fruits of anticipated persuasion, and might be operated by the mere forces of imagination."

The commission carried out a large number of experiments to support their contention. These generally involved blindfolding the subject or putting him or her in a different room from the mesmerizer and then leading the subject to believe mesmeric passes were being made when in fact they were not, or performing mesmeric passes without telling the subject. The commission found that the mesmeric phenomena occurred whenever subjects believed they were being mesmerized, regardless of the activities of the mesmerizer, and that no effects occurred if the subject was ignorant of the magnetic passes.

The commission performed similar experiments on the higher phenomena of mesmerism, the most famous being carried out in the garden of Franklin's house at Passy, outside Paris. Deslon came with one of his best subjects, a twelve-year-old boy. In the absence of the boy, Deslon "magnetized" an apricot tree, for mesmerians claimed that contact with a magnetized tree should produce mesmeric effects. The commission members were shrewd enough to shield Deslon from signaling to the boy when he was brought into the garden. The subject was led to several trees, none of them the target, and he embraced each tree. At the

fourth tree, twenty-four feet from the magnetized tree, the boy con-
vulsed, collapsed, and fainted. The commission concluded that it was
the boy's expectation that he would be led to a "magnetized" tree that
produced the convulsions; in their words it "is to be attributed solely to
the influence of imagination." Other experiments on the higher mesmeric phenomena produced similar results.

In their report, the commission members stated "the experiments
which are reported are uniform in their nature and contribute alike to the
same decision. They authorize us to conclude that the imagination is the
true cause of the effects attributed to the magnetism." When the mesmerist touched the patient, these maneuvers together with the imagination produced unusual sensations that were labeled effects of "animal
magnetism." In the public séances, where the effects were greater, imitation aided the imagination, as a group psychology similar to that of
crowds and rebellions took hold. One woman felt convulsions that
quickly spread to others, and the whole scene fed back on the individual.
Finally, the commission alluded to a practice effect. Habitués of the
séances learned how to behave mesmerically and felt the effects and experienced the convulsions more easily with each visit.

The commission argued that animal magnetism had "no existence"
and was "no more than an old falsehood," repeating the "by no means
novel" idea of a universal fluid, an idea no less erroneous for being old.
In addition, magnetism was calculated to lead us back to "astrology,
since its professors have been desirous of connecting it with the celestial
influences." Medically, they argued, mesmerism is dangerous. They
admitted that healing by faith, that is by imagination, did indeed take
place but that "when the imagination produces convulsions, the means
it employs are almost always destructive," and that, through learning,
convulsions might become habitual. In their last sentence, the commission members concluded that "consequently, every public exhibition,
in which the means of animal magnetism shall be employed cannot fail
in the end of producing the most pernicious effects."

They also filed a briefer, secret report on magnetism[16] "designed only
for the eyes of the king." The secret report "concerns morality." The
commission members observed that most mesmeric patients were
women, and that they were more prone to the mesmeric convulsive crisis than men. This was attributed to women's "more lively imagination," which in turn was caused by their "more mobile nerves" and
consequent "exquisite delicacy [of] the senses" so that "in touching

any part, it may be said that they are touched all over the body."
Women, they said, are also more prone to imitation than men. The commission members went on to observe the physical intimacy between (male) magnetizer and (female) patient, which excited "the reciprocal action of the sexes." The magnetizer kept "the patient's knees enclosed within his own" so that "all the lower parts of the body are in close contact." The mesmerist had to touch the afflicted part, "so that the touch is exerted at once on many parts of the body." The woman was drawn to the magnetizer as he made passes behind her back, "the two faces almost touch, and the breath is intermingled." The woman's face "becomes gradually inflamed, the eye brightens, and this is the sign of natural desire."

The commission members' graphic description of what ensued appears to be of an orgasm: "The eyelids become moist, the respiration is short and interrupted . . . convulsions set in," terminating in "the sweetest emotion" followed by languor and repose. The women found "nothing disagreeable" in their experience and were willing "to enter anew into the same state." The commissioners remarked that "we can understand why the magnetizer inspires such an attachment."

Because of all this, "the magnetic treatment must necessarily be dangerous to morality," as even magnetizers such as Deslon were aware. The unscrupulous magnetizer could take advantage of his patient, while the obvious desires of his patient might inflame him.

In the secret report, the commission was even harsher than in the public report. "There are no real cures, and the treatment is tedious [!] and unprofitable." Mesmer's alleged "heavenly influences are only a chimaera." Mesmer's "whole theory may be condemned beforehand, since it is based on magnetism; and it has no reality, since the animal magnetic fluid has no existence." The convulsions produced by both Deslon and Mesmer may "become habitual," "produce an epidemic," and even be "transmitted to future generations," in addition to their "injurious effect upon morality." The practices of both Deslon and Mesmer were pronounced "dangerous."

As the most interested party, Deslon quickly published a reply to the public report.[17] His major complaint was that the commission had ignored the cures he had effected, and he reported several new cases. He alleged that the immediate physical effects of magnetism were too weak and transitory to provide the basis of scientific investigation.

Deslon rejected the commission's conclusion that imitation was the major ingredient in mesmerism. He attempted to refute the experiment with the boy and the magnetized tree by maintaining that the convulsion caused by the unmagnetized tree was the result of "a development initiated perhaps in the car in which he came with me, or perhaps in the treatment of preceding days." Deslon also quibbled with the commission's failure to explicitly define "imagination" and maintained, without real argument, that imagination is too weak an agent to produce the strong physical effects produced by mesmeric practice.

As to the effects of touch, Deslon denied that the physical contacts of mesmerist and patient were "vulgar gestures" and claimed, without citing evidence, that "it is not the patient I touch who feels the effects so much as another whom I do not touch." With regard to imitation, Deslon conceded that it did indeed augment the effects of magnetism, but added that it could not account "for the great variety of reactions observed among the patients," since not all the patients at the same séance act the same way. Finally, Deslon found himself unjustly persecuted and in danger of being forced to deny succor to the sick. He concluded that scientific reasons did not lead the commission to reject mesmerism but suggested instead that "it is not easy to renounce accepted ideas—the principles of one's education, the efforts of one's youth, the reputation one has made growing old. These sources of resistance seem to me the true enemies of animal magnetism," a Kuhnian statement that could be made by many innovative scientists as well as by all pseudoscientists.

The government did not use the reports as the basis for prohibiting mesmerism, although the Faculty of Medicine at the University of Paris did forbid its members to use the technique, provoking thereby only a handful of resignations.[18] Mesmer protested because the commission had based its report on work of his renegade pupil, Deslon, rather than on his own work. Through his politically active follower, Bergasse, Mesmer got the Parlement of Paris to appoint another commission of inquiry, but it never met. Nevertheless, the support of this representative body helped protect the mesmerists from police action and forged a link between mesmerism and prerevolutionary politics.[19]

Despite the absence of official government action, the effect of the commission's report was devastating. Added to the satirical attacks just then reaching their height, it tipped the scales against mesmerism. To respectable thinkers, "Animal magnetism [is] dead, ridiculed," as Thomas Jefferson, then visiting Paris, observed in his journal on February 5, 1785.[20] In that same year, Mesmer quit Paris. Until the Revolution, French mesmerism lived an underground existence as mesmerism turned from medicine to the occult, especially outside of Paris, where mesmerism was dead. In the countryside

> mesmerists tended increasingly to neglect the sick in order to decipher hieroglyphics, manipulate magic numbers, communicate with spirits, and listen to speeches like the following, which reportedly introduced a discourse on Egyptian religion, to the Society of Harmony at Bordeaux: "Take a glance, my brothers, at the order's harmonic tableau, which covers this mysterious tub. It is the Isaic table, one of the most remarkable antiquities, where mesmerism is seen at its dawning, in the symbolic writing of our first fathers in animal magnetism, to which only mesmerists have the key."[21]

Mesmer's Followers: The Society of Harmony

Even before the report of the 1784 commission, the rebuffs of the scientific and medical establishments caused Mesmer to turn elsewhere for recognition and financial support. After Deslon left Mesmer's circle to found his own clinic, Mesmer began increasingly to rely on Nicolas Bergasse, a wealthy lawyer from Lyons, assisted by Bergasse's friend, Guillaume Kornmann, a banker from Strasbourg. In March of 1783, Bergasse and Kornmann organized a secret society devoted to Mesmer and mesmerism, called the Society of Universal Harmony.

In its charter, the society undertook to enlist 100 members, to pay dues of 100 louis each, these monies to belong to Mesmer. Dues collected after the first 100 louis would belong to the society. The society grew rapidly, even after 1784, testifying to the continued popular interest in mesmerism even after the commission's report. By 1789 the Paris organization had 430 members, with affiliated chapters all over France.

Although mesmerism was becoming politically suspect, the society, "far from harboring a revolutionary cabal . . . provided a sort of fashionable parlor game in the wealthy and well-bred."[22] This was especially true of the Paris society, whose membership included some of the greatest nobility of France, including the Marquis de Lafayette. The high membership fee ensured that nonaristocratic members were at least from the ranks of the most respectable bourgeois, such as lawyers, physicians, bankers, and clergymen. The provincial societies were more bourgeois and less aristocratic but still excluded the hoi polloi.

In return for the money, which he used to set himself up in sumptuous style, Mesmer undertook to teach the secrets of mesmerism to his disciples on condition they keep them secret. Mesmer himself was a poor speaker. Although in fact he did reveal all he knew, he always left hints that greater secrets remained, in order to bind his followers personally to him. Bergasse was a more effective speaker, using charts, diagrams, and models to impart a scientific and professional atmosphere to his addresses. He came to enjoy being Mesmer's chief lecturer and first among the supposed equals of the society.

As with Deslon, however, Mesmer could not tolerate the growing independence of Bergasse, just as Freud could not tolerate the independence of his followers Adler, Rank, and Jung. A break was inevitable, and when it came in 1785 it threw the society into schism. The issue was secrecy. As Bergasse and others understood their agreement with Mesmer, they were enjoined from public lecturing only until the sum of money to be paid to Mesmer was handed over. As they saw it, secrecy was a temporary measure to ensure membership in the society and support for Mesmer. Consequently, when the sum was paid, Bergasse began to lecture publicly on animal magnetism. Mesmer thought, however, that the oath of secrecy was permanent. After heated arguments, Bergasse and Kornmann, as well as the most prominent and politically active members, withdrew from the society but continued to meet at Kornmann's home. The rump society continued, but Mesmer abandoned it too that same year, and it became a virtual shadow that vanished altogether in the Revolution.

With the breakup of the society, three directions were taken by Mesmer's followers. One, pursued by Bergasse and his circle, was to use mesmerism as a philosophy of social change. Another, pursued by the Count Amand de Puységur, was the continued use of mesmerism as a healing tool; Puységur was the real discoverer of the "magnetic" trance that became the tool of hypnotism. The remaining mesmerists, mostly in provincial branch societies and especially at Lyons, took the path of true occultism into the fantastic realm of "higher mesmerism."

Political Mesmerism

Jacques Pierre Brissot, future leader of the Girondists in the Revolution, joined Beragasse's group. This description shows Bergasse's intentions:

> Bergasse did not hide from the fact that in raising an altar to mesmerism, he intended only to raise one to liberty. "The time has

now come,'' he used to say to me, ''for the revolution that France needs. But to attempt to produce one openly is doomed to failure; to succeed it is necessary to wrap oneself in mystery, it is necessary to unite men under the pretext of experiments in physics, but, in reality, for the overthrow of despotism!''

In Brissot's view, Bergasse's group ''contributed singularly to speeding up the revolution,'' for ''it was from this source that almost all the work published against the ministry in 1787 and 1788 were released.''[23] For Bergasse, Kornmann and others who joined them (including Lafayette), the fight against the scientific establishment was only one part of a larger fight against an oppressive political establishment, and they all were disappointed when Mesmer gave up his fight.

For Bergasse, as for the bourgeois in general, the closed worlds of science and politics were obstacles to success based on merit. ''What a source of power is ambition! Happy is the state, where, in order to be first it is necessary only to be greatest in merit. . . . All careers must be opened up to us.''[24] For Bergasse, mesmerism revealed the Natural Law, distorted by aristocratic society, and provided ''simple rules for judging the institutions to which we are enslaved, certain principles for establishing the legislation appropriate for man in all given circumstances.'' Bergasse used mesmerism as a deliberate cover for ideas like those of the more openly revolutionary Rousseau. Bergasse, like Rousseau, wanted society to return to its natural state, ''society as it ought to exist . . . the one that results from the relation that our own natures, when well-ordered, must produce.'' According to Bergasse, ''The guiding rule of society is harmony,'' just as it is in bodily health. Sickness in the body arises from blocking the natural flow of animal magnetism, sickness in society from blocking ''artificial moral magnetism.'' In each case, treatment is restoration of harmony.

This attempt to make natural physical law the foundation of man-made societal law is similar to the later doctrines of Spurzheim and Combe. Bergasse and his followers were also like the moderate reforming phrenologists in rejecting atheism and materialism. The existence of Natural Law and of the fluid demonstrated to Bergasse the existence of God and His ''profound wisdom''; just so did Natural Law and the organ of Veneration prove God's existence to the phrenologists. The Society of Universal Harmony required its members to swear belief in God and the immortality of the soul, and it excluded from membership ''creatures so deprived of sense as to be materialists.''

Bergasse's call was not for immediate revolutionary action, however. Like the later reforming phrenologists, he wanted to change society indirectly through education. He believed that the animal magnetic fluid passed from individual to individual and that a growing child's development would be determined by the moral and physical health and sickness of those around him. The child surrounded by depraved, aristocratic, French "civilization" would in turn grow up ruined and depraved. The child of the countryside, exposed to more benign effluences, would be far sounder. Sound education and treatment of the wicked, as well as treatment of the sick, were to be effected by surrounding the subject with benign influences. Echoing Rousseau's *Emile,* Bergasse said of the properly raised child: "In harmony with himself, with everything around him, he develops within nature . . . like a shrub that extends its fibers in a fecund, workable soil."

Indirectly, then, by correctly raising a healthy generation of adults, would Bergasse's revolution come about:

> If by chance animal magnetism really existed . . . I ask you, sir, what revolution should we not of necessity expect? When our generation, exhausted by ills of all kinds and by the remedies supposed to deliver it from those ills, gives way to a vigorous, hardy generation, which knows no other laws of self-preservation than those of Nature: what will become of our habits, our arts, our customs? . . . A more robust constitution would make us remember independence. When, with such a constitution, we necessarily would develop new morals, how could we possibly put up with the yoke of the institutions that govern us today?[25]

In the Bergasse-Kornmann group there were other political mesmerists, but their ideas were substantially the same as Bergasse's, whose works provide the most extensive application of mesmerism to social reform. Political mesmerism was the least durable form of mesmerism. It had its appeals, but the political situation changed so much during the upheavals of the Revolution that mesmerism simply became irrelevant to political action. Mesmerism as a reform movement was therefore weaker and less influential than reforming phrenology.

Artificial Somnambulism

> Picture to yourself the village *place.* In the middle is an elm, with a spring of clear water at its foot. It is a huge old tree, but still green and vigorous; it is a tree held in respect by the elders, who are wont

to meet at its foot on holiday mornings to talk over the crops and the market prospects. It is a tree dear to the young folk, who assemble there on summer evenings for their rustic dances. This tree, magnetized from time immemorial by the love of pleasure, is now magnetized by the love of humanity. M. Puységur and his brother have given it a healing virtue which penetrates everywhere.[26]

In this open and cheerful atmosphere, contrasting strikingly with Mesmer's séances, mesmeric healing was practiced by Amand-Mari-Jacques de Chastenet, Marquis de Puységur (1751–1825) on his family estate in Buzancy. The marquis was the eldest and most important of three brothers who were followers of Mesmer. They came from one of France's oldest aristocratic families, and they practiced mesmerism out of a sense of noblesse oblige. The practice was begun in the military by the youngest brother, Viscount Maxime and continued on behalf of the peasants of their estates by the marquis.

But the marquis was more than a follower of Mesmer, for he put the mesmeric phenomena on the road to modern hypnotism, coming gradually to discount the theory of animal fluid. Central to Mesmer's practice was the convulsive crisis experienced by his patients. The crisis was supposedly the manifestation of the increased flow of magnetic fluid within the patient, and following the seizure the patient was expected to awaken cured. While we have seen that Mesmer could induce a trance, it was of no real importance to his theory.

Converted to magnetism by the middle brother, Antoine-Hyacinthe, Amand began to practice in a small way, but his fame spread quickly and he found he had too many patients for individual therapy. So, he "magnetized" the stately old elm tree and organized group sessions around it. Patients would gather together within ropes tied to the tree, the marquis would mesmerize his subjects, and induce crises, and in this way he cured sixty-two to three hundred patients in one month.[27]

The marquis's most important subject was a twenty-three-year-old peasant named Victor Race, of a family that had long been in service to the Puységurs. Amand wrote:

> These small successes tempted me to try to aid a peasant, a man of twenty-three, bedridden with pneumonia for four days. I went to see him this past Tuesday, the fourth of the month, at eight in the evening. The fever was making him weaker. After helping him up, I magnetized him. To my surprise, at the end of a quarter of an hour he quietly fell asleep in my arms—without convulsions or pain! I

continued the treatment and he began to tremble. He spoke frankly
about his private affairs. When I saw his thoughts were having a
bad effect on him, I stopped them and tried to make him think of
more pleasant things. It did not cost me much effort to achieve this.
He imagined himself winning a prize, dancing at a fête, and so
forth. I encouraged these images.[28]

Puységur had discovered an unusual state of consciousness in which
the subject is asleep yet aware, capable of talking, yet not awake. Moreover, Victor's character was changed by the trance:

When he enters the magnetic state, he is no longer an ignorant
peasant who can scarcely speak a word in response to a question.
He is a different being whom I do not know how to identify. . . .
When somebody else enters the room, he sees that person *if I wish
him to*. He speaks to that person, saying the things *I wish him to
say*, not necessarily word for word, but substantially the same.[29]

Elsewhere, Puységur distinguished two distinct states of mind, the ordinary waking state and the state he first called "the perfect crisis" and
later, on the analogy of natural sleepwalking, "artificial somnambulism." "The line of demarcation is so complete, that these two states
may almost be described as two different existences," for the waking
subject remembers nothing that occurs in trance, while in trance the
subject remembers everything in or out of trance, including occurrences
in earlier trance states.[30]

Whatever its name, Puységur's discovery changed the course of mesmerism. In the passage above the key phrase is *"I wish."* While he
sometimes adhered to the fluidic theory, in 1785 Puységur told a Ma-
sonic society in a lecture on mesmerism: "The entire doctrine of Animal Magnetism is contained in the two words: *Believe* and *want*. . . .
Believe and *want*, sirs, and you will do as much as I."[31]

The royal commission had explained animal magnetism as a psychological phenomenon, attributing it to imagination. Puységur, too, began
to see somnambulism as a distinct psychological state rather than as a
state of the body caused by a fluid. He stated the essentially correct theory, that the trance state depends on the subordination of the will of the
subject to the will of the mesmerizer. In this state, every wish of the
mesmerizer is carried out; the trance is simply heightened suggestibility.

Puységur found that by using artificial somnambulism he could cure without convulsions or crisis, and his new method spread swiftly. He even founded his own *Société Harmonique* at Strasbourg, which set up treatment centers throughout Alsace. The "higher phenomena" of mesmerism also occurred during the "perfect crisis." Specifically, Puységur claimed that in the trance state patients became clairvoyant about their own diseases and about the diseases of those with whom they were put in rapport. This occult idea has lasted well into this century. Edgar Cayce, for example, started by diagnosing and treating his own laryngitis while in a hypnotic trance and later made a thriving business of the practice of clairvoyant medicine, continuing it until his death in 1945.

Somnambulism drove a theoretical wedge between the two camps of mesmerists. Mesmer himself was unhappy about the spread of Puységur's curing techniques and argued that the trance was a minor part of animal magnetism. It was also dangerous to his fluidic theory, for the trance cured without producing the phenomenon that revealed the fluid at work, the mesmeric crisis. Opposed to Mesmer and the diehard fluidists were the animists, whom Puységur did not completely join; they believed that there was no fluid at all and that the phenomena of mesmerism, while real enough, were purely psychological in origin.

The most interesting objection to artificial somnambulism is one that is still not settled. Puységur called wakefulness and somnambulism "two different existences." The waking Victor could not recall what the somnambulistic Victor had said or done, and the characters of the two Victors were quite different. Yet there were those who, "after having been convinced of the reality of these phenomena," remained skeptical about the cause, "preferring to suppose that there was some secret mainspring in this affair which produced illusion adroitly."[32] They suspected fraud. By asserting the probity of magnetizers, the sincerity of their patients, and the variety of manifestations, believers in artificial somnambulism attempted to refute the charge.

But proof is hard to come by, and in altered form the debate continues between those who believe the hypnotic trance to be a "different existence" from sleeping and waking and those who view it as no more than compliance with the hypnotist's demands. Skeptics claim waking subjects told to feel no pain, not to hear, or to carry out posthypnotic suggestions do these things at least as well as hypnotized subjects. Believers counter with arguments similar to those of the magnetizers.[33]

Whatever the outcome of this old debate, historically Puységur's isolation of the trance state was most significant. It began to detach the valid phenomena of mesmerism from Mesmer's insupportable theory of the universal fluid. This development opened the way for later workers to habilitate the trance as a legitimate object of scientific investigation and an accepted medical tool. The battle was not won by Puységur or the animists, however. The Revolution intervened and arrested the development of somnambulistic study. The hiatus, however, did much to strengthen the already lively occult branch of mesmerism.

Spiritual Mesmerism

Rejection of Mesmer's fluid theory by the animists did not necessarily lead them to Puységur's theory that desire and belief were the springs of mesmerism. Most moved away from Mesmer's own commitment to Enlightenment rationalism, in which the fluid was a physical force following physical laws. They turned instead toward the occult, by viewing mesmerism as a spiritual phenomenon rather than as a physical or psychological one. The Chevalier de Barbarin founded his Animist Society of Harmony, rejecting the physical fluid and accepting faith healing. He, his followers, and his patients prayed for divine help in curing sickness, retreating from Mesmer's original commitment to Enlightenment naturalism.[34]

The possibility of an occult development of mesmerism was present from the start in the "higher phenomena" of mesmerism accepted by all the early mesmerists. Mesmerized subjects could describe what was not present to the senses, could detect "magnetized" objects, could read thoughts, and could communicate with the dead. Phrenology's tendency, despite the intentions of its leaders, was ever toward materialism. Mesmerism's tendency, despite Mesmer's commitment to a materialistic theory of a physical fluid, was ever towards spiritualism.

In the fermenting decay of the Enlightenment before the Revolution, the spiritualistic seeds of mesmerism found rich soil and blossomed forth in lush profusion. The center of prerevolutionary spiritual mesmerism—if such a confused jumble may be said to have a center—was at the Society of Universal Harmony's Lyons branch, headed by Jean-Baptiste Willermoz. Mesmer himself visited the lodge in August, 1784, in order to mesmerize (unsuccessfully as it turned out) Prince Henry of Prussia, then at Lyons on a tour of France.

The Lyonnaise believed not only in mesmerism but also in almost any occult system going, including Rosicrucianism, Speculative Freemasonry, and Hermetic, alchemical magic. Willermoz's good friend and fellow mesmerist (twenty-seventh member of the Paris society) was Louis-Claude de Saint-Martin. He believed continued emphasis on the physical fluid theory could lead to materialism and find mesmerists threatened by evil "astral intelligences." Saint-Martin and Willermoz were admirers of Martine de Pasqually, founder of a spiritualistic creed called Martinism, which mixed together Cabalism, mystic Catholicism, and magic. Saint-Martin pictured a revived Neoplatonic universe in which the material world was inferior to a more perfect and more real spiritual world. Modern man was in danger of turning away from the spiritual world, and mesmerism offered Saint-Martin new hope. The clairvoyant trance of the somnambulists put them in touch with the spirit world and opened the possibility that man could be spiritually whole once more.[35]

The spiritual mesmerists were all over France, coming to dominate both Puységur's Strasbourg society and Mesmer's original Paris society after the departure of the political mesmerists. The movement also spread outside France into Germany and Scandinavia, where mesmerized mediums were produced. In 1788, for example, a philosophical society at Stockholm sent a letter to Strasbourg describing how a female somnambule had broken through to the spirit world and talked with the spirits of several deceased persons.[36] Such ideas had a long history in Scandinavia (see chapter 6).

Instead of being devastated by the Revolution, spiritual mesmerism was sometimes strengthened by it. Mesmerism was a part of the mix of occult ideas accepted by mystic revolutionaries called the *Cercle Social.* Their foremost spokesman was Restif de la Bretonne, "The Rousseau of the Gutter." He postulated a bizarre neo-Neoplatonic universe held together by a universal spiritual fluid: "God is the material and intellectual brain of the single great animal, of the All, whose intelligence is an actual fluid, like light, but much less dense, as it does not touch any of our external senses and acts only on the inner sense."[37]

More significantly, spiritual mesmerism appealed to those who were terrified by the Revolution and felt the need for a new religion after Christianity had been ravaged by Enlightened rationalism. Christianity had been discredited by reason; reason by the terror. Spiritual mesmerism offered a new truth. P. S. Dupont de Nemours, for example, was quite up-to-date on science and understood Newton's "watchmaker God." Yet at the same time his cosmic world-system was similar to Restif's and in fact went beyond to posit two universal forces, Oromasis, the good spirit, and Arimane, an evil one. Expecting, falsely as it turned out, to lose his head in the Terror, Dupont wrote all this down as a legacy to his friends: "Such is *my Religion.*"[38] Many of Dupont's contemporaries shared his need and some version of his new religion.

Thus, like phrenology, mesmerism was a response to the crisis produced by the Enlightenment. But phrenology as it developed remained more within the circle of reason. It was based on a reasonable theory of brain physiology and preached secular reform and social progress based on science. Phrenology appealed to those people who were products of the Industrial Revolution that accompanied the Enlightenment, that is, to the middle class and upwardly mobile operatives. Phrenology was a comfortable secular religion well suited to the Victorian age.

Mesmerism's new religion, on the other hand, appealed to those who were starkly terrified by the loss of feudal order and the general breakdown of traditional beliefs. In some respects, the generally bourgeois political mesmerists were like the phrenologists in using science as the foundation of a new social order. But the spiritual mesmerists were altogether different. Many of them were aristocrats or at least very well-to-do, the very people, like Dupont, who had most to fear from the Terror. The aristocrats were at the top of the Neoplatonically justified feudal order that was crumbling before the onslaught of Newton, Voltaire, and the Revolution. Spiritualism, supported by somnambulistic reports of the beyond, appealed to anyone who could no longer believe in heaven but feared imminent death.

Spiritual mesmerism passed directly into the occult underground of the nineteenth and twentieth centuries, providing a basis for cults and religions from Theosophy to Christian Science. Should hypnotism cease to be regarded as a real entity, spiritual mesmerism will have proved the most durable offspring of Mesmer's animal magnetism.

Mesmerism after Mesmer

Magnetizing the Brain: Phreno-magnetism

> When certain subjects are thrown into the mesmeric sleep, it is
> found, on trial, that by touching certain parts of the head, marked,
> and sometimes violent, manifestations of certain mental faculties
> occur. It is further observed, that these manifestations correspond,
> in their nature, to the part of the head touched, on the principles of
> Phrenology.[39]

It was inevitable that the two foremost rejected sciences of the nineteenth century should find common supporters, such as Alfred Russel Wallace, codiscoverer of evolution. In America, the Fowlers published works on animal magnetism and regularly included it in the *Phrenological Journal.* In England, *The Zoist,* too, devoted its pages to both mesmerism and phrenology. But the true hybrid offspring of phrenology and mesmerism was phreno-magnetism (or phreno-mesmerism), described above by Dr. William Gregory, professor of chemistry and student of the higher mesmeric phenomena.

The basic idea of phreno-magnetism is simple. If the brain is divided into distinct organs and the mind into corresponding faculties, it ought to be possible to activate each separately in a mesmerized subject: "If Tune be the organ touched, the subject forthwith breaks into song. If it be Self-Esteem, he throws back his head, struts with immense dignity. . . . Touch the organ of Love of Children, and he dandles an imaginary babe . . ."[40] and so on through the phrenological faculties.

Phreno-magnetism was a popular, if short-lived, movement. In both England and America there were phreno-magnetic societies and publications. What is interesting about phreno-magnetism is its appeal to different kinds of mesmerists, including both proponents and opponents of fluidism. Gregory, for example, recognized the role that suggestion played in mesmerism but was nevertheless a fluidist. He adhered to Reichenbach's concept of the Odyle, a universal fluidic influence Gregory thought was identical to Mesmer's universal fluid.[41] He was primarily interested in the higher mesmeric phenomena, investigating clairvoyance, apparitions, visions, crystal gazing, and Egyptian magic. Gregory contrasts markedly with the physician James Braid, who coined the term hypnotism. Braid did more than anyone to extract the mesmeric trance from its magical and wonder-working context, and the new name accompanied the new understanding. He did not believe in the higher mesmeric phenomena, but he did practice phreno-magnetism, calling it "phreno-hypnosis," his techniques being the same as those used by Gregory.[42]

The difficulty with phreno-magnetism was that it alienated not only the establishment, but phrenologists and mesmerists as well. John Elliotson's adherence to mesmerism was one reason for the schism between the major English phrenological societies of London and Edinburgh. Among phrenologists, mesmerism was often thought a very dubious science, especially by the staid Scottish phrenologists. On the other side, Harriet Martineau, for example, was cured of certain complaints by mesmerism and took it up herself, but, despite recognizing phrenology's influence, she did not believe in it. Despite the first reaction of mutual interest, therefore, phreno-mesmerizers were abandoned even by their fellow rejectees, and the doctrine drifted into oblivion.

The Lower Phenomena of Mesmerism:
From Artificial Somnambulism to Hypnosis

In the first decade of the nineteenth century, following the hiatus caused by the Revolution, the practice of mesmerism was resumed in France by the surviving original mesmerists, including Puységur. They attracted the interest of a new generation of physicians and others who had not known Mesmer or the conflicts of 1779–89. New and impressive demonstrations of mesmeric phenomena were given at several French hospitals.

Among the new mesmerists was the physician Alexander Bertrand, who was skeptical of the higher mesmeric phenomena but recognized the validity of the lower. He explained the trance as the result of imagination and heightened suggestibility, dismissing altogether any magnetic fluid. He participated in investigations of "lucid somnambulism," in which the higher phenomena occurred, but was generally able to show that these depended on subtle sensory cues. Precisely because the trance makes a subject highly suggestible, he or she may unconsciously respond to cues sent out, often unwittingly, by the mesmerizer through tone of voice, gesture, and other channels of nonverbal communication.

Bertrand's work could have formed the basis for a practicable and scientifically acceptable theory of mesmerism as a psychological phenomenon had French mesmerists not ignored him. Instead, they accepted the higher mesmeric phenomena of clairvoyance and extrasensory perception and tried to use them to persuade the scientific and medical establishments of the reality of mesmerism.

More committees and commissions were appointed to investigate the alleged wonders. The first, established in 1826, delivered a generally favorable verdict even on clairvoyance in 1831. But the report was greeted with derision in medical and scientific circles and did nothing to advance the cause of mesmerism in France. Another committee issued a report in 1837. It had witnessed two kinds of phenomena. It had heard of cases of surgery performed painlessly on mesmerized subjects but dismissed these as fraudulent, claiming the patients felt pain but did not report it. Clairvoyance experiments carried out before the committee failed miserably, and its published report was unfavorable.

Following mesmerists' objections to the 1837 report, a member of the Academy of Medicine put up a 3,000-franc prize for the first somnambule who could read without using the eyes. Only two candidates came before the academy. One withdrew because of rigorous conditions not to her father's liking; the other simply failed. The report of the committee assigned to investigate these cases was the last issued by French science on the subject of mesmerism. It concluded that the academy should refuse all future demands for investigation, and its conclusion was accepted.[43]

Despite Bertrand's promising beginning, French mesmerists persisted in chasing after the wonders of clairvoyance and extrasensory perception. Their demands for investigation of these phenomena were repeatedly met, to the eventual discredit of all mesmerism. Lost to view were the therapeutic and anesthetic powers of artificial somnambulism, as these were buried by controversial reports of mesmeric miracles. By mid-century, mesmerism as a medical tool was in disrepute.

But it was taken up by a courageous country doctor at Nancy, August Liébault (1823–1904), who accepted only voluntarily given fees from his patients. Liébault induced trances in his patients and simply told them they were better. This often worked, and Liébault achieved a reputation among the people as a great healer—and among physicians as a great quack. But he attracted an already established physician, Hippolyte Bernheim, who used Liébault's techniques more carefully. Bernheim (1837–1919) developed Liébault's idea that mesmeric sleep was like normal sleep except that it was induced by suggestion, with the consequence that the sleeper remained under the control of the mesmerizer. The result was a systematic position that viewed the mesmeric trance as a normal, rather than pathological, state that could be exploited for medical ends, particularly for treating hysteria.

Opposed to the Nancy School of Liébault and Bernheim was the school of Jean-Martin Charcot (1835–93) of the Salpêtrière Hospital in Paris. Charcot was already the greatest neurologist of his time before he took up mesmerism. In some ways Charcot was a throwback to Mesmer. He had an autocratic and quarrelsome personality. He continued to induce crises in patients as the highest stage of the mesmeric trance, and he sought a physiological explanation of mesmerism. Like the Nancy physicians, Charcot used mesmerism to cure hysteria by countersuggestion. As a neurologist, however, he viewed hysteria as the breakdown of a pathologically weak nervous system subjected to stress. Charcot concluded that, since the trance could be used to treat hysterics, it operated on, and revealed, a deranged constitution. Therefore, to Charcot, mesmerism was an abnormal, pathological phenomenon associated with disease or the predisposition to disease.

Charcot and Bernheim carried out a protracted and often bitter feud, won eventually by the Nancy school as it became apparent that the mesmeric trance could be induced in almost anyone and was therefore a normal, albeit unusual, mental state. Charcot's reputation crumbled when it emerged that he had been duped by his own staff and patients. As a demanding figure in supreme authority over the hospital, who had no contact with his patients except in the demonstration chamber, he seemed an inevitable victim. His staff, wanting to please him, rehearsed the patients in the hospital wards that Charcot never visited. The patients learned how to produce any manifestation Charcot asked for, from simple sensory disorders to the grand crisis. It remains unclear how deliberate the deception of Charcot was, but the incident does reveal the pitfalls of research on mesmerism.[44]

But it was in England that mesmerism finally won respectability as hypnosis, making possible the rivalry of Nancy and the Salpêtrière as scientific schools rather than as occult factions.

The introduction of mesmerism to England got off to a bad start, and again the culprits were the fluid theory and the higher mesmeric phenomena. A French mesmerist, the Baron Dupotet de Sennevoy, brought mesmeric healing to London and attracted the interest of an eminent but innovative physician, John Elliotson (1791–1868), then at the peak of his career at University College Hospital. Elliotson was popular with the students, had abandoned fashionable knee breeches for workmanlike trousers, and, to the ridicule of some colleagues, had been the first to use the stethoscope on its introduction to England. Now he took up mesmerism in the wards of the hospital.

Unfortunately for his career, Elliotson was more interested in figuring out how mesmerism worked than in quietly using it to heal patients. Elliotson was a phrenologist of a radically materialist bent (although he does not seem to have practiced phreno-magnetism). His materialism led him to search for a physical cause for mesmerism, and he accepted the idea of a magnetic fluid. To prove the existence of the fluid, he demonstrated the higher magnetic phenomena with two easily mesmerized adolescent girl patients, Elizabeth and Jane Okey. Like Mesmer, he "magnetized" water and found that the girls could detect it. As with Deslon's trees, he found they could pick out the "magnetized" gold sovereign in a run of eight. Like Puységur's lucid somnambules, the Okeys could diagnose disease and predict its course, even in other patients. Although he championed mesmerism for use as surgical anesthesia, Elliotson's interest was not in the trance and its uses but in demonstrating the existence of the fluid and establishing its laws. Unfortunately, his critics accepted Elliotson's ground.

Elliotson attracted publicity to mesmerism by lecturing and demonstrating the Okeys' talents at the hospital to large audiences filled with eminent personages. The publicity was his undoing. The *Times* of London, once sympathetic to mesmerism,[45] demanded the lectures be stopped.[46] Sensing fraud and delusion, the radical physician and outspoken member of parliament, Thomas Wakley, had his medical journal, *The Lancet,* look into Elliotson's practice. Early reports in *The Lancet* were sympathetic, but Wakley himself came to the conclusion that mesmerism was nonsense and the Okey sisters frauds.

The key test came at Wakley's home in August, 1838, where Elliotson once more demonstrated Elizabeth Okey to a group of ten people that was equally divided between mesmerists and skeptics. Wakley carried out some experiments that recall those of the 1784 commission. Part of Elliotson's fluid theory held that some metals were better conductors of animal magnetism than others. Lead was poor, nickel good. Touched by a piece of "magnetized" nickel, Okey would go into a trance; touched by "magnetized" lead nothing would happen. Wakley had Elliotson magnetize a piece of nickel, but when he got it back Wakley secretly substituted lead for the nickel. The lead was then handed to a confederate, while another said not to apply the "nickel" too hard. Touched by the lead she believed to be nickel, Okey fell into convulsions, and Elliotson came forward triumphant. Triumph turned to ashes, however, when he learned what Wakley had done. Further experiments of a like nature with metals and cups of water repeated the result: Okey only recognized "magnetized" objects when she thought them "magnetized"; no physical effect of "magnetizing" could be found. *The Lancet* denounced mesmerism as a delusion and the Okeys as frauds.[47]

Both Elliotson and his critics were trapped by the fluid theory. Elliot-

son believed in the magnetic fluid and sought the same evidence for it
the French mesmerists had sought. Wakley disbelieved the fluid theory
and concluded that if there were no fluid there must be fraud. Elliotson,
the materialist, and Wakley, the crusader, between them failed to understand mesmerism as a mental phenomenon, and Elliotson's attempt
to make mesmerism respectable was doomed.

Like Puységur, Elliotson tried to use his mesmeric subjects for prog-
nosis. Already under a cloud, Elliotson brought Elizabeth Okey to the
men's ward one evening (in itself an indecent thing to do) in order to ask
for her clinical predictions about the patients. At one bed she saw
"Great Jackey," the "angel of death," which "threw the ward into a
great flurry."[48] The governors of the hospital asked Elliotson to cease
practicing mesmerism, but Elliotson refused and resigned.

Elliotson thus failed to gain the favor of established medicine for mesmerism. He was later brought back to grace by being asked to deliver
the prestigious Harveien oration, which, characteristically, he delivered in English rather than in the traditional Latin. Still, Elliotson went
public with mesmerism. He opened his own mesmeric hospital and
started his own journal, *The Zoist*, devoted to mesmerism and phrenology. Although *The Zoist* gave Herbert Spencer his journalistic start
through articles on phrenology, it remained a marginal journal and
failed to win acceptance for mesmerism. That accomplishment was left
to James Braid, who happily renamed it hypnotism, got it accepted, and
earned the wrath of *The Zoist*.

James Braid (1795–1860) was a Manchester physician who attended
demonstrations there by a French mesmerist in 1841. Braid started as a
skeptic, denouncing mesmerism as fraud. He became convinced, nevertheless, that there was something real in the mesmeric trance. As E.
G. Boring remarks, Braid must have been thrown into a dilemma. He
had publicly denounced mesmerism but could not altogether dismiss its
ordinary, or lower phenomena. The way out for him was to rename
mesmerism and give it a plausible physiological explanation. In this
way Braid could continue to attack mesmerism while advocating his
own practice of hypnotism.[49]

In his first publication on the subject, *Satanic Agency and Mesmerism
Reviewed*,[50] Braid defended himself against a sermon accusing him of
"necromancy" and quietly introduced his new term, hypnotism, and
his physiological theory of the trance. The new name severed his rela-

tions with the miracles of mesmerism, and the new theory showed that the trance was perfectly natural and not the work of Satan.

Braid elaborated his practice and theory in his major work, *Neuryp-nology,* where he was careful to distinguish himself from the mesmerists. Instead of using magical passes, Braid induced the state by having a subject simply stare with fixed attention at a small, luminous object. The resulting trance Braid termed ''nervous sleep'' and its associated doctrine neuro-hypnotism (from Greek *neuron,* ''nerve,'' and *hypnos,* ''sleep''), conveniently shortened to hypnotism. Braid also did away with the fluid:

> The phenomena of mesmerism [are] to be accounted for on the principle of a derangement of the cerebrospinal centers, and of the circulatory, and respiratory, and muscular systems, induced . . . by a fixed stare, absolute repose of body, fixed attention, and suppressed respiration. [Induction of the trance] depends on the physical and psychological condition of the patient . . . and not at all on the volition or passes of the operator, throwing out a magnetic fluid, or exciting into activity some mystical universal fluid or medium.[51]

While the vague reference to ''derangement of the cerebrospinal centers'' reveals continued ignorance, Braid's new theory and practice successfully extricated the hypnotic trance from the occult surroundings of mesmerism. Braid put hypnosis forward as a natural, unmysterious state that could be exploited by physicians as an anesthetic and as a treatment for certain diseases. Unlike Elliotson and so many others, Braid never appeared as a wild enthusiast. He never claimed too much for hypnotism, advocating it not as a panacea but simply as a new tool for the medical art. Cautious and conservative, Braid succeeded where the more headstrong Elliotson failed; Braid made hypnotism respectable.

As he overcame his orthodox critics, Braid secured the enmity of *The Zoist* and other occult mesmerizers. Braid systematically attacked any fluid theory, including Reichenbach's Odyle, soon to be a fixture in Spiritualist circles. Reichenbach had passed magnets over the bodies of mesmerized subjects, who reported feeling pleasant cold sensations that followed the magnets as they moved. In this reversion to Mesmer's earliest practice, Reichenbach thought he was establishing the ability to influence Odyle in the human body. But in *The Power of the Mind over the Body* Braid, like the French commission, showed that such occult phenomena are the product of suggestion only rather than of any fluid. For example, he replicated Reichenbach's experiment with a young man, hypnotized but allowed to watch the magnet. Later, Braid repeated the procedure but with the subject's eyes closed. The gentleman vividly reported feeling the same sensations, and even approached a magnetic crisis. Braid, however, never used the magnet during the second session.[52] Braid was seen as an enemy of mesmerism and reviled by *The Zoist* as "a quack," advertising hypnosis "with the hope of turning *something into profit.*"[53] Assailed by preachers with the *odium theologicum,* Braid found himself subject as well to the *odium mesmericum* of *The Zoist.*[54]

In the end, Braid's naturalistic view triumphed, and the empirically demonstrable lower mesmeric phenomena were accepted by orthodox medicine. Braid's accomplishment was to remove the higher phenomena from mesmerism, leaving hypnosis. At the same time, however, he unintentionally reversed the formula: Mesmerism minus the lower phenomena (hypnotism) equals Spiritualism.

The Higher Mesmerism: From Mesmerism to Spiritualism

Although Spiritualism began, in one sense, in 1848 with the Fox sisters' spirit rappings in Hydesville, New York, the basis for Spiritualism had been prepared by the higher mesmeric phenomena. Mesmer and his followers attributed clairvoyance and unusual sensory powers to entranced subjects, and the most occult mesmerists believed the trance opened clairvoyant vision to the spirit world.

In the first decade of the nineteenth century, German mesmerists discovered subjects who strikingly anticipate spiritualist mediums. German physicians used mesmerism freely, but their interest quickly concentrated on the higher phenomena. A leading German mesmerist believed, for example, that in the highest stage of the mesmeric trance time and space disappeared, the subject perceiving past and future, here and there. The most famous mesmeric medium of the time was Friedericke Hauffe (1801–29), the "Seer of Prevorst."[55]

In 1826 Hauffe became the patient of Justinus Kerner (1786–1862), a poet, physician and friend of Mesmer, who dedicated himself to her and made her famous. Kerner found that when in a deep trance Hauffe could converse with the dead, cause mysterious rappings to be heard and objects to fly around the room, and speak in a strange language. Hauffe's abilities interested many theologians and philosophers who took them seriously as possible evidence of an immaterial life.[56] Similarly, in

France, shortly before the advent of Spiritualism, the somnambules of the mesmerizing cabinetmaker Alphonse Cahagnet described seeing God and the inhabitants of the spirit world.[57]

Old parallels to recent psychical phenomena also presented themselves in this mesmeric era. The 1840s produced their own Uri Geller in Alexis Didier who gave sittings in France and England for a fee of five guineas. Didier could play cards blindfolded, read hidden pages in books and the values of hidden cards, describe the contents of sealed envelopes, and describe people by holding a personal object. Like Geller, Didier was highly publicized and convinced many eminent men. Unlike Geller, Didier performed for conjurers and succeeded in amazing even Robert Houdin, the founder of modern professional magic.[58]

The more-occult mesmerists embraced phenomena such as these and left extensive records of them. William Gregory, a phreno-mesmerist, described numerous cases of clairvoyant phenomena in his *Animal Magnetism*. The physician and mesmerist Joseph Haddock titled his work *Somnolism and Psycheism, The Science of the Soul*. Besides discussing mesmerism as a medical cure, Haddock presented higher mesmeric phenomena ranging from the clairvoyant recovery of lost property to visions of heaven and conversations with the angels.[59]

While the occult mesmerists accepted such phenomena, they preferred to give what they believed was a scientific account of them. Gregory adhered to the fluidic theory as expounded and renamed by Reichenbach as the "od force" or "Odyle." Haddock thought the higher phenomena of mesmerism could lead to an increased understanding of physiology and to a science of the mind, called psycheism. He coined another interesting word, parapsycheism, which referred to the healing influence of mesmerism.

All these phenomena and ideas were in place when the Hydesville rappings broke out. Combined with mystical Swedenborgianism by Andrew Jackson Davis, mesmeric clairvoyance and teenage trickery gave birth to Spiritualism. Not content to remain passive conduits of information about the beyond, American mediums, carrying on the traditions of evangelism, aggressively carried these beliefs over several continents. When they arrived in England, even the occult mesmerizers were shocked. Two articles in *The Zoist* of 1853 and 1854 are representative.

The first article, signed only "N.E.E.N.," dismissed spirits as "bottomless fancies" and staunchly defended materialism as the only philosophy acceptable to "a strong, deep-thinking mind." Even a Christian, said the writer, should find conversing with spirits for money "outrageous and revolting." He recounted several séances in which spirits answered sitters' questions by rapping yesses and noes, which N.E.E.N. alleged were produced by the foot of the seer tapping a leg of the séance table. One who attended séances, N.E.E.N. concluded, was "only the secret sport and victim of the most mendacious trickery."[60]

A lengthier and more sympathetic account of Spiritualist séances and manifestations was offered by J. W. Jackson, although he also aimed to discredit Spiritualism. Jackson accused Spiritualist mediums, not of being tricksters, but of being unknowing somnambules, and he professed himself disgusted at "the perversity of mind which could refuse mesmerism as a science and receive it as a wonder." Both Spiritualists and their critics misunderstood what happened at séances, for both were captives of "modern civilization . . . become so utterly devoid of the least pretensions to soul." The Spiritualists were reacting against the "tyranny of an antecedent materialism," according to Jackson, and wished to believe in an afterlife that was "an indication of universal progress" from the material world through the seven levels of the spirit world. Consequently in "ignorance of mesmeric facts, and of the results of spontaneous extacy [sic] in other ages, the Spiritualists "completely misinterpret" their achievements. Equally ignorant, their critics "deny facts which nearly every age has witnessed, and which science is now perfectly competent to reproduce."

Jackson explained Spiritualistic phenomena according to the fluidic theory. Raps were "produced by the powerful radiation of nervous energy, from a system in a state of exalted action." This state also, mesmerists believed, resulted in "lucidity or clairvoyance," "hence the high-wrought and supersensuous intelligence" occasionally displayed by mediums. In short, the medium deluded herself in thinking she communicated with spirits; in reality, according to Jackson, she communicated clairvoyantly with other minds, bodies, and places. The physical phenomena of the séance, such as table lifting and the moving of small objects, Jackson also explained as due to the medium's radiating "a force which, like that of a magnet in relation to iron, can attract or repel various substances, such as articles of furniture." The spirits did not lift the table, the medium's Odyle did.

Unfortunately for Jackson, Elliotson, Haddock, Gregory, and the other fluidic mesmerists, the fluid theory was on the way out. Braid, and the general advance of physics, ruled it out of court for scientists, who refused to accept the higher mesmeric phenomena in any case. So these phenomena were taken over by the Spiritualists, who replaced the magnetic fluid with the more religiously appealing spirits of the dead. Moreover, the spirits opened up the prospect of eternal progress on earth and then in heaven. Battered by scientists, the fluid theory could not compete with the immortal soul.

In the work of the fluidists, we can see the birth of psychical research (later parapsychology) with its precarious attempts to maintain its balance between science and religion. Jackson must dismiss the mediums as ignorant fools, yet must acknowledge that what he offers as a scientific explanation "will of course be laughed to scorn by all who are ignorant of or disbelievers in the higher range of mesmeric phenomena." He anticipated J. B. Rhine by over seventy-five years when he claimed that "science is now perfectly competent to reproduce" the clairvoyance of mediums. Jackson knew he was trapped between the ignorant gullibility of the masses, who saw in the higher mesmeric phenomena spiritual wonders and a new religion, and the implacable hostility of the skeptics who dismissed such phenomena as foolishness and mock science. Nevertheless, Jackson retained the optimism that has ever marked the psychical researcher. At the end of his articles he promised that the mesmerist will "do battle with the host of misunderstood phenomena. These men will in the end doubtless prevail to sift the facts from the fallacies, the true from the false; and I suspect that, when this shall have been accomplished, the world (embracing even our American cousins) will find that the *ghost*, which has occasioned so much disturbance, was, after all, only *mesmerism in disguise*! come in this Puck fashion to laugh at a generation which, having refused the sage clothed in wisdom and beneficence, was nevertheless but too happy to receive the fool clad in his motley and bells!"[61]

Spiritualists seem to have remained sympathetic to mesmerism despite Jackson's attitude. For example, Gregory's book was reprinted in 1909, more than half a century after his death, under the auspices of the Spiritualists, for mesmerism, said the foreword, is "the keystone work of all the occult sciences."

CONCLUSION

The Significance of Mesmerism

The cultural meaning of mesmerism has been best stated by Robert Darnton in his appropriately titled book, *Mesmerism and the End of the Enlightenment in France*. Darnton argues persuasively that mesmerism connected the Age of Reason and the nineteenth-century fascination with the occult. Echoing James Webb, Darnton perceives a current of the irrational that "flowed through the age of reason . . . like an underground stream. When it broke through to the surface after 1789, it had been swollen by Swedenborgianism, Martinism, Rosicrucianism, alchemy, physiognomy, and many other currents of spiritualism; but the mesmerist current was one of the most powerful."[62]

Mesmer knew that what he was doing had long been the province of priests and mystics. As a good man of the Enlightenment, however, he tried to naturalize the supernatural. Faced with the exorcist Gassner, who was convinced of his own magical powers, Mesmer saw only an unwitting tool of nature. Mesmer's superiority, in his own scientifically trained mind, lay in his witting use of nature. However, Mesmer's direct links with the mystical and religious path cannot be dismissed. His doctoral thesis sought the hidden truth of astrology, and his fluid theory always smacked of alchemy. Mesmer was not content, as most Enlightenment philosophers were, to simply denounce and dismiss every trace of superstition. Instead, like William James a century later, he claimed that there must be some element of truth in things that people had long believed.

Therefore, what Mesmer brought to Paris, capital of the Age of Reason, may be regarded as the first parapsychology. It recognized the validity and importance of certain unusual human experiences and strove to bring them to the attention of established science, by then steeped in the tradition of Newton. But animal magnetism could not escape its association with the occult. While mesmerism revolted physicians and scientists, it also titillated and attracted bored nobles and suffering peasants, neither of whom knew much of science. Science was an earnest occupation for Franklin and Lavoisier, but it was a trendy parlor game for aristocrats, and a wonder-worker for the uneducated.

The earnest men of science could not avoid condemning animal magnetism. Science was only just emerging in its modern form. Newton had dismissed the angels from the heavens, and Lavoisier himself was just then dismissing the last vestige of alchemical meaning from terrestrial chemistry. While Mesmer's fluid theory was not impossible in view of Newton's invisible ether, his practice was undeniably sensational and mysterious. Its very popularity marked it as suitable only for the hoi polloi and bored aristocrats, not for emerging scientific professionals.

And to earnest men, proto-Victorians, the obvious sexuality of the magnetic rapport was both offensive and shameful, fit only to be condemned in secret.

Where phrenology was progressive, mesmerism was conservative. Phrenology found its audience among the increasingly secular bourgeoisie and rising artisans. Mesmerism appealed to the other classes: to aristocrats it was a fad, to peasants a return of pre-Christian religion. As Henri Ellenberger has noted, the trees mesmerists such as Puységur chose to magnetize were the same kinds worshipped by local cults rooted in ancient Gaul. Puységur would have made a good Druid. When his tree was uprooted by a storm in 1940, local farmers immediately took pieces as curative talismans.[63]

As mesmerism developed after the French Revolution, materialism emerged as the central issue, as it had for phrenology. Phrenology had been condemned for its tendency toward materialism. In the 1840s phrenology was beginning to fade as materialism became respectable; man would soon be pronounced a mere ape. At the same time, mesmerism began its rise to popularity, culminating in Spiritualism. The extraordinary powers of Mesmer seemed, contrary to Elliotson, the clearest refutation of materialism possible. Braid killed the fluid theory for scientists and abandoned the higher mesmeric phenomena to the Odylists and then the Spiritualists. Entranced mesmeric visions evidenced the immortal soul, and mediums described a world of spirits progressing to seventh heaven.

In one important respect, however, the positivistic attitudes of science, if not the scientists themselves, won. The visions of the lucid somnambules were taken as evidence for the existence of an afterlife and a refutation of materialism. Materialism was being met, not with faith, but with a challenge based on the empirical and observable. The occult mesmerists, like the phrenologists and most early Victorians, believed in Baconian, personal, individually experienced and proven faith. The Enlightenment philosophes, encouraged by Newtonian science and its philosophy of Baconian inductivism, had become unwilling to accept a world order based on faith. Now the philosophes' heirs, the men of establishment science, found themselves challenged by people whose motto, *See for yourself*, derived from science. The higher phenomena of mesmerism that meshed with Spiritualism seemed to offer tangible evidence that the soul does not die, that the cosmos contains more than the atoms and the void. The Enlightenment taught people to look for themselves, and it seriously undermined Christianity. Now its own faith in Reason was smashed by the Revolution with its Reign of Terror, leaving people to search on their own for something transcendent in which to believe. As early as 1784, a mesmerist proclaimed:

> [the reign of] Voltaire, of the Encyclopedists, is collapsing; that one finally gets tired of everything, especially of cold reasoning; that we must have livelier, more delicious delights, some of the sublime, the incomprehensible, the supernatural.[64]

The fundamental difference between phrenology and mesmerism is underlined by their wider cultural ramifications. Phrenology's tendency to materialism tied its adherents to this world. Phrenologists were consequently active in aggressive and realistic, if not revolutionary, social reform. The Spiritualistic tendency in mesmerism led its adherents to the next world where, released from the body, the progress of the soul would begin. When mesmerism appeared in politics, it involved unrealistic and revolutionary yearnings for man's primitive state of nature, taught through mesmeric table turning.[65] Mesmerism's most important cultural impact was not on politics or society, but rather on literature. The romantics, disenchanted with sterile reason, wanted to penetrate material reality and attain transcendent wisdom and truth. The mesmeric trance was a window on the spirit world and provided what the romantics craved, "the fantastic, the mysterious, the occult, the inexplicable."[66] Mesmerism was used by Hoffmann, Balzac, Hugo, Stendhal, Dumas, Browning, and, best known today, Poe.[67]

Phrenology was a unique product of its time and place. Its central idea was correct and eventually found its way, unacknowledged, into established science. Its facts were silly, amusing but wrong, capable of sustaining only a short interest in the public mind. Mesmerism, on the other hand, was an eruption into the Age of Reason and into comfortable Victorian science of something deeper, older and probably permanent. It treated of experiences known in every time and place and called divine everywhere until the Enlightenment. It appealed to people's need to believe in more than atoms and the void and to find meaning as well as predictable order in the universe. But it placed on these needs the stamp of science. Mesmerists claimed to *prove* the survival of the soul. The Enlightenment's science killed religion but could not kill the religious impulse and so left people with only that same science to justify morality and immortality.

Was Mesmerism a Pseudoscience?

Mesmerism was a much simpler doctrine than phrenology. It had fewer pretensions to being a systematic science, and criticisms of it are correspondingly simpler. Two major scientific questions were asked about animal magnetism: Are the phenomena real; and, Does the fluid exist? In fact, the questions are intertwined. We must separate mesmerism into the lower phenomena, consisting of the trance and simple cures, and the higher, clairvoyance and precognition. When we do this, we find that the question of the reality of the fluid and the higher phenomena go together, while the trance and the cures are similarly linked.

Mesmer himself acknowledged that cures were poor evidence for animal magnetism and dismissed the trance as a minor phenomenon of little interest. So beginning with Mesmer and the commission of 1784, the main object of scientific investigation was the direct, physical effects of the magnetic fluid, that is, of the higher phenomena. These later included clairvoyance, after Puységur and the 1784 commission. The fluid and the higher phenomena were always the sticking point for critics and complicated the issue tremendously.

In a sense, the 1784 commission conducted the first investigation into parapsychology. It had to rule out fraud, conscious or unconscious collusion, suggestibility, and subjective judgments, just as parapsychological researchers do today. But manifestly, investigation of the higher phenomena is not over. The 1784 commission dismissed them, Whatley and *The Lancet* dismissed them, but parapsychologists today are still convinced, contrary to established science, that they are real. Even the fluid theory still has its adherents.[68] The higher phenomena and the fluid have all along led to mesmerism's rejection, but unlike the case of phrenological bumps, not all parties yet accept the negative verdict.

The trance and the cures have had an up-and-down existence. Braid, Bernheim, and Charcot made the trance a respectable medical tool and legitimate object of scientific study. But its widespread application has been repeatedly thwarted. Its use as an anesthetic, demonstrated by Elliotson and James Esdaile, was obviated by the appearance of more reliable chemical agents at about the same time. As a treatment for neurosis, demonstrated by Charcot, the use of hypnotism was obviated by psychoanalysis. Sigmund Freud briefly studied with Charcot and used hypnosis in his treatment but abandoned it as unreliable and unnecessary given his new method of verbal free association.

Despite these checks, hypnosis has continued as a medical technique and an object of psychological inquiry. Although it has its own division in the American Psychological Association, it remains controversial. Theories about the real nature of the trance abound.[69] Even the existence of the hypnotic trance is doubted by some. Theodore Barber, for example, writes that, " 'Hypnosis' may eventually go the way of 'ether' in physics and 'phlogiston' in chemistry."[70]

Mesmerism as expounded by its adherents is too simple a hypothesis to fit the demarcation criteria proposed by philosophers of science. The fluid theory was probably not falsifiable, but in the context of its time it was not unreasonable. It was not until the Michelson-Morley experiments in 1887 that Newton's ether began to be seen as illusory, and even then it retained adherents into the twentieth century. The lower phenomena could, and did, provide the basis for sound research programs, and these continue to the present day. The trance, however, was not an important part of mesmerism, being discovered (or rediscovered) by Puységur but not separately studied until Braid investigated it. At any rate, the trance was such an inessential part of Mesmer's doctrine that its truth or falsity would not have meant anything to the scientific status of Mesmer's system. His twenty-seven propositions might have formed the basis for a more general paradigm, but no one, not even Mesmer, did anything more than announce them. The higher phenomena were the main object of controversy. For our present purposes, however, as long as their reality remains problematical, to speak of falsification or verification is meaningless.

Altogether, mesmerism remained too undeveloped to be called either a science or a pseudoscience, and, indeed, this was never an issue between mesmerists and their critics. Mesmerism is better regarded as the flamboyant beginning of Spiritualism, which produced scenes as outré as anything at Mesmer's séances, and of psychical research, which sometimes induces numbing boredom. For Spiritualism and psychical research continue mesmerism's grappling with unmet religious needs and mystic experiences. Psychical research in particular carries on the mesmerists' attempt to naturalize the supernatural, to accept what materialistic reason denies without giving up on science.

Six

Spiritualism

The fantastically different church where worship is a pleasure.

New Age Temple—Where Miracles Abound! The Religion of the New Age in an Old World Atmosphere.

A male medium was suffering sexual frustration, mainly because he never gave private sittings; it is during these, as a rule, that the medium does his seducing. His frustration became acute the day he and I were acting as co-mediums in a group séance of about thirty-five sitters, mostly women. Among them was a woman he had had his lustful eye on for quite some time. He decided to strike now or never.

The séance was in darkness, of course. Through the trumpet my spirit voices were droning on when the other medium quietly took his intended seducee by the hand and led her to a corner of the room. With whispered instructions to be quiet so as not to disturb the others, she was told that she was going to receive special spirit ministrations to "open your psychic center."

While the rest of us, including me, continued with our séance the woman had a thrilling spiritual experience all her own. Her psychic center opened very satisfactorily. The medium had sexual intercourse with her.

Later he told me about it with a coarse laugh. And the woman?

> She remained thrilled by what had happened and, we discovered, had rushed out to tell her equally pleased (well, almost) husband that the spirits had chosen her for a "wonderful" experience.

> When Mary Hunter's [a medium] husband and his remains were on view in the casket in Camp Chesterfield Cathedral, she ran to the front and pulled at the corpse, begging him to come out. That shows the depth of faith of one who has been marketing it to others.

> There *are* sitters, real sickies, who actually believe—or delude themselves into thinking they believe—that a spirit can draw ecto-plasm from the medium and produce the complete body (and I do mean complete) of a dead spouse or lover. The sitter has carnal intercourse with this spirit body which is as satisfyingly solid and responsive as the physical and goes on his or her way rejoicing in the reality of sex after death.[1]

These statements were made by M. Lamar Keene, a former Spiritual-istic minister, in his autobiography. The church where worship was a pleasure was his church. He was on the board of directors of Camp Chesterfield, the largest gathering place for Spiritualists in America, and was also a trustee of the Universal Spiritualist Association. Thus he is a knowledgeable witness to the frauds of Spiritualism.

He confessed and retired in 1976.

Spiritualism, despite repeated exposures, is not dead. When Keene retired, he compiled a list of likely devotees of spiritualism (or "sitters" in mediumistic jargon) in the Miami area, comprising more than four hundred names. And these were by no means only the lonely, the ne-glected, and the desperately bereaved. Keene says, "I know scores of people, professionals such as doctors and teachers who were so enam-ored of the fantasies of spiritualism that they tore up roots and relocated halfway across the country to be near a favorite medium."[2] Many are very well off. One Sunday alone, for example, Keene collected $18,000, mostly in cash, for a fictitious building fund. His church sported several crystal chandeliers and expensive oil paintings, as well as two concert grand pianos, a spinet, and a harp. "The music was heav-enly even if the spirit phenomena weren't. We created an atmosphere in which the dead could return in style."[3]

Keene's congregation was rich—and so was he:

> As a medium, money never concerned me.
> I mean that I didn't bother to think about it; there was no need.

Money was simply there. More than enough for everything I desired.

We didn't concern ourselves with bookkeeping. If we wanted anything, we just took the money. We lived, as they say, high on the hog.

The good things of life abounded. Fancy clothes are a weakness of mine, and I had more suits than Liberace. I ate at the best restaurants and attended the best clubs. When I took out a girl, it was to the swankiest nightspots. It wasn't unusual to spend five hundred dollars for an evening on the town [in the 1960s].[4]

The most ridiculous way Keene describes of making money is selling astral development lessons. For fees up to $1,000, the medium's spirit guide would "minister to him or her in the sleep state when the astral self is opened up to such instruction."[5] Thus the medium himself does nothing, and the client cannot tell if his astral self has learned anything!

What is it these clients are paying for? Minor miracles. If you lose your driver's license, your library card, the ring your grandmother left you, the key to your jewelry box—the spirits will "apport" it from thin air into your lap. Thus you feel sure that the spirits take a flattering interest in even the smaller matters of your life. If you think that apports sound similar to a conjurer removing a quarter from your ear, you are right. Prestidigitation and sleight of hand are a major part of the Spiritualist minister's repertoire. The Spiritualists have also taken over the clairvoyant acts of magical mentalists.

On top of the thrill of receiving an apport, you may also see the ectoplasmic materialized spirit of some deceased relative or friend, who will console you for his or her death with platitudes straight from the higher astral planes. Such spirits may also offer you financial advice and exhortations to support the church generously.

Is there any method in this folly? On the whole there is. Spiritualism appeals to people's hopes and fears, especially to those pan-human hopes and fears of death. It offers supposedly scientific, empirical evidence that there is life—and even sex—after death. Like Scientology, therefore, Spiritualism tries to unite religion and science. It also embodies the modern faith in progress. Far from sharing the fundamentalist's fear of Darwinism, Spiritualism has provided a religious parallel to Darwinism, spiritual evolution. According to Spiritualism, there are seven astral planes, stages of spirit life through which all spirits can pass. There is no hell, and Summerland, or the seventh astral plane, can be attained by everyone. Spirits of bad people take longer to attain this joy, but all can make their way there eventually.

This new pilgrim's progress is well suited to modern society. An eternity of afterlife spent in one spiritual state, whether in heaven or hell, made sense when the whole of creation was seen as static, unchanging, set until the Second Coming in one divine mold, and thereafter into another. Our modern society, on the other hand, is based on change, progress, and evolution. To us, continuous change and growth seem natural. The sinners in Dante's *Inferno* are forever frozen in the sins they represent; no chance of repentence exists, for their very being is inextricably bound up with their sins. To us this seems unlikely. Surely, after spending a few centuries meditating on your sins, you should be able to move on to purgatory. The fixity of souls is to us no more believable than the fixity of species.

Thus, combining as it does empirical verification and evolution, Spiritualism is indeed a Religion for the New Age. Unfortunately it is based largely on fraud.

Mediums pick their clients' pockets to provide apports "that never leave my wallet." They keep files, called Poems, on all their clients, which they exchange among themselves. Thus a medium in a city you have never visited before can, if warned in advance of your visit by your usual medium or minister, readily tell you your maternal grandmother's maiden name or the nickname only your dead brother called you. The Spiritualist churches have hidden peepholes, sonic listening devices, tape recorders . . . ad nauseum.

At a séance the room is always dark. The sitters sit in a circle, holding hands. The medium may be part of this circle, may sit inside the circle, or may be put in a cabinet. The cabinet is supposed to serve as "a kind of condensing chamber for the psychic forces and ectoplasm [spiritual matter that is drawn from the medium] . . . which enables the spirits to materialize."[6] In reality this cabinet is a dressing chamber for the medium. The medium smuggles compressed chiffon into the cabinet in his underwear or body cavities, or the cabinet attendant, usually a woman with a large handbag, smuggles it in for the medium. The medium wears black on any parts of his or her body that will not be covered by the chiffon and is therefore invisible in the dim, red light that is all the spirits will deign to be seen in. Weird effects can be created by a deft medium.

> Standing in the séance room in my invisible outfit I would deftly
> unroll a ball of chiffon out to the middle of the floor and manipulate

it until eventually it enveloped me. What the sitters saw was a phenomenon: A tiny ball of ectoplasm sending out shimmering ten-
drils which gradually grew and developed into a fully formed materialized spirit. . . . The variations were endless. By standing in
front of the cabinet and pulling the black curtains out and around
me then manipulating them I could create the illusion of the spirit
form *undulating;* varying in width from a mere inch to many
inches; shooting from two feet to six feet . . . and then crumpling
back to four feet, three, two, one . . . and through the floor. A
whooshing sound added to the illusion of the form melting through
the floorboards. . . ."[7]

After going into a trance, the medium starts talking in a different
voice, that of his or her spirit guide. The spirit guide then serves as a
"switchboard operator," so that any spirits who wish to communicate
with people at the séance speak through the medium. The medium is
supposed to be just that, an unconscious conductor similar to the
speaker on a telephone or radio, the medium through which spirits can
speak and materialize. Undoubtedly some people really go into a trance
and "speak in tongues," as happens frequently in such emotionally
charged situations as revival meetings. Professional mediums, however, must generally fake it. Altered states of consciousness, and paranormal abilities if they exist, cannot be counted on to perform six days a
week and twice on Sunday.

Spirits that are too weak to materialize completely generally make
their appearances talking through the medium's mouth, or through
floating trumpets (megaphones), or playing musical instruments. These
props are worked by the medium or by black-clad assistants.

One more anecdote of Keene's will serve both to describe a séance
and to show why it works:

A near-escape we had once in a house sitting taught Raoul and me
never to lose our nerve in the face of apparent exposure. If nothing
else, the bad eyes of the faithful may save you.

In this particular séance in a private home, I had moved, in pitch
darkness, to the piano to provide some spirit background music
while Raoul spoke through the trumpet. A split second after I returned to my place, someone going to the bathroom flipped on a
light. I was safely seated, though just in the nick of time, but Raoul
was caught standing, the trumpet held to his lips.

In an instant I grabbed him and pulled him down next to me, and
as I did, he dropped the trumpet.

The hostess (as it turned out, the only one who was looking) didn't see that. What she saw, she said, was the most amazing sight her eyes had ever beheld.

"There was the trumpet suspended in mid-air," she told the others, "and when the light came on it just fell to the floor."[8]

Origins

But where did this bag of tricks come from? From upstate New York, where in 1848, two mischievous girls tried to play a prank on their superstitious mother.

Margaret and Kate Fox discovered that they could make spooky noises by cracking their toe joints. After several days of this mild poltergeisting, they tried questioning the "spirit" and ascertained that it was the ghost of a peddler who had been murdered in the vicinity of their cabin before they had moved in. Word of these amazing events soon spread. So many visitors came to their cabin that their older sister, Leah Fox Fish, noticed the financial possibilities of going into the ghost business.[9]

Of course, this is only one, limited answer to the question of the origin of Spiritualism. There would have been no financial opportunities to be seized if Spiritualism had not been fully gestated and slouching towards New York to be born.

One should remember that 1848 was the year of revolutions. All Europe was in a political ferment. Ideas such as Owenism that were visionary or rebellious in Europe were being put into practice in America. It was a time when society seemed about to explode, and many people confidently expected the end of the world. Thus it was into a wildly gyrating milieu that Spiritualism erupted.

Spiritualism's intellectual antecedents are Swedenborgianism and Mesmerism. Emanuel Swedenborg (1688–1772), from whom Spiritualists drew directly, had published his *Arcana Coelestia* in 1749. In it he described his visionary conversations with angels. He claimed that the Age of the Christian Church was about to be overthrown, as had been foretold in Revelations. Soon the New Age would begin. Ten years after his death, in 1782, the Church of the New Jerusalem was founded to preach his revealed truths.[10] Keane's New Age Temple, a common Spiritualist name, was, ultimately, named after Swedenborg's post-Christian New Age. Thus Spiritualism, like Mormonism as well, was not the first religion to claim a new revelation.

Mesmerism also gave Spiritualism several of its distinctive traits. The performing mesmerists who toured America magnetized their clairvoyant maidens. Some maidens even described trance journeys to spiritland. The scientific vocabulary and scientific rational of magnetized trances was easily adapted to the spirits' uses.[11]

These features were first combined by Andrew Jackson Davis, the "Seer of Poughkeepsie." In 1843, Davis heard about mesmerism from an itinerant lecturer, one Professor Grimes. He was subsequently mesmerized in December of that year by a local tailor named Livingston and started to give demonstrations of his clairvoyance while in a trance— demonstrations such as reading a newspaper while blindfolded. This is one of the easiest mentalist tricks to learn; just peer down the side of your nose. No blindfold can be completely effective. Davis soon progressed to being bodily transported around the countryside and being taught medicine by spirits. He then opened two successful clairvoyant clinics where he diagnosed the patient's diseases while in a trance. His prescriptions, however, well predate Mesmer: put a frog skin on a poisoned finger; to cure deafness, put behind your ears rat skins or oil from the legs of weasels.

In 1845, Davis dictated, while in a trance, *The Principles of Nature,* a "compendium of poor philosophy and ecstatic language" that reveals Davis's conscious or unconscious debt to Swedenborg.[12] Davis soon became the leading theorist of the Spiritualist movement. His clairvoyance developed to such an extent that he was able to report the geography of Summerland, home of the spirits. At first he thought it might have a real, physical existence in the Milky Way. However, this physical basis of the six spheres through which the soul ascends to the godhead was soon discarded.[13]

Davis thus coalesced several new religious trends, offering in Spiritualism a scientific religion whose audible, palpable miracles could answer all the qualms and doubts of the Victorian crisis of conscience. To believe or not to believe—as man's learning became more and more the learning of scientific fact rather than of received wisdom, Sunday school religion became harder and harder to believe. And there were doubts too among many believers, doubts as much about the social order as about any realm of faith.

Davis himself was a social revolutionary, expecting the imminent dawn of the religious and social millennium of the New Age. Such a combination was by no means uncommon. Phrenologists, Owenites,

Spiritualists all overlapped.[14] The Fox sisters lived in the "Burnt-Over District," an area stretching from the western part of upstate Vermont, across New York State from Albany to Buffalo, and on to the Great Lakes. This region was called burnt-over because of the spiritual fires of Christian revivalism and many obscure cults that had ravaged the area. The Millennarianists who expected the Second Coming in 1843 originated there, as did Mormonism. These larger cults also had some more obscure competitors, such as the vegetarian-nudist Darrilites and Bullard's Pilgrims, who refused to bathe and wore only bearskin tunics.[15]

This area was also burnt over by the fires of Christianity. During the eighteenth century there had been a gradual falling away from the pilgrims' faith, until in 1789 the Presbyterian General Assembly warned against "a general defection from God." A year later, however, they saw signs of a revival. The first of the long series of American revivals lasted from 1800 to 1803, with revived Christians experiencing convulsions, trances, visions, and a tendency to bark like dogs. By 1803 this revival had covered most of the union. It then declined in 1804, and was quiescent by 1805—quiescent but by no means extinct.[16] Millennarianism, in the 1830s and 1840s, was the next major attack of religious fervor experienced in the Burnt-Over District, closely followed by Spiritualism.[17]

RECEPTION

The year 1848 brought revolutions in Europe and the beginning of Spiritualism in America. "On the one hand the furnace of revolution; on the other, the blackness of the void. God was dying, but Nietzsche had not yet officially erected his tombstone."[18] All this witch's cauldron needed was the addition of two toe-cracking girls to produce the heady brew of Spiritualism.

Spiritualism was received in several differing ways. Mrs. Underhill, an early supporter, described the cabin where Spiritualism was born:

> The humble frame dwelling at Hydesville looms up into the proportions of a gigantic temple whose foundations are laid in the four corners of the earth, and the rough and ragged path which the bleeding feet of the Hydesville mediums seemed doomed to tread amidst tears, shudderings and nameless horror, has now loomed out into the splendid proportions of the bridge which arches over

the awful chasm of the grave, affording a transit for millions of aspiring souls into the glorious realities of eternity.[19]

On the other hand, T. H. Huxley offered the following reason why he did not want to bother investigating séances:

> . . . I take no interest in the subject. The only case of "Spiritualism" I have had the opportunity of examining for myself was as gross an imposture as ever came under my notice. But supposing the phenomena to be genuine—they do not interest me. If anyone would endow me with the faculty of listening to the chatter of old women and curates in the nearest cathedral town, I should decline the privilege, having better things to do.
>
> And if the folk in the spiritual world do not talk more wisely and sensibly than their friends report them to do, I put them in the same category.[20]

The Imperial Archduke Johann was also worried about the spread of Spiritualism on the continent:

> . . . this modern superstition flourishes not only among the weavers of the Braunauer country, or among the workmen and peasants in Reichenberg, but it has also fixed its abode in numerous palaces and residences of our nobility, so that in many cities of the monarchy, and especially in Vienna and Buda-Pesth, entire spiritualistic societies exist, carrying on their obscure nuisance without any interference.[21]

With the help of Baron Hellenbach, an Austrian Spiritualist, the archduke arranged a series of unsatisfying séances at his palace with Harry Bastian, an American materializing medium. These ended when he caught Bastian disguised as a spirit, "half Roman knight, with bare head, draped in white, perfect in every way, and refulgent."[22]

Harry Houdini, the great magician, was sufficiently upset at the spread of Spiritualism that he spent much time and effort combating its fraud. He always hoped to get in touch with his "sainted mother," but never met a medium he could trust. On the subject of Spiritualism, he wrote:

> The great wave of Spiritualism which is sweeping the world . . . has caused many deep thinkers to go into the subject. . . . When in 1848, the Fox Sisters started the mythical snowball of Spiritualism rolling down the snowclad mountain of Time, there was no thought

that it would survive seventy-five years of criticism, exposure, and
consequent opposition, and would have developed to the stupen-
dous proportions made manifest by careful observation in this year
1923.[23]

Between February 26 and May 21, 1926, Houdini testified four times
before a congressional committee that was investigating Spiritualism,
particularly in the District of Columbia. During these hearings it was
reported that several members of Congress frequently went to mediums
and astrologers for advice.[24]

Established churches considered belief in spirits heretical.[25] By claiming to produce empirical evidence of survival, Spiritualism denied the
need for faith. By claiming that there was no hell, and that a pleasant
afterlife was in store for everyone, it denied the fear of God and of hell-
fire on which organized Christianity depends. Not only did Spiritualism
claim to demonstrate the immortality of the soul, it also promised that
that immortality would be spent in Summerland, the spiritual equivalent
of a Manhattan penthouse.

Spiritualism enjoyed a tremendous vogue during the 1850s. Many
people besides the Fox sisters discovered that they were mediums. The
job was especially appealing to women. Since a medium is only an unconscious telephone, mediums could not be held responsible for what
happened during séances. Like hysteria, another common female complaint of the time, the trance excused all sorts of sexual or masculine
activities otherwise closed to women.

The famous Margery the Medium (really Mina Crandon), for example, was a normal, pretty, demure, upper-middle-class Boston woman,
married to a doctor. During her séances she generally performed in the
nude—which was supposed to preclude fraud. In the darkened séance
room, sitting in the circle with her sitters, she would become very active
during her trances. Sometimes her head would lie in one man's lap and
her feet in another's.[26] Her ectoplasm also tended to come out of her
vagina. Another turn-of-the-century medium, Eusapia Palladino, had
orgasms during her séances.[27]

Such orgiastic carryings-on were certainly not available to most Victorian or Edwardian women. Spiritualism also opened various masculine activities to women. The medium, for example, could preach
sermons—or rather, her spirit guide and assorted Master Teachers from
the seventh astral plane could preach sermons, an activity still not generally open to women. Similarly, male and female mediums both could
give learned lectures during trances, as Davis did, although they had

had little education. Thus they could win respect, money, and power over people's lives. Clearly it was a job with great appeal to the downtrodden.

After the initial amazement at spirit rapping and table turning, the popular interest in Spiritualism died down. The Civil War, however, with half a million dead, revived interest in the movement. Such sources of religious doubt as Darwinism also sent many people to Spiritualism as an empirically verifiable religion. Robert Dale Owen, for example, writing in the *Atlantic Monthly,* explained his belief in the biblical account of the risen Christ by saying that recently he had himself "seen and touched and conversed with a materialized spirit."[28]

By the 1860s new phenomena appeared to whet the appetite of a public grown bored by rapping. These included materialization, the planchette (precursor of the ouija board), and the "trumpet" or megaphone, through which the spirits were supposed to speak. Kate Fox produced the first full-form materialization. Meanwhile the Davenport brothers (who neither claimed to be mediums nor denied it) invented the spirit cabinet to protect themselves from aggressive skeptics. They were tied up inside the cabinet, it was closed, and then the spirits played on musical instruments and showed their faces in small windows. By 1871 "spirits," wearing white robes, started seeping out of the cabinet to be seen, heard, and even embraced by the sitters—as they have done ever since.

The movement went through various ups and downs as it was repeatedly exposed. The Fox sisters, for instance, publicly confessed to fraud by exhibiting their rapping toe joints—but later, when they needed money, claimed that the confession was a fake due to pressure from the press. And there were, and still are, many who believed this explanation of the confession.

Spiritualism was once more revived by World War I, along with other supernatural beliefs. During the war the British reported that St. George had intervened on their side. The French marched under the standard of Joan of Arc, while the Russians were encouraged by visions of Mary and a fiery cross.[29]

World War I destroyed a whole generation in England, France, Italy, and Germany. The casualty rate was appalling. J. B. Priestley, writing in 1932, described the war and its aftermath:

> The re-union battalion dinner, which had brought me here when I ought to have been continuing my journey elsewhere, was held at a

tavern on Saturday night. The battalion was the 10th Duke of Wellington's, of the 23rd Division, which did good work in France and then in the later stages of the war did equally good work on the Italian Front. It was not specifically a Bradford battalion. Most of the fellows I had known as a boy had not belonged to it, but had joined a Bradford ''Pals'' battalion that had been formed rather later. There were a number of these ''Pals'' battalions, and as a rule the young men in them were well above the average in intelligence, physique and enthusiasm. They were all sent to the attack on the Somme on 1 July 1916, when they were butchered with remarkable efficiency. I spent my boyhood in a rapidly growing suburb of Bradford, and there was a gang of us there, lads who played football together . . . and sometimes made plans for an adventurous future. If those plans had been more sensible, they would still have been futile; for out of this group there are, I think, only two of us left alive. There are great gaps in my acquaintance now; and I find it difficult to swop reminiscences of boyhood. ''The men who were boys when I was a boy,'' the poet chants; but the men who were boys when I was a boy are dead. Indeed, they never grew to be men. They were slaughtered in youth; and the parents of them have gone lonely, the girls they would have married have grown grey in spinsterhood, and the work they would have done has remained undone. . . .

I knew that I should not see the very ones who had been closest to me in friendship, for they had been killed: though there was a moment, I think, when I told myself simply that I was going to see the old platoon, and, forgetting the cruelty of life, innocently hoped they would all be there, the dead as well as the living. After all, there was every excuse that I should dream so wildly for a moment, because all these fellows had vanished from my sight for years and years and in memory I had seen the dead more often than the living. And I think that if, when I climbed the stairs of the tavern, I had seen my friends Irving Ellis and Herbert Waddington and Charlie Burns waiting at the top, grinning at me over their glasses of ale, I would not have been shocked nor even surprised, would not have remembered that they had returned from distant graves. Sometimes I feel like a very old man and find it hard to remember who still walk the earth and who have left it: I have many vivid dreams, and the dead move casually through them: *they pass and smile, the children of the sword.*[30]

It is not surprising that Spiritualism did well in a world so full of ghosts. Such brutal facts require some sort of explanation, and many besides Spiritualism were offered. Sir Oliver Lodge, whose book *Raymond, on Life and Death,* went through twelve editions in six years before being revised in 1922, considered World War I to be part of a divine evolutionary plan. Only such a plan could justify the carnage and despair of the Great War.[31]

Another man with a personal religious synthesis was Dr. Evans-Wentz (1878–1965), an American who studied under William James and Andrew Lang. His field of graduate study was social anthropology, and in 1931 Oxford University gave him the honorary degree of Doctor of Science in Comparative Religions. He was the first American to win this degree, and only six other people had the great honor of receiving it from Oxford.[32] What makes Evans-Wentz of great interest is the fact that, notwithstanding his academic qualifications, he believed in fairies. However, his conception of fairies has little relationship to Tinkerbell:

> . . . if fairies actually exist as invisible beings or intelligences, and our investigations lead us to the tentative hypothesis that they do, they are natural and not supernatural, for nothing which exists can be supernatural; and, therefore, it is our duty to examine the Celtic Fairy Races, just as we examine any fact in the visible realm wherein we now live, whether it be a fact of chemistry, of physics, or of biology.[33]

He started out studying the Fairy-Faith among the Celts in Ireland, Scotland, Wales, and Brittany as well as transplanted, citified Celts. He found the belief in fairies to be flourishing:

> Old and young, educated and uneducated, peasant and city-bred testify to the actual existence of the Celtic Fairy-Faith. . . . What poets have said agrees with what is told by business men, engineers, and lawyers. Even in many cases where Christian theology has been partially or wholly discarded by educated Celts, in the country or in the city, as being to them in too many details out of harmony with scientific truths, the belief in fairies has been jealously retained.[34]

His most interesting finding was that fairies are often considered to be the spirits of dead people, a conflation that has since been documented over much of northern Europe. Fairies may not all be spirits of the dead, but many of the dead are among the fairies. As one Irish informant put it:

> People killed and murdered in war stay on earth till their time is up,
> and they are among the good people [fairies]. . . . [At the same
> time] the opinion always was that they [fairies] are a race of spirits
> for they can go into different forms. . . .[35]

In many studies of British folklore, people reputed to have second
sight (clairvoyance) have said that they saw recently dead friends or relatives in the company of the fairies, frequently inside a mound or tumu-
lus. Such mounds are generally supposed to contain the court of the local fairy king and queen, or to give entrance to the fairy realm under the
earth. Since many of these mounds are the barrow graves of pre-
Christian kings and queens, the connection of fairies with the dead is
reinforced. Similarly, mortals who eat fairy food cannot return to the
world of the living—just as Persephone had to stay half of each year in
Hades, the Greek realm of the dead, after eating six pomegranate seeds,
one for each month.

Out of this connection of fairies and the dead, Evans-Wentz constructed his personal religious synthesis, which he called the Celtic Esoteric Theory of Evolution, or the Celtic Doctrine of Rebirth. He thought
that psychical research had proved that the spirits of the dead existed
invisibly all around us, as fairies were thought to do. He also thought the
Celtic Doctrine of Rebirth revealed a mystical belief in both spiritual
and physical evolution. Like the Spiritualists, he sought to combine
Darwinism and religion, to save the latter from destruction by the
former:

> Scientifically speaking, as shown in the Welsh Triads of Bardism,
> the ancient Celtic Doctrine of Rebirth represented for the priestly
> and bardic initiates an exposition of the complete cycle of human
> evolution; that is to say, it included what we now call Darwinism—
> which explains only the purely physical evolution of the body
> which man inhabits, an inheritance from the brute kingdom—and
> also besides Darwinism, a comprehensive theory of man's own
> evolution as a spiritual being both apart from and in a physical
> body, on his road to the perfection which comes from knowing
> completely the earth-plane of existence. And in time, judging from
> the rapid advance of the present age, our own science through psy-
> chical research may work back to the old mystery teachings and
> declare them scientific.[36]

He further concluded that we continue to evolve spiritually after
death, that eventually we will all become divine:

> Man now stands related to the divine and invisible world in precisely the same manner that the brute stands related to the human race. . . . Hence the gods are beings which once were men, and the actual race of men will in time become gods.[37]

This Celtic Esoteric Theory of Evolution is similar to Spiritualism in several ways. Both assume continual spiritual development for all, development that will end only when each spirit has attained complete, divine wisdom. Spiritualism based its claims on spurious, fraudulent, "empirical demonstrations," while Evans-Wentz's scholarship has never been impugned. By fair means or foul, however, they arrived at similar conclusions. The Mormons, another cult that started in the Burnt-Over District, also believe in continual spiritual evolution. The doctrine of fixity of souls was clearly becoming less and less acceptable to people grown used to progress.

EARLIER ORIGINS

The similarities of Spiritualism and Evans-Wentz's ideas also reflect their similar folk origins. The time was ripe for the reassertion of some very old pagan beliefs. Evans-Wentz may or may not be right about the existence of fairies, but he was certainly right about the popular belief in a non-Christian afterlife, an afterlife where spirits linger near their homes and families and, talking through sibyls or dreams, reveal their continuing interest in the living. These pagan beliefs continue to this day in ballads and folk tales. The dead mother who comes back to comfort her children, especially when they are suffering under an evil stepmother, is quite a common motif. A variation on this theme is offered in the tale of Cinderella, where the fairy godmother can easily be seen as the ghost of her real mother. Similarly, the various brownies, pucks, and other household spirits may well be ancestral spirits.

If you think that these ideas linger on only in fairy tales, consider the following turn-of-the-century lawsuit. In Marggrabowa, in East Prussia, a farmer named Frederik Rick complained to the magistrates that he had been defrauded by a witch who had undertaken to bring him prosperity. The witch told Rick to write with honey on a thin cake of bread the magic words, "Adonis dear, Adonis my own! Thou canst do all. Thou art friendly and thy goodness is eternal. Help me this once. Thou art the Lord!" Then, after washing his hands and face with water on which the sun had never shone and praying to Adonis seven times, he was told to tie a cake of bread around his neck. He also had to lend the witch his carriage and put the heart of a white toad and three feathers under the seat of a bicycle he had bought for a wizard who was supposed to be assisting the witch. To darken the room where the witch called up the spirits, he bought thirty yards of English cloth. After this séance was over, he found that he had lost 1,200 reichsmarks, which seems to have finally made him suspicious. The witch and wizard were sentenced to three months and six months imprisonment respectively.[38]

There is no reason to assume that Americans are any less superstitious than their European relatives. Many Celts, Germans, and Scandinavians settled in America, and it would seem reasonable to assume that they brought in their mental baggage a belief in fairies/spirits of the dead hovering about mortals. Germans and Scandinavians probably held beliefs very similar to those Evans-Wentz found among the Celts, for Dr. Ellis-Davidson has shown that the Norse also believed in family spirits, often called elves, and in reincarnation.[39]

The Wagnerian Valhalla seems to be a confusion of several Norse views of the afterlife: a hall of the Lord of Hosts, Odin, to which only the most valorous and noble warriors were admitted; bewitched, zombielike dead warriors who could fight forever; a land of the dead, ruled by Odin in his aspect as god of the dead, to which entrance was gained by cremation or by sacrificial death by hanging. And this list by no means sums up the various Norse views of the afterlife.

The Valhalla confusion involves only the possible afterlife of votaries of Odin, usually nobles. Farmers and traders were more likely to be followers of Thor. Some families of Thor worshippers expected to "die into the hills." Second-sighted people in the sagas occasionally said they had seen a sacred hill open, revealing the dead family welcoming the newly deceased member of the family. Most followers of Thor, however, expected to live on in their burial mounds, or howes. Good friends were sometimes buried next to each other so that they could talk together after death.

Sometimes these howe-dwellers took on a ghastly animation, similar to that of the vampires of Eastern Europe. These walking dead—not incorporeal ghosts—were called *draugar* (pl.; *draugr* sing.). Sometimes, like many ghosts in folk tales, they were seeking a just revenge for their death. Usually, however, they had been obnoxious people in life and simply continued to be obnoxious, with preternatural strength, in death. Those howe-dwellers who stayed peacefully in their mounds could also become *draugar* when a mortal entered their mounds to steal the treasures buried with the dead. A vivid image of the *draugr* is offered in *Egils Saga ok Asmundar,* where a foster brother of the dead Aran voluntarily stays in Aran's mound for three nights to fulfill a vow. He fights the howe-dweller—no longer a being with the mind or soul of Aran—when the howe-dweller, on the third night, tries to devour his companion as he had previously devoured the horse, hawk, and hound that had been buried with him.[40]

Howe burial was also associated with the cult of the Vanir, the second family of gods. Odin, Thor, and the rest of the Wagnerian deities were the Asir, the gods of the life and death of humans. Odin, the father of the other Asir, was the god not only of war and death but also of mead, poetic inspiration, and magic wisdom. Thor protected the world from the depredations of giants and was the everyday god before whom oaths were sworn and whose hammer hallowed weddings.

There was another whole family of gods, however, the Vanir, who were concerned with the fertility of the earth. The main deities of the Vanir were Freyr and Freyja, whose names mean simply Lord and Lady. In *Gylfaginning* (XXIV) Freyr is said to control "rain, sunshine and the fruitfulness of the earth."[41] They are the only deities of whom stories of love and lust are told. Freyr gave up his magical sword to win the love of a giantess. Thus he will have no weapon when Ragnarok, the last battle of the gods against the giants and monsters, arrives. In *Lokasenna,* Loki's scabrous tirade against the gods, he accuses Freyja of having love dealings with her brother, Freyr, and of taking all the gods and elves for lovers. Myths dealing with such episodes have not survived, however. She was the goddess of love, and some sort of ritual marriage formed a major part of her cult and of her brother Freyr's. We know of this sacred wedding because Gunnar Helming, a follower of the Christian king, Olaf Tryggvason, took advantage of the mock wedding to have some fun. Having made friends with a priestess of Freyr, who was called Freyr's wife, Gunnar accompanied her when the statue of Freyr was taken around the countryside in a wagon to bless the crops. The priestly party was caught in a snowstorm and all fled except the priestess and Gunnar. He pulled the wagon for some time and then sat down to rest. The priestess threatened that Freyr would attack him if he did not go on, and it is said that the image of Freyr got down from the wagon and did indeed attack him. The fierce fight was ended only when Gunnar remembered the Christian god of King Olaf and called upon him for help. The "fiend" fled, and Gunnar destroyed the statue. Then he dressed up in the god's finery and proceeded on the god's route. This new Freyr who could eat and drink with his followers was very popular. His preference for gifts rather than human sacrifices added to his popularity. His reputation was further increased when his priestess-wife became pregnant. This idyll ended when King Olaf heard of it and recalled Gunnar to his court. Gunnar and the priestess left secretly, taking the gifts Freyr had received with them.[42]

This story, beneath its humor, shows that Freyr was a fertility deity, associated with the fertility of both crops and people. Freyja, then, was the embodiment of the female half of fertility. Other Vanir seem to have been deities of the sea, on whose fertile supply of fish the Norse depended. The elves (*alfar*) were also associated with the Vanir, and with the dead. They were fertility spirits who lived in hills or mounds, like the British fairies. They were propitiated with libations of milk, as brownies occasionally still are, and, for exceptional assistance, libations of bull's blood were poured on their mounds. The fertility of the earth is easily interwoven with the dead buried in the earth, and, as in Britain, the elves were often considered to be the dead.

The different cults had each its own view of the afterlife—with Odin, or in the howe with Thor, or with Freyja. Burial in the howe seems closely related to belief in reincarnation. Cremation, on the other hand, meant that the dead would not be born again.[43]

This triad of beliefs—in spirits of the dead, in elves, and in reincarnation—is similar to Evans-Wentz's conclusions about the Celtic Fairy-Faith. The interrelations of this triad are illustrated in an incident in Norwegian history.

Reincarnation was thought to work by name; newborn children were commonly named after a dead ancestor rather than after living relatives so that the spirit of the dead could return to life. Dying men are frequently reported to have asked that the next son be named after them. Thus many Norwegian kings were named Olaf, one of whom was Olaf the Holy, an aggressive Christian. Despite his efforts to destroy paganism, he was generally thought to be a reincarnation of King Olaf Geirstadaalfr, Olaf the Elf of Geirstad. The earlier Olaf was not called the Elf during his lifetime. The title was given to him posthumously when people took to offering sacrifices at his howe in hopes of getting a good harvest. This shows that elves were associated both with the dead and with fertility.

According to *Flateyjarbok* (II, 106) Olaf the Holy rode past the howe of Olaf the Elf one day, and one of his bodyguards said:

> "Tell me, lord . . . were you buried here?" The king replied: "My soul has never had two bodies, it cannot have them, either now or on the Resurrection Day. If I spoke otherwise, there would be no common truth or honesty in me." Then the man said: "They say that when you came to this place before, you said—'here we were once, and here we fare now.' " "I have never said that," said the king, "and never will say it." And the king was much moved, and clapped spurs to his horse immediately, and fled from the place as swiftly as he might.[44]

This story offers proof that a belief in reincarnation lasted in the North until at least the eleventh century. Furthermore, the forerunner of this story may well offer an explanation of the *draugar*.

Olaf the Elf appeared in a dream to a man named Hrani, begging Hrani to break into his howe, to fight with the howe-dweller there and cut off its head (which treatment, along with burning, was a frequently reported way to really kill a *draugr*). Then Hrani was to take Olaf's ring, belt, and sword and go to Queen Asta who was in labor:

> Then you must ask to go and speak with her, saying that it is quite likely that she will be eased thereby. You must ask to decide the name if a boy is born. Then you must put the belt round her. I think it is very probable that there will be a rapid change in her condition. She will give birth to a child, and it will be a boy, both big and thriving. You shall have him named Olaf. I give to him also the ring and the sword Besing. . . .

Olaf the Holy was the son born to Queen Asta.[45]

As noted earlier, the characters of *draugar* may have little similarity to their characters when alive. Here the spirit, Olaf the Elf, is clearly separate from the howe-dweller, whom he wishes destroyed. Thus there is some possibility that "the continued animation of the restless *draugr* is caused because the soul cannot be freed until it is born into the world."[46] As comprehension of this idea waned, the *draugr* became a vampiric favorite of the storyteller.

All of this offers us the earliest direct sources of Spiritualism. The worship of the Vanir continued well into the Christian era, which did not reach the North until the eleventh century. As the Spiritualists know well, there seem always to be people who want occult assistance on matters of love and prosperity, and the priestesses of Freyja offered such help long after Christianity had become the established religion of the North. Reincarnation may have been forgotten, but spirits still clustered as close around the Norse farmhouses as around the Foxes' cabin in Hydesville.

The population of the Burnt-Over District was originally English, with a continuing, westward-bound influx of Irish, Scandinavians, and Germans. That Celtic faith in fairies still found by Evans-Wentz would have been present as well, in an only slightly different form, in the Scandinavian and German immigrants. Until recently many Irish families left a bowl of milk each night for the fairies, as the Scots did for the brownies. Similarly, the Scandinavians left milk out for the elves. These old ideas die hard, as the German legal case cited earlier also showed. Anyone in the Burnt-Over District could have heard stories of ghosts, witches, and many other relics of old religions.

The next two quotations come from old sagas, describing two kinds of séances held among Christian Scandinavians. They illustrate the sort of ideas, lying fallow in many minds, that once more bore fruit, this time in the form of Spiritualism.

In the *Vinland Saga,* the story of the Norse discovery of America, a public séance is held by a priestess of Freyja.[47] (Freyja's animal was the cat. Her cart was pulled by cats,[48] and here her priestess wears cat-fur gloves. Perhaps this is the origin of the typical witch's black cat.)

> At that time there was severe famine in Greenland. Those who had gone out on hunting expeditions had had little success, and some had never come back. There was a woman in the settlement who was called Thorbjorg; she was a prophetess, and was known as the Little Sybil. . . . It was her custom in winter to attend feasts; she was always invited, in particular, by those who were most curious about their own fortunes or the season's prospects. Since Thorkel of Jerjolfsness was the chief farmer in the district, it was thought to be his responsibility to find out when the current hardships would come to an end. . . .
>
> She arrived in the evening . . . dressed like this: she wore a blue mantle fastened with straps and adorned with stones all the way down to the hem. She had a necklace of glass beads. On her head she wore a black lambskin hood lined with white cat's-fur. She carried a staff with a brass-bound knob studded with stones. She wore a belt made of fouchwood, from which hung a large pouch, and in

this she kept the charms she needed for her witchcraft. On her feet were hairy calfskin shoes. . . . She wore catskin gloves, with the white fur inside.

When she entered the room everyone felt obliged to proffer respectful greetings. . . .

Late next day she was supplied with the preparations she required for performing the witchcraft. She asked for the assistance of women who knew the spells needed for performing the witchcraft, known as Warlock-songs; but there were no such women available. So inquiries were then made amongst all the people on the farm to see if anyone knew the songs.

Then Gudrid said, "I am neither a sorceress nor a witch, but when I was in Iceland my foster-mother Halldis taught me spells which she called Warlock-songs."

Thorbjorg said, "Then your knowledge is timely."

"This is the sort of knowledge and ceremony that I want nothing to do with," said Gudrid, "for I am a Christian."

"It may well be," said Thorbjorg, "that you could be of help to others over this, and not be any the worse a woman for that. But I shall leave it to Thorkel to provide whatever is required."

So Thorkel now brought pressure on Gudrid, and she consented to do as he wished.

The women formed a circle round the ritual platform on which Thorbjorg seated herself. Then Gudrid sang the songs so well and beautifully that those present were sure they had never heard lovelier singing. The prophetess thanked her for the song.

"Many spirits are now present," she said, "which were charmed to hear the singing, and which previously had tried to shun us and would grant us no obedience. And now many things stand revealed to me which before were hidden both from me and from others.

"I can now say that this famine will not last much longer, and that conditions will improve with the spring; and the epidemic which has persisted for so long will abate sooner than expected.

"And as for you, Gudrid, I shall reward you at once for the help you have given us, for I can see your whole destiny with great clarity now. . . . You will start a great and eminent family line. . . . And now farewell, my daughter."

Then everyone went over to the prophetess, each asking her whatever he was most curious to know. She answered them readily, and there were few things that did not turn out as she had prophesied.[49]

This passage shows that around A.D. 1000 white witchcraft was still in good repute in the North. It also shows several similarities to a Spiritualistic séance. The medium answers questions about health, prosperity, and love with the help of spirits, while sitting inside a circle of sitters. It is unclear whether Thorbjorg goes into a light trance, or, like the second-sighted, sees the spirits all the time. The Spiritualistic deep trance may owe something to the social discipline of the nineteenth century, when women especially needed an excuse for acting as mediums do. Since the trance is a worldwide religious phenomenon, however, it seems likely that Thorbjorg did go into some sort of a trance.

The next passage does mention the medium, a man this time, going into a trance. In the *Fareyinga Saga* Thrándr uses full-form materialization to solve the mystery of who killed Sigmundr Brestison. Whether Thrándr cheated as completely as modern materialization mediums do does not really concern us here. What does concern us is the evidence that belief in such manifestations goes back much further than the late nineteenth century.

Thrándr sets the scene and then goes into a trance:

> Then Thrándr had great fires made up in the hall, and had four hurdles set up to form a square. Then he marked out nine enclosures from the hurdles, in all directions, and he sat on a stool between the fire and the hurdles. Now he forbade them to talk among themselves, and they obeyed him. Thrándr sat thus for a while, and when some time had elapsed, a man came into the hall, soaking wet. They recognized him as Einarr the Hebridean. He went to the fire and stretched out his hands to it for a little while, and after that turned and then went out. After a while a second man walked into the hall; he went to the fire, stretched out his hands to it and then went out; and they knew that this was Thorir. Soon after a third man came into the hall; he was a tall man, much covered in blood, and he held his head in his hand. They all recognized him; it was Sigmundr Brestison; he stood still on the floor for a little while, and then went out. And after that Thrándr drew a deep breath [coming out of the trance] and said, "Now you may see how the man has met his death." . . .
>
> Thrándr went on to explain that the men appeared in the order in which they died: "Einarr died first, and either froze to death or was drowned," then Thorir, and finally Sigmundr, who had clearly been killed on land "since he appeared to us covered with blood, and headless. [Thrándr later proved that his words were true by finding Sigmundr's ring in the house of the man who killed him].[50]

This account traces the origins of Spiritualism as far back as historically possible. Another kind of theory about the origin of all religions is offered by Eugene G. d'Aquili in ''The Neurological Basis of Myth and Concepts of Deity.''[51] He suggests, in brief, that the brain automatically constructs models of reality, including answers to scientifically unanswerable questions. Our brains are programmed to come up with answers to the whys as well as to the hows of life, although there is no scientific way to answer most whys. Thus, as materialism in general and Darwinism in particular undermined Christianity, a new religion was needed. Spiritualism, despite its many frauds and exposures, continues to meet the religious needs of many people.

This human need to make sense of things is well illustrated in an experiment done by Dr. Joseph Weizenbaum of M.I.T. (1976). While trying to get computers to understand ordinary language, he programmed a computer to talk like a Rogerian psychotherapist. Weizenbaum named his program ELIZA. There follows a typical conversation between ELIZA and a young woman, who speaks first. ELIZA's lines are in capitals.

My boyfriend made me come here. He says I'm depressed much of the time.
I AM SORRY TO HEAR THAT YOU ARE DEPRESSED
It's true. I am unhappy.
DO YOU THINK COMING HERE WILL HELP YOU NOT TO BE UNHAPPY
I need some help, that much seems certain.
WHAT WOULD IT MEAN TO YOU IF YOU GOT SOME HELP
Perhaps I could learn to get along with my mother.
TELL ME MORE ABOUT YOUR FAMILY
My mother takes care of me.
WHO ELSE IN YOUR FAMILY TAKES CARE OF YOU
My father.
YOUR FATHER
You are like my father in some ways.
WHAT RESEMBLANCE DO YOU SEE
You are not very aggressive, but I think you don't want me to notice that.
WHAT MAKES YOU THINK I AM NOT VERY AGGRESSIVE
You don't argue with me.
WHY DO YOU THINK I DON'T ARGUE WITH YOU
You are afraid of me.
DOES IT PLEASE YOU TO THINK I AM AFRAID OF YOU
My father is afraid of everybody.

What else comes to your mind when you think of your father
Bullies.
Does that have anything to do with the fact that your
boyfriend made you come here[52]

Eliza works largely by using standard, stock phrases such as, "I am
sorry to hear that . . ." or, "Tell me more about your family." These
stock phrases are combined with phrases copied from what the patient
said, such as, "What makes you think I am not very aggressive," or,
"Your father." Eliza can also refer back to a previous statement, as in
"Does that have anything to do with the fact that your boyfriend made
you come here."

Coolly considered, this is quite a simple program. Yet even patients
who were told a computer was "talking" with them became emotionally involved. Many insisted that there must be a sympathetic person
controlling the other end of the teletype machine.

This clearly illustrates the expectation of sympathy on which mediums play, the fundamental and necessary egocentrism without which
humankind would wither and waste away. We must have a feeling of
order in our lives. This need for order, however, is not only emotional
but intellectual as well. We do not suffer confusion gladly. This "universal adaptive drive related to problem solving" is called by d'Aquili
the cognitive imperative, "an effect of the neural mechanisms . . . op-
erating within the dominant hemisphere of the brain."[53]

All creatures need to order their environments, to make sense of the
blooming, buzzing confusion available to the senses. The more complex the organism is, the more sensations are available to it, and, therefore, the more complex is the ordering system the organism requires.
Frogs, for example, only see things that move. They are blind to mo-
tionless ones, being interested only in things to eat or mate.[54] A frog is
simple, fitting neatly into one specific environmental niche that requires
only a simple perceived world. Much higher up the phylogenetic scale
are chimps, who see not only food in the foreground but the background
as well. This background is not merely scenic. To chimps, as to people,
awareness of things other than food is useful. Jane Goodall has reported
chimps making tools to fish for termites, blades of grass that they stick
into termite mounds. One male chimp in Goodall's group even took to
using empty oil drums to enhance his ritual charges and, thereby, to

raise his status. Thus chimps perceive much more than frogs, and they can, to a small extent, order their environment to suit their needs. That it is only to a small extent is shown in a classic experiment by Wolfgang Köhler.

Bananas were placed, out of reach, near a chimp. Also left in the cage was a stick with which a person could easily reach the bananas to knock them down. The chimp did indeed use the stick to get the bananas, but only when he saw both the bananas and the stick at the same time.[55]

Thus chimps can order their world to fit their needs, but far less than even a three-year-old child can, who will look all over the house for a stepladder when bananas, or lollipops, are out of reach. Without this ability to order our world, we hominids would have a range not much larger than that of chimps or gorillas. Without the ability to make clothes, houses, and fire, we would probably be filling a hunter-scavenger niche on the Serengeti Plain, a niche very like that of hyenas. Ordering and fabricating are so firmly entrenched in the human mind that the attempt to stop us from coming up with religious answers to rationally unanswerable questions is probably doomed to failure.

Another study that illustrates the human propensity for making sense out of nonsense was done in 1955 by N. D. Sundberg. He had two psychologists prepare personality descriptions based on the Minnesota Multiphasic Personality Inventory (MMPI) scores of twenty-five female and nineteen male subjects. Then he made up a personality description for each subject using sentences from an astrology book. Each person was given his or her MMPI description and a copy of the astrological description. They were then asked two questions: "Which description is more accurate?" and "One is not yours; which one is that?" The subjects also were asked to get their friends to evaluate the descriptions. Finally, all the descriptions were given to a new group of subjects, who were asked to decide which one fit them best.

None of the questions was answered significantly above chance. Subjects were just as likely to pick the astrological descriptions as the MMPI descriptions. In answer to the first question, eighteen of the forty-four subjects chose the MMPI as more accurate. Twenty of the forty-four subjects picked the MMPI as the correct description of them, and six subjects preferred neither description. Of eighty-two friends, only forty-two chose the MMPI. Results were much the same for the new subjects, even though none of the descriptions were based on tests of these new subjects.[56] Thus the client may be just as happy with a drug-store astrology book's description as with that of a trained psychologist—although the astrological analysis naturally will be of less use to therapists and counselors.

Another version of this study was done in 1975 by Snyder and Shenkel. They used a single astrological description:

> Some of your aspirations tend to be pretty unrealistic. At times you are extroverted, affable, sociable, while at other times you are introverted, wary, and reserved. You have found it unwise to be too frank in revealing yourself to others. You pride yourself on being an independent thinker, and do not accept others' opinions without satisfactory proof. You prefer a certain amount of change and variety, and become dissatisfied when hemmed in by too many restrictions and limitations. At times you have serious doubts as to whether you have made the right decision or done the right thing. Disciplined and controlled on the outside, you tend to be worrisome and insecure on the inside. Your sexual adjustment has presented some problems for you. While you have some personality weaknesses, you are generally able to compensate for them. You have a great deal of unused capacity which you have not turned to your advantage. You have a tendency to be critical of yourself. You have a strong need for other people to like you and for them to admire you.[57]

Some of these statements are contradictory: you are both extroverted and introverted, controlled and insecure. The rest of these statements rely on a carefully calculated vagueness and ambiguity. Even those that sound specific prove not to be on closer consideration. Whenever someone abuses your trust, for example, you have, by definition, been too frank. Anyone can claim to be an independent thinker, but the amount of proof required varies greatly from one "independent thinker" to another. Anyone prefers "a certain amount" of change, but again the qualifier, "a certain amount," allows for great differences. "Too many restrictions" is similarly vague, potentially fitting even the most authority-craving individuals; there can always be "too much" of anything. And so on.

Still, sixteen out of thirty-nine students in this study considered it a perfect description of their personalities, and of the others, only five considered it merely average. None thought it really bad. The present author also finds it quite a good fit, as most readers probably do too. We all are contradictory and confused and therefore welcome any seemingly authoritative description/explanation of ourselves. We need order and sense, and if we cannot find them in external or internal nature, we create them.

This need for order can affect the medium too. Ray Hyman, in his article " 'Cold Reading': How to Convince Strangers You Know All about Them," in *The Zetetic,* gives an example of such an effect:

> I started reading palms when I was in my teens as a way to supplement my income from doing magic and mental shows. When I started I did not believe in palmistry. But I knew that to "sell" it I had to act as if I did. After a few years I became a firm believer in palmistry. One day the late Dr. Stanley Jaks, who was a professional mentalist . . . tactfully suggested that it would make an interesting experiment if I deliberately gave readings opposite to what the lines indicated. . . . To my surprise and horror my readings were just as successful as ever. . . .[58]

M. Lamar Keene offered a more striking example of this effect:

> Once during a backroom discussion, when I used the word fraud, a woman medium whose materializations were as phony as a three-dollar bill whirled and said, "Don't use that word when I'm around. I certainly believe in what I'm doing."[59]

Thus all such "psychic" readings have a certain validity. People accept them and believe in them, occasionally even those who know full well on one level that they are frauds. How much difference is there between a palmist and Eliza? Both are accepted by many of their clients. Both could be helpful and therapeutic. The following example shows how a character reader can give authoritative, helpful advice just as a therapist can:

> A good illustration of the cold reader in action occurs in a story told by the well-known magician John Mulholland. The incident took place in the 1930s. A young lady in her late twenties or early thirties visited a character reader. She was wearing expensive jewelry, a wedding band, and a black dress of cheap material. The observant reader noted that she was wearing shoes which were currently being advertised for people with foot trouble. . . .
>
> By means of just these observations the reader proceeded to amaze his client with his insights. He assumed that this client came to see him, as did most of his female customers, because of love or financial problems. The black dress and wedding band led him to

reason that her husband had died recently. The expensive jewelry suggested that she had been financially comfortable during marriage, but the cheap dress indicated that her husband's death had left her penniless. The therapeutic shoes signified that she was now standing on her feet more than she was used to, implying that she was working to support herself since her husband's death.

The reader's shrewdness led him to the following conclusions—which turned out to be correct: The lady had met a man who had proposed to her. She wanted to marry the man to end her economic hardship. But she felt guilty about marrying so soon after her husband's death. The reader told her what she had come to hear—that it was all right to marry without further delay.[60]

Thus Sherlock Holmes's detective abilities can be turned to therapeutic uses as well as to the solution of crime. In trying to allay his client's doubts and feelings of guilt, this character reader was doing much the same job many therapists do.

A trance medium also could be a good therapist. What could be more consoling to the bereaved than the assurances of their dead that there was a happy afterlife where all would be reunited? A medium who gave no more than two or three sittings to any one client, who refused to let the client get hooked, would be rendering a good service—and is rare. Usually, instead of helping the bereaved and neurotic, Spiritualism preys on their worries, hopes, and fears. Instead of building up the competence and independence of their clients, most mediums use their dependence to swindle a good living. As Keene said, "the services of a phony medium do not help the sitter—they hinder him or her in developing the inner resources to face life realistically."[61]

Spiritualism has offered the materialistic, convincing evidence of a happy afterlife to millions of worried people who no longer find established religions believable. Just as Margaret Fox's confession is still considered fake by modern Spiritualists, so Keene's followers refused to give up their faith in Spiritualism. He confessed to the board of directors of his church, and all but one were determined to stay on with his former partner. The one who left with Keene, however, was no less credulous than the rest: "Well, I agree with you. If it isn't right, my spirit people have taught me through you that I shouldn't be any part of it."[62]

A strong wish to believe is a part of human nature. Fake mediums exploit this emotional and cognitive imperative, but they also debase it.

"The Religion of the New Age Presented in an Old World Atmosphere," where lost rings and library cards are returned by spirits, where mediums do mind-reading acts and seductions, is no religion. It is an X-rated nightclub act. While no doubt interesting, such magic tricks are not the stuff that dreams of spiritual immortality are made of. Nor is the giving of spiritual financial advice to rich widows the high and glorious destiny of a spiritually rich faith.

The only truly spiritual aspect of Spiritualism is its apparently Phoenix-like ability to rise refulgent from its ashes after every exposure. Ever since the well-contrived hoopla of the Fox sisters, Spiritualism has been at least as much cynically exploitative show business as religion. All the well-known mediums have been exposed as frauds. But the urge to believe is strong, as is the desire to find answers to the unscientific whys of life as well as to the scientific hows. The desire for a scientific religion, for a synthesis of the two major antitheses of the modern world, is strong. As we have seen, the attempt to concoct such a synthesis started far back with the alchemists. It has continued into the twentieth century in the forms of parapsychology and various cults.

Seven

Psychical Research

Phenomena such as mesmeric clairvoyance and mediumistic manifestations obviously could not escape the scrutiny of scientists and other investigators, sometimes sympathetic, sometimes hostile. As Spiritualism grew, investigations proliferated and eventually became organized. This happened in 1882 with the formation of the Society for Psychical Research in Great Britain. Its founding inaugurated the systematic study of paranormal phenomena with the explicit goal of scientific acceptance of the results of such study. Psychical research merged eventually into parapsychology, a term coined by J. B. Rhine to describe the scientific study of extrasensory perception and psychokinesis.

With psychical research we come to a possible pseudoscience that, unlike phrenology or mesmerism, is still alive after a controversial century. During this time we have seen, in a characteristically modern way, an explosion of information about the paranormal, which makes a complete history impossible in one chapter.[1] For our purposes what is important is the kind of controversy that has surrounded psychical research from the beginning. One of the most interesting characteristics of the field is its static quality. Attacks on it, and its defenses, have changed little over the years. Beginning with the royal commission of 1784, attacks on paranormal phenomena have repeated themselves ad nauseum, as, necessarily, have parapsychologists' replies. Therefore, following a brief historical sketch of the development of psychical research, we will organize this chapter topically, around the basic accusations leveled against psychical research.

DEVELOPMENT OF PSYCHICAL RESEARCH

Three broad periods in the development of psychical research are usually distinguished. The first period is that of Spiritualism. This is usually said to have begun in 1848 with the Fox sisters, but broadly viewed it may be taken to extend back to the occult mesmerists of the *ancien régime.* Then follows the era of psychical research proper, formally beginning with the founding of the Society for Psychical Research in 1882. The modern era of parapsychology began in 1934 when Joseph Banks Rhine published his book *Extra-Sensory Perception.*

After 1848 Spiritualism was a rapidly growing movement that appeared to many to be a distinct competitor to orthodox Christianity. It appealed to the temper of the age, offering ''scientific,'' empirically verifiable faith and another focus for the Victorian reformist urge. Mediums conveyed messages from dead abolitionists, and Spiritualist conventions provided forums for radical political speeches. Spiritualism provided an ideology for advocates of ''free love,'' those who sought the union of souls, not of bodies, even if the beloved soul did not belong to one's spouse. It likewise provided moral support for women who had learned to hate their sexuality, and it opened up for some women an independent, paying career: mediumship.[2]

Such radical-reformist associations were noted by contemporary opponents of Spiritualism. The *New York Times* reported on a convention of Spiritualists in Chautauqua County, New York, which adopted the usual Spiritualistic resolutions: Evil is to be cured by man's development of his internal and external faculties. Like so many other Americans before and since, the Spiritualists resolved to found a ''moral society,'' free from the world's evil, where they could raise a better generation and ''redeem humanity.'' This ''Divine Social State upon Earth'' would be ruled by an assembly of experts, including Electrizers, Healthfulizers, Educationizers, and Governmentizers, to the ultimate attainment of ''perfect bliss on earth.'' Despite these fine intentions, the *Times* was not pleased. It called the Spiritualists ''fanatics'' bent on releasing themselves from all ''the restraints which virtuous society imposes [in order to] adopt practices at which state and conscience'' revolt. The Spiritualists' "vaunted self-development consists in the unlimited gratification of passion and appetite."[3]

Similarly, English Utopians were attracted to Spiritualism. We have already seen how certain followers of Robert Owen turned to phrenology in the later stages of the Owenite movement. Others, including Owen himself late in life and his son Robert Dale Owen, turned to Spiritualism. Owen chanced to meet Mrs. Hayden, the first American medium to visit Great Britain, and soon found himself conversing with the spirits of Thomas Jefferson, Benjamin Franklin, and the Duke of Kent. He became "compelled, contrary to my previous strong convictions, to believe in a future conscious state of life, existing in a refined material, or what is called a spiritual state." Owen did not give up his plans for a new moral world, however, for the spirits supported this idea. Many other Owenites had similar experiences. Some followed Owen in receiving spiritual encouragement for their earthly plans; some planned for the millennium, when Owen's ideas would be implemented by spiritual, rather than political, power; and some waited for the new moral world beyond the grave. Spiritualism bucked up the discouraged reformer and held out promise of ultimate victory for the despairing.[4]

Investigation of the claims made for mediums and mesmeric somnambules began with the French royal commission of 1784, and therewith began psychical research. The commission investigated the extrasensory powers of Deslon's subjects, such as clairvoyance and prognostication, powers claimed also by such occult mesmerists as Gregory and Haddock. Systematic research on the reality of paranormal powers did not begin until the 1870s, however, from which time the enterprise is formally called psychical research.

In the nineteenth century many people began to suspect that something was seriously wrong with the orthodox scientific world view. The Newtonian world-machine left out of account human experiences, beliefs, and hopes that had been around for millennia. But science had destroyed traditional Christian beliefs for many. As Frederic Myers (1843–1901) put it, "Never, perhaps, did man's spiritual satisfaction bear a smaller proportion to his needs. The old world sustenance, however earnestly administered, is too unsubstantial for the modern craving." Consequently, the second half of the nineteenth century was marked by "deep disquiet" and "the decline of any real belief in the dignity, the meaning, the endlessness of life."[5]

To Myers the central loss of science was belief in an afterlife. He wanted desperately to establish the existence of eternal life and felt that "the discovery that there was a life in man independent of blood and brain would be a cardinal, a dominating fact in all science and in all philosophy." Religion was dead, but he hoped that "the authority of creeds and churches will be replaced by the authority of reason and experiment."[6] Science had killed religion, but its methods could be used to establish the truths it sought to deny.

A broader view was taken by William James, pragmatist, philosopher, and psychologist, who found the orthodox scientific conception of the world false to human experience. James believed that modern science had turned its back on its original mandate—to accept immediate human experience as the touchstone of truth, to grapple with experience and finally explain it. Instead, confronted with "exceptional observations," such as those of mediumship, science found it easier to ignore them than to attend to them. For James, "divinations, inspirations, demonical possessions, apparitions, trances, ecstasies, miraculous healings and productions of disease and occult powers" were long-standing facts of experience; consequently, "science, so far as it denies such exceptional occurrences, lies prostrate in the dust for me."

In James's view it was entirely illegitimate for science to continue to adhere to its mechanistic laws in the face of contrary facts: "If you wish to upset the law that all crows are black, you must not seek to show that no crows are; it is enough if you prove one single crow to be white. My own white crow is [the medium] Mrs. Piper." But, like Myers, James did not turn his back on science. Science was not established truth, but, "mere affairs of methods; there is nothing in them that need hinder science from dealing, successfully, with a world in which personal forces" are effective. "The most urgent intellectual need which I feel at present is that science be built up again in a form in which such things may have a positive place."[7] James's view was broader than Myers's, however. He believed personal consciousness to be the "primal curse" of man and so found abhorrent Spiritualism's insistence on the eternality of one's personal spirit.[8] What James found exciting in Spiritualism was its contemporary illumination of the hidden recesses of the mind, glossed over or denied by psychology, philosophy, and biology.

There were many like-minded men of the time, and it was natural that they should come together to pursue their research on a continuing basis. Thus was founded first the English Society for Psychical Research (known as the S.P.R.) and then the American Society for Psychical Research. These groups were eclectic, bringing together scientists (e.g., the physicist Oliver Lodge), philosophers (e.g., Henry Sidgwick), psychologists (e.g., James), scholars (e.g., Myers, a classicist), and even politicians (e.g., Arthur Balfour). They were united, not by profession, but rather by the desire to provide "one means of bringing science and the occult together in England and America."[9]

The Societies initiated research in such spontaneous phenomena as hauntings, poltergeists, and the manifestations of the séance, and in the experimentally induced phenomena of extrasensory perception. Carrying on from the occult mesmerists, the bulk of the work of the societies was of the former sort. They wrote about mediums, apportings, and hauntings, as well as such ordinary although abnormal phenomena as multiple personality, hypnosis, and hysteria.

At the same time, controlled experiments were performed to study thought transference. Senders would attend to such standard "targets" as playing cards, while a receiver, or percipient, attempted to name or reproduce the target. Researchers then tried to establish whether the percipients' number of "hits" (correct namings of the target) was greater than that expected by ignorant guessing, i.e., by chance.

The societies did what established science would not: systematically investigate the elusive, yet humanly significant, phenomena listed by James. With firm evidence in hand, they hoped to go to science and win acceptance of psychical research and recognition of its problems as scientific ones. No longer desiring to enter a discredited church, they wanted recognition from its rival.

But recognition and acceptance did not come. Despite its eminent membership, the work of the English S.P.R. and the A.S.P.R. in America received only mixed reviews. An anonymous writer in *Science* found it exciting and hoped for progress in hitherto unrespectable fields, and *Scientific American* welcomed it as the new science of the modern age.[10] Others, such as Andrew Lang, found it "sound but boring."[11] But too many scientists agreed with the psychologist Joseph Jastrow, who lumped psychical research with alchemy and astrology as "deviations from the normal progress of knowledge," and castigated its "morbid pseudo-scientific spirit [that] apes the manners of the true goddess, and by such disguises sues the favor of the world."[12]

There was a young botanist who, early in the twentieth century, became persuaded that there was truth in psychical research, but who

wondered if "scientific recognition would ever come." J. B. Rhine believed that psychical research had shown that psychic phenomena occur
but had failed "to show what might be the nature of such unorthodox
phenomena, to find their relations or laws, or even the conditions under
which they may be demonstrated." Rhine wanted to add scientific plausibility to the facts of psychical research: "To make plausible a new and
strange type of phenomenon, it must be connected with the already
known; in other words, it must be naturalized."[13]

To naturalize the supernatural, Rhine named psychical research
"parapsychology" and concentrated on experimental control of paranormal phenomena to the exclusion of spontaneous phenomena. Rhine
began his famous research in 1930 when he was brought to Duke University by William MacDougall, a famous psychologist, head of the department of psychology there—who firmly believed in psychical research. Rhine quickly became the leader of the field, establishing not
only his own laboratory but also his own journal (*The Journal of Parapsychology*), and his own popular fame with general-audience books
such as *New Frontiers of the Mind,* a Book of the Month Club selection.

The motivation behind Rhine's parapsychology was the same as that
of the founders of psychical research. Rhine found society in 1937 "dis-
illusioned and floundering [and needing] a profounder kind of self-
knowledge than any former age has had." To fill this need, Rhine said,
we needed to attend to "the *un* recognized and the *un* usual," which
would be the job of parapsychology.[14] In the past, man had created his
"whole ethical structure [on] faiths and doctrines which 'endowed' man
with those unusual capacities with which we are dealing in this research."[15] Echoing James, Rhine saw parapsychology as bridging "the
cult of Spiritualism and the mechanistic philosophy of science."[16] Like
the psychical researchers, Rhine believed that only science and its methods were competent to establish the former truths of religion,[17] to refute
materialism and the dangerous doctrines of communism.[18]

Rhine's work completely reshaped the field. In place of exciting sittings with gifted mediums came the drudgery of collecting thousands of
card-guesses by ordinary subjects. In place of the séance room came the
laboratory. In place of ectoplasm, apports, and apparitions came statistical tests to see if 54 correct guesses out of 200 chances revealed ESP.
In place of the amateurism of the psychical researchers came the professionalism of the parapsychologists. The study of the occult donned the
complete garb of science.

But parapsychology has achieved only the same equivocal status that afflicted psychical research. On the one hand, parapsychology is discussed in standard introductory psychology texts, has seen the Parapsychological Association accepted as an affiliate of the American Association for the Advancement of Science, and sees an occasional article printed in an established journal. On the other hand, most psychology faculties are "inclined to disbelieve" in ESP, and parapsychology is attacked as "anti-humanistic" and "a reversion to a pre-scientific religio-mystical tradition," leading to "maladaptive and anti-social effects."[19] *The Humanist* magazine regularly assaults parapsychology as a pseudoscience and in 1976 spun off *The Zetetic* to specialize in bashing the occult, including parapsychology. Some in the field argue that parapsychology is preparadigmatic (in Kuhn's terms, prescientific)[20] and have become depressed by parapsychology's failure to gain acceptance despite "a hundred years of herculean effort."[21]

ARGUING THE PARANORMAL

Controversy has surrounded the scientific study of paranormal phenomena since its mesmeric beginnings. There has been continual conflict between advocates of psychical research and skeptics, the issues raised having altered little since 1784. At the same time, psychical researchers and parapsychologists have debated among themselves the meaning and significance of the phenomena they accept. In this section we will briefly examine each field of controversy.

Given the large amount of controversial literature in, on, and around parapsychology, it is hopeless to try to digest it all. Instead we will describe the major categories of skeptical attack on parapsychology, briefly noting some of the points made on each side.

Fraud and Deception

The oldest, most persistent, and ultimately perhaps the most damaging attacks on psychical phenomena have maintained that they are not phenomena at all, but only the mundane, if titillating, effects of fraud and deception. Accusations of fraud range from the mild to the serious. At worst, one can allege that a given result was the conscious product of fraud by all parties involved, not excepting the researcher. At best, one can claim that everyone was sincere and honest, but that they all deluded themselves. The most usual charge is that the psychical researcher, because of eagerness to believe, has been taken in by unscrupulous subjects.

Accusations of fraud may be pursued along two main lines. First, the skeptic may seek to expose fraud directly, for example by catching a medium in the act of cheating. The other line of attack is to provide a "rational reconstruction" of a paranormal achievement, showing by argument or replication how the effect *could* have been achieved by trickery, collusion, or unconscious, but not paranormal, means. This line of attack is especially popular with skeptical conjurors.

Either argument can be exploited by skeptics in three ways. Most obviously, proof of fraud, or even establishing its probability, takes evidence away from the psychical researcher. More generally, demonstration of fraud or its possibility supports a skeptical position borrowed from David Hume's rationalist dismissal of miracles: it is easier to believe in lying and cheating than in suspension of the laws of physics. If skeptics can show repeatedly that demonstrations of paranormal powers can be explained normally, they weaken the claim of parapsychology to be a legitimate science. Finally, establishment of fraud can be used to brand psychical researchers as charlatans, if they themselves cheated, or as fools, if they were cheated. Ridicule is an especially important weapon for popular, rather than professional, attacks on parapsychology.

Allegations of deception began with the Commission on Mesmerism of 1784. It was a mild allegation; the commission did not accuse Deslon or his subjects of conscious fraud but only of unwittingly falling victim to imagination, suggestion, and role playing. Similarly, Wakley never accused Elliotson of cheating, only of misinterpreting the abilities of the Okeys, although the popular press regarded the girls as scheming fakes.[22] More recently, in Spiritualism, numerous mediums have been exposed or have confessed to fraud.

The psychical researchers, too, often found themselves with fraudulent mediums. Perhaps the most famous case was that of Mrs. LeRoi Crandon (Margery the Medium), including as it did skeptics from outside psychical research and massive publicity. *Scientific American* became sympathetically interested in psychical research in 1922, and in December of that year announced a $5,000 prize for "conclusive psychic manifestations." The magazine put together an eminent committee consisting of the psychical researchers Walter Franklin Prince and Hereward Carrington; William MacDougall, famous psychologist and later Rhine's mentor; Daniel Frost Comstock, physicist, and advisor to the ASPR; and magician Harry Houdini. The secretary, and effective leading investigator, was J. Malcolm Bird,[23] associate editor of *Scientific American* and avid spiritualist.[24]

The crop of candidates was distinctly disappointing, even to Bird, who noted their "lack of quality."[25] In 1924, however, Margery came forward, and Bird's reports on her were favorable. Margery's specialties were the physical phenomena of spiritualism: under control of her dead brother Walter, Margery could apparently move furniture and extrude ectoplasm.[26] The committee, however, was divided. Houdini pronounced her a "deliberate and conscious fraud," Prince and Comstock said her claims were not proven, and Carrington believed she had powers but cheated on occasion.[27] Sittings continued, and finally all save Carrington gave up believing in Margery; the case and contest were closed in April, 1925.[28] *Scientific American* later launched an equally unsuccessful search headed by the magician Joseph Dunninger, in 1941–43, with a $10,000 prize.[29]

Others, however, considered the Margery case still open. A young psychologist, Hudson Hoagland, organized a Harvard investigation of Margery. The committee members included psychological historian E. G. Boring, astronomer Harlow Shapley, and a magician. The Harvard group secured damning evidence against Margery, and the magician duplicated her feats. While calling her a fraud, Hoagland considered her an unconscious one, hypothesizing that Walter was a secondary personality that emerged in trance, so that Mrs. Crandon was not responsible for her tricks.[30] Margery continued to have defenders, at least her husband and members of the ASPR, though most outside observers, including J. B. Rhine in 1927, thought her a fraud.[31]

Obviously, investigating mediums is fraught with the dangers of deception. The researchers are denied full control of the situation, and the medium usually has a financial interest in success. These dangers, coupled with the repeated exposure of mediums, particularly physical mediums, contributed to the acceptance of Rhine's laboratory-based, controlled experiments with ordinary subjects. This work, although taking place in the bright laboratory instead of the dark séance room, has also attracted cries of "fraud" from skeptics.

The skeptics' case was forcefully stated by George R. Price in 1955. Writing in *Science*, Price argued that accepting ESP meant overthrowing all of established science—an absurdity. He had once been impressed by Rhine's work, he said, but his confidence had evaporated when he read Hume on miracles; he also quoted Tom Paine's pithy restatement: "Is it more probable that nature should go out of her course, or that a man should lie?" Price provided rational reconstructions, involving fraud, of some parapsychological experiments. Naturally, parapsychologists responded with alarm to Price's article, although Rhine at least welcomed Price's argument on the revolutionary implications of parapsychology.[32] Many years later Price briefly apologized for his slur on Rhine's character and on that of the English parapsychologist, S. G. Soal, whose experiment he attacked.

Price's banner was picked up by the English psychologist C. E. M. Hansel in his *ESP: A Scientific Evaluation* of 1966, revised and extended in 1980 as *ESP and Parapsychology*. Hansel's approach was to assume that positive ESP results had to work by trickery, and then to figure out what the trickery might have been—an approach that, while interesting, is hardly conclusive. In this way he provided rational reconstructions of the experiments most widely touted by parapsychologists themselves as the best evidence for ESP.[33]

Recently, research conducted with supposedly gifted people has been making a comeback, especially with Uri Geller.[34] Like Margery, Geller finds his committed enthusiasts and his detractors.[35]

These references are only the tip of the iceberg of accusations of fraud and deception made against mesmerists, psychical researchers, and parapsychologists. To these old charges, proponents of the paranormal have had to reply. Of course, they have replied to specific challenges, such as Price's or Hansel's, but broadly speaking, three kinds of replies have been forthcoming. Continuing to collect data demonstrating paranormal powers under better-controlled conditions has been a common reply. Much of the work reported in the parapsychological literature is of this kind, designed to firmly establish the existence of ESP or psychokinesis.

Another reply to skeptics is the parapsychological community's vigilance against fraud and acknowledgment of it when proved. On the whole, psychical researchers have been good at discovering false mediums. The most recent scandal, involving the falsification of records at Rhine's laboratory, was discovered and made public by parapsychologists themselves.[36] Similarly, parapsychologists have recently started to accept the likelihood of fraud in S. G. Soal's classic experiments.[37] And of course they can point out that fraud is not unknown in accepted scientific fields.[38]

The most radical reply parapsychologists can make to skeptics is to dismiss charges of fraud as themselves unscientific. A chemist does not allege fraud when someone else's findings upset him; so why should critics of parapsychology get away with such a lack of scholarly courtesy and of the scientific, enquiring spirit? A corollary of this position is that parapsychology is strong enough to ignore its critics and live its own life.[39] This radical view does not seem to be shared by many parapsychologists. Although it is an understandable reaction to a century of rejection, it would tend to force parapsychology to fully enter the occult underground and become "a self-satisfied cult."[40]

Violations of Accepted Law

The impetus behind accusations of fraud is, explicitly or implicitly, that ESP and psychokinesis are so at variance with well-established scientific law that they simply cannot occur. If they are impossible, then all apparent instances of psychic powers are necessarily fraudulent. This argument is scattered liberally throughout the skeptical literature.

Response to this criticism has divided the parapsychological camp. Much of the appeal of psychical research has always been exactly that it *does* challenge the prevailing materialistic-mechanistic world view based on science. From this standpoint, parapsychology is exciting and important precisely because it demands fundamental change in Western orthodoxy. As R. A. McConnell put it recently, the parapsychologist and the skeptic agree that "if ESP is a real ability, it will change our outlook and our ways of behaving more radically than any discovery in the history of science."[41] The natural reply to the skeptic is indictment for dogmatism—for sticking to orthodox science in the face of the facts of parapsychology. Popperian falsification is next invoked: the facts of ESP refute materialism and mechanism, so these traditional views must be abandoned. This argument makes the skeptic rather than the parapsychologist look unscientific.

But other, often younger, parapsychologists disagree with the conventional view of the significance of ESP. They maintain: "Strangely it does not seem possible to find the scientific laws or principles violated by the existence of ESP."[42] This viewpoint seems to be growing. The *Journal of Parapsychology* now regularly prints contributions that adopt a highly technical, information-processing, mechanistic approach to parapsychological problems, and there are repeated attempts to show that modern quantum physics is not incompatible with ESP.[43]

Proponents of this view accuse the skeptics of double dogmatism in stubbornly clinging to a world view refuted not only by ESP but also by modern physics itself.

Simple Prejudice

Some people simply refuse to believe in psychic phenomena. Although this opinion is rarely expressed in print, it was once, in a passage that has become famous among parapsychologists. In 1951, Donald O. Hebb, one of the leading psychologists of the century, wrote:

> Rhine has offered us enough evidence to have convinced us on almost any other issue . . . . Personally, I do not accept ESP for a moment, because it does not make sense . . . my own rejection of his views is—in the literal sense—prejudice.[44]

Parapsychologists regularly report similar, if unpublished, remarks indicating hostility or at best indifference. Targ and Puthoff claim to have been told by a journal editor, "This is the kind of thing that I would not believe in even if it existed."[45] Such reactions are similar to Newtonians' rejection of the Master's alchemical interests.

The reaction of blank indifference or prejudice is not new. Andrew Lang found psychical research to be tedious and uninteresting. During the era of Spiritualism, it was often observed that the spirits of even the greatest seemed dull or silly. The *New York Times* in 1859 called the spirits "unmistakable blockheads [uttering] rubbish."[46] Cyril Burt recorded the reactions of two colleagues:

> When we turn to the accounts given by these disembodied spirits of the life they now live in their new celestial environment, the descriptions prove to be so banal and so crude as to provoke almost every critic to scornful ridicule. As Professor Broad sarcastically observes, life in their new abode appears to resemble an unending sequence of "Pleasant Sunday Afternoons at a nonconformist chapel: its nearest earthly analogy would probably be a Welsh university, and the more religious-minded members who pass from one institution to the other must hardly notice any difference." Joad similarly remarks that, "if our departed relatives still possess souls, it is all too clear that they no longer possess brains."[47]

Parapsychologists usually stand aghast at sentiments like Hebb's and fall to accusing such skeptics of narrow dogmatism. These reactions are sometimes accompanied by despair at ever changing such admittedly closed minds. Their despair is entirely justified. If large numbers of scientists are coolly indifferent or hostile to parapsychology simply because it seems silly, no pile of cards guessed correctly will be high enough, no logical argument will be forceful enough, no stories of survival will be strong enough to move parapsychology from the margins of science.

Theological Arguments

Occasionally psychical researchers are accused of doing evil. We have seen how Braid was attacked as an instrument of Satan for practicing mesmerism; it was in replying to the charge that he coined the term *hypnosis.* In the early twentieth century some Catholics found psychical research to be dangerous. Dr. J. Godfrey Raupert, despite working for the Society for Psychical Research, was sent by Pope Pius X on a lecture tour of Roman Catholic seminaries in America to warn of the hazards of psychical research. Writing in the *New York Times Magazine* in March 1909, Raupert declared that "nothing but evil can result from our efforts to solve these mysteries of life." While he did not doubt that mediums can contact spirits, he believed them to be evil, malicious spirits rather than the souls of the beloved dead.[48]

The publication of such charges seems to have ceased, and in any case the parapsychological community does not seem to have concerned itself with refuting them. Apparently there are some things in heaven and earth that are not dreamed of even in parapsychology's philosophy.

Philosophical-Methodological Arguments

Now we come to a collection of highly technical objections to psychical research that involve questions of philosophy, proper conduct of science, and experimental methodology.

Some philosophers have raised various problems for different aspects of psychical research. For example, it has been maintained that the notion of "survival of death" is incoherent. We know what it means to survive a plane crash, and we never call the dead "survivors." Nor can I imagine my own funeral, according to these philosophers, without logical absurdity: how can I watch myself be placed in a coffin and buried? (To the more spiritually inclined reader, this argument may seem incoherent.) Another example of these ordinary language philosophers' attacks on parapsychology concerns precognition: How can I "see" an event that literally does not yet exist? While these controversies have often generated much philosophical heat, they seem not to have shed much light on parapsychology, which has generally ignored them. Philosophers have arisen to argue both sides of such questions, and in the absence of a resolution, parapsychology has continued little disturbed.[49]

More serious are objections that directly challenge the status of parapsychology as a science and, in fact, frequently trouble parapsychologists as well as their opponents. There are two main objections of this sort. First, parapsychology has no repeatable experiments. Second, there are no adequate theories to explain the various paranormal phenomena.

The problem of the repeatable experiment is a crucial one for modern parapsychologists. The whole reason for moving from the séance room to the laboratory was to make psychic phenomena controllable and repeatable, thereby winning the approval of established science. As Rhine put it in 1937, spontaneous experiences "leave nothing but memory [so] there is no way of coming to grips with them." What is needed to give them the "broad reality of a meteorite or a fossil?"

> The answer of science is this: When a group of facts or of alleged facts can be checked, reproduced at the will of an experimenter, varied and measured and tested, they take on an enormously increased reality. In this day of experimental science nothing so penetrates the skepticism that safeguards one's belief as the ability to produce at will, and to vary at will, the phenomena about whose objective reality there is doubt.
>
> For this reason, then, if a scientific investigator—a psychologist or anyone else—wants to find out whether the human mind can upon occasion know things in a psychic or extra-sensory manner, he must turn from spontaneous cases of psychic occurrences, regardless of how interesting and dramatic they are, to definite, systematic experimentation. He must try to discover by repeated test, by careful laboratory techniques, whether there is anything behind the circumstances related in these stories. In short, the material within this field must be taken from the anecdotal stage to that of experimentation before it can be classified as scientific knowledge.[50]

Rhine is quite emphatic: scientific status depends on experimental control of psychic phenomena, that is, on the production of a repeatable experiment. But by the continued admission of many parapsychologists, the needed repeatable experiment has not been found. In 1948, the first two numbers of the *Journal of Parapsychology* (vol. 12) were given over to a symposium on the needs of parapsychology for the coming ten years. Gardener Murphy stated that, without a repeatable experiment, there is not "even the beginning of a science of parapsychology" (p. 19). D. J. West said that the lack of a repeatable experiment is "the main reason why parapsychology is not a generally accepted science," and J. L. Woodruff maintained that "the central problem of parapsychology still remains . . . the creation of a repeatable ESP experiment" (p. 124).

Things did not improve. In 1972, John Beloff wrote, "if we want to be treated on a par with the other sciences, then we cannot flout the very criteria that are used to distinguish genuine from pseudo-science," and these include experimental control and repeatability. Even more recently, in 1977, R. A. McConnell, in arguing that parapsychology is preparadigmatic, attributes much of the resistance to accepting paranormal phenomena to the problem of nonrepeatability.[51]

The failure to produce a repeatable experiment has led some parapsychologists to question the importance of doing so. Rhine himself in 1962 dismissed the "bugaboo of repeatability" as irrelevant to a young field like parapsychology, and he encouraged parapsychologists to be less defensive. By 1975 Rhine was arguing that paranormal abilities are deeply unconscious and beyond scientific control, rendering impossible the construction of a repeatable experiment in principle. More constructively, Robert Thouless has argued since 1948 that exact repeatability is unnecessary. No amount of data will, in his view, ever persuade the skeptic, although general repeatability, the repeated demonstration of clairvoyance or precognition, has been shown. Instead, parapsychologists need to make ESP more reliable so that its laws become more obvious. Recently some parapsychologists, such as Lawrence Leshan, have dismissed repeatability as irrelevant to scientific status. Many established sciences, including geology, astronomy, and their subspecialties, are observational, unable to exercise control over their subjects. Vulcanology is not called a pseudoscience because volcanoes do not erupt on cue. Similarly, if psychic powers are capricious and unpredictable, then they must be accepted as a fact of nature rather than rejected as a symptom of pseudoscience.[52]

Lack of a theory also troubles parapsychologists and critics alike. Indeed, Thouless wants to abandon the search for a precisely replicable experiment in order to pursue experiments devoted to unraveling the causal patterns of psi occurrences. Similarly, K. Ramakrishna Rao, in surveying various current theories about parapsychological phenomena, maintained that only by producing a theory capable of "deductive development [and] verifiable predictions" can parapsychology be separated from the occult.[53] It is true that, although currently many parapsychologists are proposing theories, few are accepted by any but their proponents, confirming McConnell's conclusion that parapsychology is preparadigmatic.

Of course, parapsychologists could contend (although they rarely do) that their immediate neighbor, psychology, also lacks any well-defined theories. But this might well call into question the already shaky status of psychology as a science. This would not help parapsychology but would tend rather to impel critics to move the demarcation line away from both psychology and parapsychology instead of moving it nearer to parapsychology.

Parapsychologists can also be accused of using ad hoc stratagems to evade the force of experimental findings because they typically do not put the simplest interpretation on their data, twisting what seems to be evidence against psychic abilities into evidence for psychic abilities. Consider the "decline effect." Rhine and other experimenters have found repeatedly (perhaps parapsychology's only repeatable finding!) that a subject who starts out well, making many correct guesses, shows an inevitable decline in his abilities and degenerates at last to chance level. This has been interpreted by parapsychologists as showing the quirky, elusive nature of psi, as many parapsychologists now call paranormal abilities. As Thouless put it: "It appears that the subject, if he has shown psi in the early part of a run of guesses, then unconsciously covers his tracks by making an unexpected number of wrong guesses to bring his score near the expected chance total. This indeed is odd, yet somewhat resembles other apparent tendencies to avoid the appearance of psi activities."[54]

Critics disagree. They maintain that decline is "the opposite to what usually happens" in science, which is "the demonstration of a clearer" effect as obstructing variables are controlled. "If this sharpening effect does not occur, the original finding is rejected and abandoned." Decline may be explained in two ways without invoking ESP. First, the usual story of the decline effect is good performance under loose conditions followed by vanishing of ESP as controls are tightened. This is to be expected if controls are eliminating the ability to cheat. Parapsychologists counter that subjects get put off by rigorous controls and lose their fragile powers. Second, a gambler, for example, might initially win a large sum at roulette but end the night broke. Lucky early guesses are followed by unlucky ones, but in the long run losses cancel gains. Likewise, a card-guessing subject starts out lucky, but his performance declines over the long run to where it should be—chance.[55] The parapsychologists may still argue that this repeated finding is a law of ESP, not an artifact.

Statistics have played a large role in disagreements about parapsychology. At the broadest level, it can be argued that just because something is unusual or unexpected it need not be "paranormal."[56] For decades the orbit of Neptune appeared odd and at variance with Newtonian physics; finally, the discovery of Pluto showed, on Newtonian principles, why the orbit was odd. In this way, "odd" psi phenomena may prove normal sometime in the future. Here the critic and the radical parapsychologist agree: psi will be proved to be compatible with modern physics.

It has also happened that critics have tried to impugn experimental psi findings on narrow statistical grounds, accusing the parapsychologists of using incorrect mathematical procedures. Generally, parapsychology has been cleared of these charges, but they still crop up occasionally.[57] These issues involve technical aspects of statistics that it would be pointless to review here. A general statistical problem with ESP findings can be reviewed, however.

Suppose you wanted to show that men are more extroverted than women. You could test the hypothesis by giving twenty men and twenty women a test for extroversion-introversion and comparing the results from the two groups. Suppose your hypothesis was not confirmed: no difference occurred. Nevertheless, to rescue your hypothesis you might allege that, quite by chance, of all the women in the world you happened to pick twenty highly extroverted ones, and of all the men, you chose twenty highly introverted ones, so that the differences cancelled. But, you might continue, had you tested everyone, there would be a difference.

Your only recourse would be to test more and more people, perhaps six hundred men and six hundred women. There still might be no obtainable difference. So you sample five thousand men and five thousand women, and finally a small difference appears. How happy should you be?

On the surface of it, you should feel vindicated—the hypothesis proved out. But, on the other hand, you found a tiny difference between two groups of five thousand people. This means that even if men are more extroverted than women, still the difference is so slight that it makes no practical difference. If you could have demonstrated your thesis with just forty subjects, you would have felt confident that the difference was large and genuine, being found in so few subjects.

Similarly, parapsychologists are proud of having conducted thousands of card guesses and of having found a few subjects whose scores are slightly above chance. They interpret this as proof of ESP. For example, out of five thousand guesses we expect by chance a score of one thousand; a subject may get one hundred more right, getting a total of one thousand and one hundred correct guesses. This indeed may prove that something is going on, but it need not convince the skeptic that this something is important or worthwhile. There are many oddities in nature, and one as slight as this cannot challenge the achievements of Newton and Einstein. A score of twenty out of twenty under perfect control, repeatable on demand, would be much more persuasive. The parapsychologist may protest that he has still proved ESP to be a fact, but the skeptic may respond that such odd, infrequent occurrences are trivial anomalies in the structure of science, meriting little, if any, attention.[58]

Association with the Occult

The argument often used first against parapsychology is its association with the occult. It is easy to link parapsychology with other rejected forms of knowledge that emphasize spirituality, psychic powers, the survival of the soul, and other traditional religious concerns. Thus, parapsychology can be castigated as "a reversion to a prescientific religio-mystical tradition."[59]

Such arguments of guilt by association are logically unfair and ad hominem,[60] but they contain a grain of truth. As we have shown, parapsychology historically developed out of Spiritualism, and much of its appeal derives from flouting the establishment. Although the typical parapsychologist may scoff at *Secrets of Miracle Metaphysics* and *Seth Speaks*, it is nonetheless true that enthusiasts of such books believe in ESP and psychokinesis. Nor do books such as *Phone Calls from the Dead* (written by an established parapsychologist) do much to enhance the scientific image of parapsychology. Thus there are links between the occult and parapsychology—historical, psychological, and sociological—and they are a factor in its rejection.

Some parapsychologists are aware of the danger. R. A. McConnell has observed that a way for parapsychology has been opened by "the disintegration of social values and beliefs that had no place for psi phenomenon." However, he sees a related danger: "We are living in a crescendo of popular superstition whose only relation to parapsychology is through the substrata of weak, sporadic, natural phenomena which both attempt to relate." McConnell documents the rise of superstition by pointing out acceptance of astrology for student diagnosis by a school board president, the commercialization of the quasi-religious mind control business with its antiscience education, "and the nonsense of psychic healing." Sounding like a contributor to *The Humanist*, McConnell fears that all this occult activity will drown the voice of scientific reason, as "our nonscientific fellow travelers . . . obscure the role of intellectual self-discipline."[61]

Parapsychologists have always feared that scientific rejection would force them into the ocean of the occult. It now appears that they may be engulfed by rising occult tides and dragged willy-nilly from the shores of science.

Tensions within Psychical Research

From the different kinds of responses parapsychologists give to their critics, it is clear that, however united they may be by bonds of rejection and by interest in the paranormal, parapsychologists do not always agree on the nature of psi. Various debates have marked the development of parapsychology, and we believe that they indicate a general retreat from the antimaterialism that imbued the founders.

The first step in this retreat came in arguments over the meaning of the communications from the dead revealed by mediums. Mediums often told their sitters facts that apparently were known only to the sitter and the deceased; that is what persuaded people that mediums were honest. But, assuming the mediums are honest, there are still two possible sources of knowledge available to the medium—the soul of the deceased or the sitter's mind, read by telepathy. Although some psychical researchers, notably James H. Hyslop, fervently upheld the spirit hypothesis and heaped scorn on the telepathy hypothesis, gradually the latter has become the dominant, but not unanimous, view. It became clear that genuine mediums were (possibly literally) as rare as hen's teeth, and that it was practically impossible to distinguish spirit communication from thought transference. So the parapsychologist need no longer believe in an immortal soul.[62]

The next step will come as a surprise to most readers: parapsychologists do not necessarily believe in telepathy, the paranormal power most associated with Duke University and Dr. Rhine. In a telepathy experiment, a sender looks at a target hidden from the receiver, who in turn tries to read the sender's thought. The trouble is that the receiver, if successful, could have read the value of the card itself by clairvoyance without reading the sender's thought. Nor was it feasible to have the sender just imagine cards, for at some point a record must be made of these choices, and the reader could, through clairvoyant precognition, "see" the record. Various unsuccessful attempts have been made to devise a "pure telepathy" experiment, but none have proved satisfactory. Today few parapsychologists try to draw the telepathy-clairvoyance distinction. Thus a parapsychologist need believe in the immaterial thoughts of an immaterial mind no more than in an immortal soul.[63]

Most recently, a generational split has developed over the very meaning of psi phenomena. Critics believe that psi phenomena cannot occur because they violate known scientific laws. Traditional parapsychologists believe that psi phenomena do occur and that known science is thereby overthrown. Younger parapsychologists believe that psi phenomena do occur but that "psi involves energies that are derived from physiological processes of the organism, are primarily brain-dependent, and are not essentially different from the psychological forces that influence behavior through normal sensori-motor mechanisms" and may be "adequately explained by the laws of physics."[64]

The new radical view distresses some of the older parapsychologists, such as J. G. Pratt, one of Rhine's earliest associates. Writing in 1978, Pratt said that parapsychology is undergoing a crisis; it remains unaccepted by established science, while at the same time its younger members embrace physics and abandon the faith of the founders. Pratt maintained that the new parapsychologists "have become, in general, very reluctant to face up to the major implications of their findings, namely that psi phenomena are a direct challenge to the mechanistic, materialistic mainstream view of the universe, the predominant view of normal science." Pratt indicates that unless parapsychologists remain true to the motives of the founders of psychical research and struggle to overthrow materialism, they will, by aping science and ignoring their critics (who share Pratt's interpretation of psi), become a mere cult. Instead, parapsychologists should struggle to force the acceptance of a scientifically established mind-body dualism.[65]

Should the younger parapsychologists win out, as seems likely, parapsychology will have completed its retreat from the antimaterialism and belief in transcendent spirit that moved its founders. The supernatural will become so naturalized that it will vanish altogether from parapsychology. True, the physical world will be mildly spiritualized, but fundamental materialism will remain. At the same time, it is likely that resistance in orthodox scientific circles will continue, and parapsychology will become a cult.

PARAPSYCHOLOGY AND PSEUDOSCIENCE

Psychical research has suffered from two difficulties. It tried to bring religious questions before the bar of science, acknowledging the failure of traditional institutions to uphold faith in "the dignity', the meaning, the endlessness of life." And it tried to turn the methods of science against the substance of science.

That the first is a difficulty was not seen by the founders of psychical research, who entered the field in order to sustain faith. But it was observed by George M. Beard in 1879:

> Modern spiritism is an attempt to apply the inductive method to religion; to make faith scientific; to confirm the longings of the heart by the evidence of the senses. In thus submitting spiritism to the inductive method its friends forgot that to prove a religion would be to kill it—to transfer it from the emotions, where it belongs, to the intellect, where it can find no home. A religion proved, dies as a religion, and becomes a scientific fact, and would take its place side by side with astronomy and chemistry, with physics and geology, in the organized knowledge of men. . . . The security of religious beliefs consists in their keeping out of range. Religion, indeed, is between two fires: Absolutely proved or disproved it is destroyed; disproved it becomes a delusion, a negative fact of science; proved, a positive fact, in both cases recognized by the intellect and appealing to it; like the horizon it recedes as we go toward it—even the attempt to submit it to scientific study causes it to disappear. No religion on the globe is strong enough to bear the shock of its own demonstration. . . . Spiritism is thus organized for failure.[66]

To use a modern term, psychical research has been guilty of scientism, the belief that only the scientific method produces knowledge, that only scientific knowledge is real knowledge. But, as Beard pointed out, religion appeals to the heart, and scientific proof of religion is heartless. Against the first burst of enthusiasm for reason and science Pascal wrote, ''The heart has its reasons which the reason does not understand.'' The psychical researchers, in their zeal, driven by the heart's desire to find meaning, rather than mere order, in the universe, easily forget this. The search for proof, for repeatable experiments, for technical theory, for scientific acceptance become paramount. In the long run, the heart will be just as unhappy with ''cognitive factors in ESP performance'' as it was with ''the old world sustenance'' of traditional religion. Like their opponents, psychical researchers believe, in Myers's phrase, that ''the authority of creeds and Churches will be replaced by the authority of observation and experiment.'' But ultimately this repeats the error of which James accused orthodox science, of denying age-old spiritual needs in favor of that which can be measured in the laboratory. In embracing physics, the newest parapsychology cuts itself off from the emotional wellspring that called forth psychical research. This may displease older psychical researchers—but the tendency was present from the moment psychical research decided to emulate science.[67]

In emulating science, psychical researchers from the beginning adopted the conventional view of science and separated science's method from its content. Parapsychologists often say things like this: ''Science is not a collection of subjects 'approved' for research. It's a process, a way of investigating, reporting, and verifying observations.''[68] They then strive to turn the methods of science against its substance, to ''investigate, report and verify observations'' of paranormal phenomena, to show (at least until very recently) that the modern scientific world view is wrong. For the traditional parapsychologists this meant proving dualism against scientific materialism; for the neoscientific parapsychologists it means finding room for psychical quirks among physical quarks. Both traditionalists and modernists call themselves scientists because they follow scientific method.

But recent studies of science, such as Kuhn's, have shown that the conventional separation of method and substance is actually impossible. In the conventional view, which owes its origin to Bacon, scientists are essentially curious individuals who ''investigate, report, and verify'' facts according to a demanding set of methodological canons. So the parapsychologist follows the canons quite faithfully and is upset when science says, "Throw the pseudos out!" But scientists are not just curious; they are committed to certain substantive views on the nature of a piece of reality, and these views, not simple curiosity, guide their research. As Kuhn points out, in normal science the scientist applies accepted ideas to ripe problems, confident of finding a solution. He is not testing those ideas against the data.

Kuhn's analogy to puzzle solving is apt. The scientist has a general view of what the world-puzzle is like, and in his own research area he is looking for pieces of information that will fit in with the parts of the puzzle already solved. That which does not seem to fit is assumed to be from a part of the puzzle not yet reached, and it is quite properly ignored. It "makes no sense," as Hebb said, but the scientist assumes it will make sense someday. So when someone comes along, as parapsychologists are wont to do, and says, "This fact shows your whole puzzle-plan to be wrong," the scientist reacts with indifference or hostility. If science is proceeding successfully from puzzle to puzzle, there is no obvious reason to abandon it, even for facts that are collected in the purest, most rigorous form possible. And when the scientist discovers that the alleged anomalous puzzle pieces are statistically marginal and sometimes fraudulent, he or she is likely to dismiss all of them as irrational.

The problem is compounded by the general unwillingness of skeptics to accept this necessary form of scientific dogmatism, which is, after all, no more than sticking with a proven idea and building on it as long as possible. Skeptics tend to believe with parapsychologists that "investigating, reporting, and verifying observations" are the essence of science. Impelled by their commitment to the substance of science, they nevertheless use methodological criteria to exclude psychical research from science. They try to dissolve the facts of psi by putting them down to bad method—fraud, deception, statistical artifact—and may accuse the psychical researchers of being frauds or fools taken in by frauds. Skeptic and parapsychologist share the same erroneous view of science.

Like our other pseudosciences, psychical research has a reforming spirit. Although it has not been as active in reform movements as phrenology, it has always (at least until recently) been activated by a moral aim—the overthrow of materialism. Fear of materialism energized the founders of psychical research. They worried that destruction of faith in transcendent and enduring values would create a world of moral relativism in which guilt becomes an illusion and powerful immoralists fear no ultimate retribution for their sins. Horrified by the implications of the materialism inherent in modern science, the psychical researchers strove, by the methods of science, to prove materialism wrong. More recently, younger parapsychologists seem far less moved by that spiritual impulse; parapsychology threatens to become paraphysics. At the popular level, however, psychical research's strength remains its proffered proof that there is more to life than pain and pleasure, suffering and death. The need to conquer death remains strong; Elisabeth Kübler-Ross, pioneer in the study of how people come to terms with death, has herself come to deny death and has accepted "proofs" that would have embarrassed the S.P.R.[69]

Also like our other pseudosciences, psychical research has sought a wider audience than professional scientists. In part, this results from need—the work of parapsychology, research and publication, cannot be met by nonexistent government grants and a trickle of professional subscriptions. In part, also, seeking a wider audience stems from the moral urge to conquer materialism. And finally, its broad base results from its appeal as a supposed scientific wonder. From the Enlightenment onward, people have expected to be amazed by science; moon shots and test-tube babies become media events. And if science should say that you have latent psychic powers and an immortal soul—so much the better. It is no wonder, then, that works by parapsychologists, such as *Phone Calls from the Dead*, should appear as popular paperbacks in bookstores' overcrowded occult sections; nor is it surprising that parapsychologists should seek such markets. Royalties from popular works can be plowed back into the work of research. Philosophically, the Baconian ideal justifies such popularization: each person, whether professional or lay, must judge firsthand the claims of science. Parapsychologists, like the Fowlers before them, want each person to test the truths of psychical research, to believe, not on authority, but on the sure foundations of individual experience.

Status of Parapsychology

Is psychical research, and its modern offspring parapsychology, a pseudoscience?

As with mesmerism, this question is difficult to answer. The usual demarcation proposals presuppose some body of theory to be falsifiable (Popper), to lead to progressive problem shifts (Lakatos), or to lead to puzzle-solving research (Kuhn). But parapsychology lacks any established body of theory, and it remains a field still searching for reliable phenomena upon which to erect a theory or paradigm.

Broadly speaking, however, there does not seem anything unscientific—or antiscientific—about psychical research and parapsychology. Reliable data is sought; fraud is rooted out; control is instituted. Some problems, such as the spirit hypothesis and telepathy, have been abandoned as pseudo questions. Specific problems are raised and addressed: Is ESP affected by distance? By physical barriers? By drugs? By subjects' personalities?

From a methodological standpoint, parapsychology cannot legitimately be called a pseudoscience. At worst, it may be accused of being an overambitious prescience, copying all the forms of physics but lacking as yet anything solid or substantial to build upon. It may turn out that paranormal phenomena are a snare and a delusion; but this does not make the search for them unscientific. There was no Northwest Passage, but this does not make those who sought it pseudo explorers. Paranormal phenomena may exist but be so quirky that they elude any systematic treatment; this possibility would mean only that parapsychology is a scientific failure, not that it is a false science. On the other hand, paranormal phenomena may eventually yield to scientific inquest, in which case parapsychology must be accepted as a science. Methodologically, then, there is no reason to fault parapsychology.

Opponents of parapsychology are on sounder footing with respect to substance. Most parapsychologists think their phenomena overthrow established science. But this claim is based on a naive falsificationism that says that one contrary fact, James's white crow, destroys a theory. Kuhn and others have convincingly shown, however, that scientists balance success and failure. A few contrary facts never deter an otherwise successful research program. And against the handful of apparitions and successful card-guesses, the modern skeptical scientist can set the triumphs of mechanistic science, from breaking the code of DNA to the flight to the moon. The success of materialistic science is undeniable, and it remains vital.

Few scientists can be expected to give up their successful world view because of a few rather odd occurrences and laboratory results. At the same time, those scientists should avoid the hubris that suggests that all is known that can be known, that no surprises are left in nature. Methodologically, parapsychology is a science; substantially, the verdict is still out.

Eight

Contemporary Therapeutic Cults

> Cult is culture writ small.
> William Bainbridge, *Satan's Power*[1]

Pseudosciences and religion seem inextricably intertwined. Phrenology began as an austere brain physiology but in the *Constitution of Man* began to function as a secular religion whose churches were the phrenological societies. Mesmer's lurid séances and occult dress appealed to the religious needs of many. Psychical research grew out of the spontaneous religious phenomena of Spiritualism. Today, we find cultic religious movements that take on the trappings of science.

Cults are, of course, much written about at present, and the usual question is whether or not they ought to be considered religions. In a country where religions are accorded special freedom from government control, this question is important, for its answer bears on issues ranging from tax exemption to parents' rights to seize and "deprogram" their adult children. But students of religious sociology and psychology have been unable to resolve the problem: some argue that cults are sham religions, while others maintain that a religion is just a respectable cult.[2] While this issue parallels the question of what defines a pseudo-

213

science—something real or just establishment power—it lies outside the scope of our inquiry.

On the one hand, then, it is difficult to separate cults from religions. On the other hand, a number of modern cults claim the status of science, generally designating themselves the one true psychology. The resemblances are clearest between cults and psychotherapies, although some cults offer general theories of mind as well as cures. What does separate therapies from cults? Both offer personality analyses, guidance, ways to change your outlook or behavior in order to improve your life. Therapies may be scientific insofar as psychology is scientific. But is there any absolute distinction to be made between therapies and cults?

Various faddish therapies seem distinguished from cults primarily by their lack of a strong organization. You do not have to join an authoritarian club in order to do Primal Screaming or to be Rolfed. The theories of these therapies and of some cults, however, are similar, as we will see. Transactional Analysis, to take a well-known example, works to overcome "parent tapes," which are very like Scientology's engrams; they are both the effects of an unhappy childhood and keep the client from living freely and fully.

There are various therapies that try to overcome the psychic scars of birth trauma. Primal Screaming, developed by Dr. Arthur Janov, offers to cure the traumas of birth and of an unhappy childhood, releasing in screams the accumulated pain of childhood. Paul Bindrim, a California psychologist, has added some new twists to Primal Scream Therapy in his Nude Marathon Regression Therapy. This is a group therapy, held in a warm swimming pool, which is supposed to recapture the sensations of life in the maternal womb. One of the clients is held horizontally by the rest of the clients, being rocked as if in a cradle. The subject is also given a bottle to suck, to stimulate memories of infancy.

These therapies have much in common with Scientology—except that Scientology has taken the next logical step and tries to exorcise the traumatic engrams left from previous incarnations. Working within the paradigm of birth trauma, this is indeed the next logical step. If your clients still do not get over their neuroses after reliving birth—well, you just tinker with the protective belt of your paradigm; this route leads first to intrauterine traumas and thence to traumas in previous incarnations.

But faddish therapies cannot be held to represent the whole field of psychotherapy. Do the established, more socially acceptable forms of therapy show any greater differences from cults than the faddish therapies do? Even our slang poses this question when we call psychoanalysts "shrinks" or "head shrinkers." Is there, then, any real difference between a fully accredited psychotherapist, a Scientologist, and a village witch doctor?

The noted anthropologist Claude Lévi-Strauss, writing in 1949, thought that there was a real, if tenuous, difference. He respected psychoanalysis and gave it scientific standing as a study of particular cases, but he refused to accept it as an absolutely true theory of mind and reality: "The fact that a certain form of integration is possible and effective practically is not enough to make it true. . . ." He feared that a distressing trend "has tended to transform the psychoanalytic system from a body of scientific hypotheses that are experimentally verifiable in certain specific and limited cases into a kind of diffuse mythology." He suggested that all magical, religious systems attempted to reconcile our need for meaning with our rational awareness of the world: "The universe is never charged with sufficient meaning and . . . the mind always has more meanings available than there are objects to which to relate them. . . . [Therefore] man asks magical thinking to provide him with a new system of reference, within which the thus-far contradictory elements can be integrated. But we know that this system is built at the expense of progress of knowledge." He feared that psychoanalysis would become so compelling a mythology that we would stop seeking knowledge, lulled by a "fabulation . . . whose function is to provide a socially authorized translation of phenomena whose deeper nature would become once again impenetrable. . . ."[3]

A lot has happened since 1949. The siren song of psychoanalysis has clearly weakened, but so has our faith in truth, in a deeper nature of reality, that is experimentally verifiable. More than thirty years later, we can only look at these ideas of Lévi-Strauss across a paradigmatic chasm. What, in these latter days when the experimental verifiability of any science is called into question, separates therapies from cults? Is there any real separation?

Ironically, perhaps, Lévi-Strauss himself pointed towards these Kuhnian questions. In an earlier, more strictly anthropological part of his essay, "The Sorcerer and His Magic," he suggested that only the relative richness of the emotional "fireworks" produced by competing shamans "makes possible a choice between several systems." Only the metaphysical artistry of the shaman ensures his success. "In contrast with scientific explanation, the problem here is not to attribute confused and disorganized states, emotions, or representations to an objective cause, but rather to articulate them into a whole system,"[4] to present a world view that explains the patient's, and the tribe's, experience. Shorn of the contrast to scientific explanation, this could stand as an accurate diagnosis of the occult and therapeutic supermarket. (Cultural relativism was clearly in the air, even if Lévi-Strauss did not entirely like it.)

But we still put movements into the different categories of therapies and cults. Do we have a reason for doing so? Psychoanalysis is still the best-known therapy. The scientific foundations of even this bastion of therapeutic respectability, however, have recently been called into question. Frank Cioffi, for example, has suggested that Freud's early patients invented their childhood seduction experiences and fantasies in order to please him.[5] These seduction episodes, which Freud later believed to be significant fantasies, are the "experimentally verifiable" basis of the Oedipus complex, the cornerstone of Freud's theory. Thus Freud's beautiful, complex, and intellectually appealing theory has been pushed a large step closer to the category of myth. Which raises the awkward question—What does separate therapy from cult? Tax exempt status aside, is there any reason to consider Scientology a church rather than a therapy? Is there any sound reason to reject, or accept, the claims to scientific status of the Maharishi International University (educationally accredited in 1980)? These must be worrying questions, not only to any clinical psychologist, but also to our culture that gives such power to anyone with a medical aura.

The Church of Scientology provides an interesting case of a therapy that became a religion. L. Ron Hubbard, a science fiction writer, published *Dianetics, the Modern Science of Mental Health* in 1950.[6] This book claimed that two normally intelligent people could cure each other of all mental and most physical ills in about twenty hours using Dianetic techniques, which were supposedly laboratory tested, scientific facts. Hubbard's system involved a fairly complex faculty psychology, with a strong computer-programming bent. The analytical mind is completely rational, it "computes perfectly on the data stored and perceived." However, this computer can be incorrectly programmed: "Incorrect data enter the human memory banks, the person reacts in an 'abnormal manner.' "[7] Such an individual will be "aberrated" due to an "engram," the recording of painful experiences that occurred while he was unconscious. These engrams are stored in the memory banks of the reactive mind, which is the irrational part of the mind that evolved to take over when shock or pain makes the analytical mind "shut off." The purpose of Dianetic therapy, called auditing, is to locate and erase engrams. Someone who has been successfully treated is a "clear," a superman of sorts, without ills, possessing psychic powers and very high intelligence. If you have bad eyes, Dianetics will incidentally improve your vision markedly: "With the removal of aberrations, repeated tests have proven that the body makes a valiant effort to reconstruct back to optimum."[8] It will also cure color blindness and ringing in the ears, as well as greatly improve the range of all one's senses.

Sense perception is fundamental to Dianetics, for it is how we "face reality": "Perception of the present would be one method of facing reality."[9] This strangely literal interpretation of the phrase "face reality" provided the basis for Dianetic therapy. The pre-clear (or Pc) is "returned," or put in a state like hypnosis without losing consciousness, so that he or she can "face yesterday" and relive all the situations that caused the engrams. Once the origins of these engrams are discovered, they will "unlock" and clear the individual.

This basic idea is similar to Freud's early work with Joseph Breuer, on abreaction therapy, where reliving a tramatic experience while under hypnosis was supposed to release the pent-up emotions generated by the experience and thus cure the hysteric symptoms. Engrams are also similar to the conditioned reflexes of the Behaviorists. A learned response that can be triggered by some specific stimulus no matter how inappropriate the resulting behavior may be—this is an engram or a conditioned response. Thus Dianetics combined two of the apparently irreconcilable schools of psychology.

Other probable influences on Hubbard were the various abreaction therapies in use after World War II. Although Freud abandoned it early in his career, abreaction therapy was popular as a treatment for shell-shocked soldiers, whose condition improved when they vented the suppressed emotions of war. A drug was used instead of hypnosis to help them relive the traumatic experiences that had left them in a state of shock. These shell-shock therapies shed an interesting sidelight on Scientology's claim to be based on laboratory-tested, scientific facts. "The technique of suggesting quite imaginary situations to a patient under drugs, leading to abreaction of fear and anger was found to be equally effective. . . ."[10]

Dianetics also claimed to cure, or clear, people by returning them to traumatic experiences so as to erase the engrams wedged in the mind during the traumatic experiences, when the Pre-clear was unconscious and the reactive mind was therefore in control.

A chronic case of sinusitis suffered by a Pre-clear will serve as an example. A man has been abused by his parents during childhood (according to Hubbard, something that most parents do). During a nasal or respiratory illness, the child was nursed by his devoted grandmother. While he was delirious or unconscious and his reactive mind was in control, his grandmother told him that she would take care of him and stay with him until he was well. Thus his reactive, unconscious mind began to correlate sickness with grandmotherly love, assuming that respiratory ailments would conjure up a fairy godmother to protect him.

Years later, the individual marries a woman whose voice or manner of speech reminds his reactive mind of his grandmother. The engram associating grandmother and illness is keyed in whenever he wants attention. His reactive mind produces sinusitis when his wife is unsympathetic, and his wife reacts to his illness unsympathetically, creating a spiraling pattern. The less sympathetic the wife is, the worse the sinusitis.[11] This interpretation of the patient's problem is similar to the psychoanalytic idea that there is "secondary gain" involved in being sick, with the difference that an engram can be formed only when a person is unconscious. Eventually this difference led Scientology to wilder terrain—the reactive mind, being completely unconscious, need not be in a person's whole body or even in one's current body.

Hubbard had at first assumed that the birth trauma was the earliest possible cause of an engram. In tracing back pre-clears' engrams, however, he frequently elicited prenatal memories, usually of the father beating the pregnant mother and yelling at her, or of the mother attempting abortion: "Dianetic therapy would demonstrate attempted abortion or an equally foul prenatal existence" for all criminals, retardates, and neurotics.[12] Whatever was said during these episodes, while the child was unconscious, was faithfully recorded and perversely interpreted by the fetus's reactive mind. To quote John Sladek, another science fiction writer, and a debunker of the occult:

> Fetuses not only have keen ears, they're fond of Freudian puns. If someone strikes the pregnant mother, saying "Take that!" the child is liable to grow up to be a kleptomaniac. Someone made the mistake of offering one American mother an aspirin, which profoundly affected her fetal daughter. The daughter grew up with an

unaccountable rash on her bottom, having believed she was offered an "ass-burn." (Presumably this wouldn't apply to an English fetus [who would pronounce *ass* as *arse*], for whom the offer of "aspirins" could only set off an uncontrollable urge to rinse out small snakes [asps]).[13]

Engrams need not be entirely personal, however. They are also inherited. The morning sickness engram, for example, started when "somewhere back in time some mother may have vomited from food poisoning being overheard by her unconscious fetal daughter and started the whole thing—perhaps in the days when man was still in the trees."[14]

Thus Dianetic therapy claimed to clear man of all personal and inherited engrams, and of all responsibility for his actions. It held out the hopes of a scientifically tested road map to happiness. As one of Hubbard's original followers said:

> There were certain people . . . I couldn't approach, or certain people on certain subjects, because I would burst into tears. . . . So I was ready for Hubbard when he came along. . . . Well, I think the reason that it seemed so important is basically . . . there was a promise . . . that I could bypass all my troubles and come out in the clear without having to face them. And there was absolution . . . the engram is something that has been done to you which determines your behavior.[15]

Dianetics appealed mostly to well-educated men, nearly all of them white, and many of them science fiction readers. The Dianetics Research Foundation, started in 1950, lasted only one year. Most people did not get "clear," and those whose symptoms did improve generally lost interest. There was also growing friction among the founding members. Hubbard's book was reviewed badly by doctors and psychiatrists, who objected strongly to his grandiose claims that Dianetics was based on laboratory-tested scientific facts and could cure anything. After the American Psychological Association, among others, objected to these broad claims and lack of scientific testing, one such test was carried out with the cooperation of the Dianetics Research Foundation in Los Angeles. A Pre-clear was rendered unconscious by the administration of sodium pentothal, since engrams are supposed to be acquired when the patient is unconscious, feels pain, and hears words. Once the patient was unconscious, pain was inflicted while a passage from a physics text was read aloud. This satisfied all the conditions for engram formation.

During six months—considerably more than the twenty hours claimed in *Dianetics*—a trained auditor did not recover any part of the passage read; the patient had formed no engrams based on the physics text.[16]

Problems such as these, combined with the members' dislike of Hubbard's increasingly authoritarian attitude, led to a sharp decline in membership and subsequent bankruptcy in 1951. Hubbard then started Scientology, working with those members who had remained loyal to him. Scientology soon incorporated to become a church, highly centralized and authoritarian, its cures, or indoctrinations, practiced in a professional manner. No more cures in twenty hours by ordinary people. Hubbard is the sole source of new knowledge and sole interpreter of all knowledge. This knowledge, the theory and methods of Scientology, is gradually revealed only to those people who have shown their commitment to Hubbard.[17] Thus in 1951 an unusual therapy became a cult.

"The Fundamental Axioms of Dianetics," on the inside covers of the 1971 edition of *Dianetics,* show the religious underpinnings of the movement:

> The dynamic principle of existence is—Survive! The absolute goal
> of survival is immortality or infinite survival.
> The reward of survival activity is pleasure. . . .

While the first and third axioms provide a rather nasty and amoral version of Social Darwinism, the second axiom reveals a religious presupposition—immortality. This idea has been more fully developed in Scientology: reincarnation has become part of Scientology's creed. This belief was one reason for the falling out of the early Dianeticists and especially for the apostasy of J. A. Winter, M.D. The Foundation did not conduct scientific research, preferring to "investigate the possible therapeutic benefits of 'recalling' the circumstances of deaths in previous incarnations."[18]

Interest in reincarnation is clearly more religious than scientific. Reincarnation can also be seen as a *post hoc, ergo proptor hoc* justification for the lack of clears, which grew out of the reactive mind's unconscious nature. When memories of conception, or even "sperm dreams," did not succeed in erasing all engrams and producing clears, some explanation was needed.[19]

The Thetan, a variety of soul, was Hubbard's answer to his unclear dilemma. Thetans are supposed to be the creators of the world, even of the cosmos, immortal beings, "omniscient and omnipotent," who have existed since before the beginning, before matter, energy, space, and time. These physical constraints on existence were invented by the Thetans when they grew bored by their immortality. "Life," Hubbard claims, "is a game." Thetans have been thus playfully reincarnated millions of times.[20] As they became absorbed in their game, attached to their works, enmeshed in matter, they became more limited and forgot their spiritual nature.

Hubbard claims that scientology can liberate Thetans, enable them to recover their awareness of their spiritual natures and, with that awareness, the super-human powers they possessed until they were debased by matter. The liberated Thetan is the ultimate clear. This idea provides an interesting groundwork to explain and support Hubbard's original claims for the miracles of Dianetics.

The dénouement of Hubbard's time and space opera has not yet come about, but it promises to be interesting. Eventually, as more Thetans are liberated, ordinary people—mere mortals, so to speak—are bound to catch on to what is happening. Then there will be a great battle.[21]

In *Dianetics,* Hubbard claims to have produced some two hundred "laboratory tested clears"[22]—who have never been produced for inspection. Given this history of failure, those now living probably need not fear a confrontation with a horde of liberated Thetans.

To liberate a Thetan Hubbard uses many techniques of Dianetics, with one interesting exception. In Dianetics, out-of-body experiences, or exteriorization, was considered an aberration. Scientology, on the other hand, considers this psychic experience to be a sign of the Thetan's liberation from its body and of its total control of its body.[23]

The theme of total control seems to be central to Dianetics. The Thetan is supposed to be in full control of its environment, of time, space, and matter. Part of the way this is achieved is by helping the pre-clear take control of his or her life by confession of sins, or "overts"—overt acts committed against other people. Failing to admit to overts leaves the Pre-clear unable to control his relationships with others, because he will be likely to treat them as if they were guilty in order to hide his own guilt, thereby committing yet more overts.[24] (I say "his" because Scientology appeals almost exclusively to men.) This adds a certain moral level to Scientology that was lacking in Dianetics, even if one is moral only in order to control others, to liberate one's own Thetan. You cannot get clear until you have confessed all your overts.

Scientology has developed a wide variety of methods for indoctrinating and clearing its followers. The auditor (therapist) uses an E-meter, for example, to tell if the pre-clear is answering truthfully. The E-meter is a crude lie detector, often made from old tomato juice cans, but it is nonetheless psychologically effective. The E-meter is used, for instance, to test whether the pre-clear is truthfully confessing to all his overts—which Scientology, unlike some other religions, considers possible.[25] Other indoctrination methods include "Being There," in which two pre-clears have to sit stock still and gaze at each other for two hours. William Bainbridge, who did participant-observer research on Scientology, describes the effects of this technique:

> TR-0 also could produce an altered state of consciousness. One time I did it with a young man from Kentucky, an English teacher I happened to like. We sat staring at each other for two hours, which is 120 minutes, which is 7,200 seconds. A long time to stare into someone's face, allowed to breathe and blink occasionally, but never look away, never smile or fidget. Afterward my partner exclaimed excitedly that he had seen me change before his eyes! I had become different persons—a savage with a bone through my nose, then a decayed corpse covered with filth and cobwebs. He was sure these were glimpses of my previous incarnations. Everyone in the Technianity [Scientology] center was pleased and complimented him on his perceptions. His interpretations fitted the cult's ideology exactly.
>
> I did not tell them what I had seen. He, too, had changed. A halo of light had grown around his face. He had become pale and two-dimensional, shimmering, covered with dark spots. Of course, I interpreted what I saw as simple eye fatigue. He and I had experienced the same stimuli but understood them differently.[26]

This is followed by "bull baiting":

> The student sits in the catatonic immobility of TR-0, and the coach tries to make him react against his will. Rogers [Hubbard] says, "This TR should be taught rough-rough-rough and not left until the student can do it. Training is considered satisfactory at this level only if the student can BE three feet in front of a person without flinching, concentrating or confronting with, regardless of what the confronted person does." In theory, the student is said to be vulnerable at certain points, to have "buttons" which if pressed will make him react. Sensitivity about being overweight, for example, may cause the person to blush when his fat is poked. These

psychological buttons are to be found and "flattened." Sometimes, it seemed to me, the student himself was flattened by bull baiting. At the very least, this and the other TRs are successful in flattening the affect of the student, reducing his emotional resistance to control by Technianity.[27]

Another indoctrination technique is the "Alice games," taken from *Alice in Wonderland*. The Pre-clear has to quote meaningless sentences as if carrying on a conversation with the auditor:

> What a number of cucumber-frames there must be. The master says you've got to go down the chimney. I didn't know that Cheshire cats always grinned. She doesn't believe there's an atom of meaning in it. However, I know my name now, that's some comfort.

I found it singularly appropriate to quote the Cheshire cat at my Technianity coach: "We're all mad here. I'm mad. You're mad." Alice asked, "How do you know I'm mad?" The cat replied, "You must be, or you wouldn't have come here." There is a subtle brainwashing and propaganda effect here. The student becomes inured to crazy ideas. He treats them as detached words, bleached of their meaning, absurd, unconnected to his surroundings. He is confronted by madness and sees it as a beneficial game. He plays the game. After he has accepted the words of Wonderland, he has no difficulty accepting the words of the cult. The student submits to the discipline of the cult, merely by going through the exercise. If he performs poorly, the coach shouts "Flunk!"

TR-2 is a reversal of TR-1. This time the coach recites a quotation from Alice, and the student tries to acknowledge it in such a way as to bring the dialogue to a full stop without encouraging the coach to continue. Acknowledgment is a means of control. The student was permitted to use one of the following five acknowledgments: alright, okay, thank you, good, fine. Rogers [Hubbard] says that a properly delivered acknowledgment is so powerful it "can take a client's head off." "An acknowledgment is a very, very powerful sixteen-inch gun . . . it actually staggers people to have an acknowledgment come to them." But, Rogers warns, "We're not trying to reach the ultimate in an acknowledgment, because that would be the end of the universe. If someone could say, "Yes"—"Good"—"Okay" with enough intention behind it, all communications of this universe from the moment of its beginning would then be acknowledged, totally.'' Technianity seems obsessed with the idea of power.[28]

Scientology clearly is not a science. Its early claims of laboratory-tested clears were probably fraudulent, although some members may have been psychosomatically "clear" for a time. And optometrists have not been put out of business by its curative side effects. Whether Hubbard believes in it, or ever has, is not known. It may be a giant rip-off as its opponents claim, or a modern attempt to produce a scientific religion, an attempt, somewhat akin to Newton's alchemy, to reconcile the religious impulse with the prevailing secular, empirical ideology. Hubbard's philosophy of science is thoroughly empirical and pragmatic: "Dianetics, as a study of function and the science of the mind, does not need any postulate concerning structure. . . . The only test is whether or not a fact works. If it does work and can be used, it is a scientific fact.''[29] This attitude is as modern and American as any pragmatist or behaviorist could wish. Yet it is allied to a system that believes in immortality and reincarnation. Scientology is a modern synthesis of science and religion, endowing the immortal soul with cybernetic jargon and embodying the neo-Darwinian acceptance of survival as the only goal of life. If offers a largely amoral, thoroughly godless, and pragmatic cure of souls, achieved by electrodes and bullying.

A relatively benign offshoot of Scientology was The Power, also studied by William Bainbridge. This "satanic" cult originated in London in 1962 and eventually had chapters in New Orleans, Boston, New York, and Toronto, until personality conflicts destroyed it in 1974. The founders of The Power, Edward de Forest and Kitty McDougle, met when they were both in training to become auditors. They left Scientology because they did not like its authoritarian nature, and "did not want to be mere robots in Hubbard's science fiction world.''[30] They added some Adlerian ideas to Scientology's techniques and started a new therapy, Compulsions Analysis. Their system was founded on the assumption that everyone has an overriding, unconscious goal in life—a compulsion. If you become aware of that goal, you can proceed to pursue it more rationally and less compulsively, gaining control over your own life. Unlike Scientology's pursuit of power and control over others, Compulsions Analysis, and later The Power, emphasized control of oneself and acceptance of others.

Compulsions Analysis was a sensible therapeutic idea, not necessarily occult. In describing their system to a reporter in 1965, Edward de Forest hit on a major difference between established therapies and fringe therapies and cults—the desire to enrich everyone's life rather than merely to cure neuroses:

> Our aim is to make people become aware of themselves, and so more responsible to themselves and to other people. We are not so concerned with healing the mentally sick as are the more orthodox psychoanalysts. We want to help people fulfill themselves.

Although it started out concentrating on helping people function in this world, "The Power never set any limit to what might be achieved. Psychiatry sets normal functioning as its limit as well as its goal. For Kitty and Edward's movement, the sky was the limit."[31]

They used E-meters and group sessions similar to Scientology's, and wound up with people discovering magical or religious goals such as "I want to be one with God" or "I want to destroy the world."[32] As the members of the Compulsions Analysis group grew closer and closer together, they started to have religious experiences as a group. For a time they retired from the world to live in a remote Mexican village, where they discovered that Jehova was God. Jehova, however, was a very strict, rigid, demanding god. So Edward de Forest found another god, Lucifer, who was more kindly, compassionate, and sensual. These gods evolved out of the personalities and interactions of the group—Jehova being like Kitty and Lucifer like Edward. They eventually settled on four "Great Gods of the Universe": Jehova, Lucifer, Satan, and Christ.

Jehova is wrathful, vengeful, and demands purity, duty, and self-denial. Lucifer is sensual, loving, and wants peace. Satan is "the receiver of transcendent souls and corrupted bodies," for he leads us either to become all soul and rise above bodily appetites, or to become all body, "to wallow in a morass of violence, lunacy, and excessive physical indulgence," which latter aspect makes him "The Adversary." Christ, not originally a God, was "The Unifier," who brings together the gods' qualities and who represents them on earth. The following diagram illustrates the unification of opposites that is the fundamental presupposition underlying all The Power's theology:

"'Christ is nailed to the cross, at the center, stapling the extremes together.''[33]

Of these gods, "Each defines a personality type, and together they expressed a sociology.''[34] Each person has primarily the characteristics of one of these gods, manifesting ''one of the patterns as an extension of its God. . . . Members often discussed each other's God patterns, considering them useful analyses of personality style.'' The exact ontological status of these gods is unclear, for they may not be gods in the usual sense: "Sister Roxan was . . . a Luciferian. 'I know that he doesn't exist as an anthropomorphic entity or as a person. To me Lucifer is a name for a whole presence, a whole force, everything that Beauty is, everything that Poetry is!' ''[35] Similarly, The Power's church services were dedicated ''to the Gods who are within us.''[36]

Of these four gods, Jehova is female and Lucifer is male, and they are ''joined in union'' of marriage. The Power expected the coming union of Christ and Satan, "The Lamb and the Goat. Pure love descended from the pinnacle of Heaven, united with pure Hatred raised from the depths of Hell.''[37] The Power saw Good and Evil as an essential duality; neither can exist alone. This implies that there must be harmony or conflict. The time of conflict is coming to an end, with the world, and a new world of peace will be reborn.

This interest in rebirth extends to the individual as well as to the world:

> Lucifer is the God of Rebirth and Immortality; have faith—in yourself, in your undying spirit, in your future, most of all in your immortality. This is what matters: that in the end, you are infinite; in God you are infinite. . . . Death is the gate to life. And no man passes through the gate, but he reaches the other side.[38]

Thus, like Scientology, The Power could not stay an empirical therapy. An answer to our chronic fear of death was needed—and answering that need may well be truly therapeutic. The Power also followed Scientology's lead into reincarnation, again in an intriguing psychological way. One kind of Power "therapy" was Mediumistics, which presupposed four levels of consciousness, or alternate personalities. These levels had different names and could carry on conversations among themselves. In some Powerites these levels were reincarnations of famous people.[39] Like the gods, however, these reincarnations seem to be at least as much terms to describe personalities as things that really exist. The Power's theology always managed to maintain this feat of juggling, combining internal and external realities—providing its members with Lévi-Strauss's "new system of reference within which the thus-far contradictory elements can be integrated."

This integration was achieved by the skillful use of Edward de Forest's therapeutic techniques. Unlike Scientology's bullying indoctrination techniques, The Power was loving and accepting. Even an aggressive, violent, or perverted person was only following his god pattern, after all. Everyone fits into the universal scheme of things. By meditations, sensitivity sessions, therapeutic sessions with the P-scope (the E-meter put to a kinder use), and Mediumistics, the Powerites tried to uncover their compulsions, later called Burdens, and replace these Burdens with the corresponding Blessing of the patient's god pattern. These Burdens and Blessings were twenty-five pairs of dualities of the human psyche, such as Unconsciousness-Awareness, Hatred-Love, Anxiety-Serenity, Insensitivity-Sensitivity.[40] Ultimately, The Power was a religious therapy that sought to free people from unconscious compulsions by acceptance.

While some of its techniques, such as "telepathy" (i.e., sensitivity), psychometry, and Mediumistics, were occult, much of its system was similar to single-patient interviews or group meetings of more conventional therapies. The Power used religious terms, ceremonies, and costumes to express psychological concepts and states. This union of psychology and religion was achieved largely by means of questioning in search of unconscious goals. Using the P-scope to judge the strength of the response, the therapist would question the "questor" about his or her goals. Bainbridge cited a sample interview:

> "What is your most intense emotional state?"
> "Paranoia."
> "Why is paranoia your most intense emotional state?"
> "I am being watched."

''What does your paranoia stem from?''
''A need to isolate myself.''
''Why does your paranoia stem from a need to isolate?''
''It keeps my attention on myself.''
''What does your need to isolate stem from?''
''My knowledge of the future.''
''Why does your need to isolate stem from your knowledge of the future?''
''I see things differently from other people.''
''What does your knowledge of the future stem from?''
''The world is ending.''
''Why does your knowledge of the future stem from the fact that the world is ending?''
''It has been revealed to me.''
''What does the fact that the world is ending stem from?''
''Nothing. It is ending.''
''Why does the fact that the world is ending stem from nothing—it is ending?''
''That's the way it is.''[41]

Thus this ''therapy'' required a religious answer by going on until it received one or, possibly, until the patient quit. The same could be said of the auditing process that led Scientology to accept reincarnation. A truly open-ended therapy, unrestricted by strong belief in the modern, secular, scientific outlook, will almost inevitably become a cult as it tries to answer the whys and wherefores that science, so far at least, cannot answer. As Bainbridge put it:

> This sequence of questions and answers is a very good example, because it shows the likelihood of a supernatural outcome in a therapy process that starts with obsessive assumptions and no antisupernatural basis. The sequence of questions forces the answerer to search for some ultimate response that can terminate the process. Any answer less than ultimate will call forth another question.[42]

So far we have seen how two therapies turned into cults. The Transcendental Meditation (TM) movement serves to give us the other side of the coin.[43] In India Maharishi Mahesh Yogi started the movement after the death of his guru and his subsequent period of solitary contemplation in the Himalayas. It did not prosper, so he decided to take his teachings to the West, ''where people are in the habit of adopting things quickly.'' TM started in the West with a traditional vedic system of meditation, dietary laws, and yoga designed to promote the soul's non-attachment to this world of illusion and eventual "liberation from the cycle of reincarnation and attainment of nirvana."[44]

This Hindu system met with very limited success in the West until the 1960s, when the Maharishi was taken over by such popular, countercul-ture figures as the Beatles. During this period, "The goal of 'cosmic consciousness' was described in terms of bliss, energy, and peace with-out reference to the loss of individual ego or serious implications of non-attachment to the relative, material realm."[45]

With the waning of the counterculture, TM changed its approach. It now produces "scientific validation" at the Maharishi International University. This institution has a staff of Ph.D. meditation researchers, some of whom have presented papers at recent meetings of the Ameri-can Psychological Association.

The Maharaj-ji of the Divine Light Mission also tried to adapt Eastern ideas to Western images: "Your mind is the best computer. . . . But this computer has gone wrong. I have the international screwdriver. It will fit any man."[46] This statement sounds cybernetically reminiscent of Scientology.

Clearly, traditional vedic thought did not do well in the West. There-fore, some brands of Eastern mysticism, especially TM, have tried to become Western science. We are too scientific and empirical a culture to accept much mysticism, although we still have a residue of the reli-gious nature, and of the fear of death, that keeps us looking for gods, or at least for scientific truths.

As we saw in the last two chapters, people require meaning as well as order. Cults, like Spiritualism, offer a new meaningful order to those who are satisfied by neither traditional, established religions nor tradi-tional empiricism. The need for order and for answers, even where these are scientifically unattainable, is strong. New cults spring up to fill this psychic vacuum every day—new cultic containers for old religious ideas. Both the religious needs and their forms of fulfillment are ancient of days.

RELIGION, SHAMANISM, AND CULTS

As we saw in the discussion of Spiritualism, the work of Eugene d'-Aquili indicates that there may indeed be something like the phrenolo-gists' organ of Veneration. E. O. Wilson, author of *Sociobiology,* has suggested that religions evolved originally because they helped bind groups of hunters, and later whole societies, in unquestioning allegiance. Thus religions that enhanced the survival of their members would survive as successful religions—and the genes that predisposed their carriers to religious commitments would also survive and propagate. Epigenetically, by interacting with the environment, these genes "constrain the maturation of some behaviors and the learning rules of other behaviors. Incest taboos, taboos in general, xenophobia, the dichotomization of objects into the sacred and the profane, nosism, hierarchical dominance systems, intense attention toward leaders, charisma, trophyism, and trance-induction, are among the elements of religious behavior most likely to be shaped by developmental programs and learning rules."[47]

This theory gets some support from the work of Mircea Eliad, the French anthropologist and historian of religion. In his book *Shamanism: Archaic Techniques of Ecstasy,* Eliad shows that ecstatic religion is found all over the world. The worship of the Vanir and of Odin by the pre-Christian Scandinavians had many shamanic elements, most notably the séances where the medium went into a trance, assisted by ritual music, and conversed with spirits. The *Edda* myths of trips to Hel made by Odin or one of his followers—trips made in an attempt to learn of the future from the dead or to rescue a soul from death—also show strongly shamanic elements.

Such rituals of ecstatic converse with spirits by mediums are also found among the Siberians, the Eskimos, the Africans, the Australians, and the American Indians. The similarities are so striking that shamanism must be ancient indeed. Shamans, often called medicine men or witch doctors, are people who deal directly with the sacred as well as the profane. They are charismatic leaders, part doctor and part priest, high in the hierarchical dominance systems of their tribes, who often are allowed to break some taboos during their séances. The characteristic Eliad considers definitive of shamanism is the ability of such leaders to induce in themselves a state of ecstatic trance, similar to the trances of mesmeric somnambules and of Spiritualistic mediums. During this trance they commune with deities, ancestral spirits, and animal spirits, covering great distances of time and space, generally in an effort to bring back the wandering or stolen soul of a sick person, to guide the newly dead to the land of the dead, or to learn the future from the spirits.[48]

Thus most of the religious characteristics that Wilson thinks are genetically shaped are to be found in an age-old, pan-human religious system. In its purest form this system is found in "primitive" cultures. Its resemblance to Spiritualism and psychic healing, however, shows that it is by no means lacking in "advanced" cultures. A hankering after the supernatural seems to be a part of human nature, although like all genetic traits and predispositions, it is expressed at different levels in different people. Empiricists and materialists would seem to have a much smaller organ of veneration than religious devotees. This paradigmatic clash of human nature appears to be built-in.

But what about the shamans themselves? Do they believe, or are they as fraudulent as most mediums? The answer seems to lie in the muddled middle. Shamans live in cultures that believe in shamanic miracles, value shamanic powers, and share a shamanic world view that includes spirits and deities of various kinds. In such a culture, most shamans would be predisposed to believe in shamanic magic. However, important parts of this magic are faked. One shamanic feat among the Samoyeds, for example, is highly reminiscent of Houdini. The shaman is tied up and left in a tent, where he or she invokes helping spirits. The audience, outside the tent, hears the animal voices of the spirits, voices that are frequently heard issuing from the shaman's mouth during a trance. When the séance is over, the shaman is found untied.[49] As any conjurer can attest, there are several natural ways to free yourself after letting yourself be tied up. When investigating cabinet mediums who were escape artists, Houdini considered a test adequate only when ankles, wrists, and knees were tightly bound with short lengths of fishing line. In other shamanic feats shamans painlessly slash themselves with knives, hold hot coals, or beat themselves on the head. The lack of pain serves to validate the reality of the practitioner's status and therefore of the whole ambient religious culture. The same could be said of Spiritualistic mediums, except that the religious culture of Spiritualism is a minority religion in our society. Such cultural validation may help the shaman forget that the miracles are faked.

On the other hand, some shamans were sure shamanism was a fake before they took it up. In the same article cited earlier, Lévi-Strauss tells of one American Indian shaman, named Quesalid, who became a shaman because he wanted to find out how the tricks were done. The method for curing disease that he was taught was elementary and is still common among psychic healers. After hiding a bloodstained feather in his own mouth, Quesalid sucked dramatically on the site of the pain, eventually producing the gory "sickness" from his mouth.

A similar operation is still performed by many so-called psychic surgeons. After palming a piece of meat, they knead the patient's flesh, making a fold in the skin. The flesh is then "cut" by hand or with a dull knife, and the "surgeon" dramatically reveals the "cancer" or other disease, enclosed in his hand. Of course there is little or no bleeding and no scar. In the early 1970s psychic surgeons were so popular in the Philippines and Brazil that Northwest Airlines and Pan-American World Airways ran special flights for those in need of such a cure. In 1974 the Federal Trade Commission banned the promoting and scheduling of these flights.[50] The Reverend Jim Jones, of Jonestown infamy, is said to have cured members of his congregation in the same way.

Quesalid, however, did not remain a total skeptic. His cures were effective. He was in fact one of the best shamans of his day and frequently cured people other shamans had failed to cure. Just as Ray Hayman became convinced that palmistry worked (Chapter 6), so Quesalid found himself believing in his own magical powers. In a culture where such cures are expected, where shamanic magic is a part of normal life, conviction would be easily acquired and maintained. The culture and its myths serve to validate the magic, just as the magic gives empirical validation to the social order and to those myths and customs necessary to maintaining that order. What is fraud to us is necessarily sacred to many other cultures.

This necessary sanctity is bolstered by the initiation ordeals the would-be shaman has to endure. As Eliad shows, these rites portray the death and resurrection of the novice. He (or she) hallucinates that he is being torn apart by spirits. He must see his own bones. Then he is remade with pure, spiritual parts of the body. He must experience all sorts of diseases so that he will know them and therefore be able to cure them. He will visit the world of the gods and the world of the dead, and he will acquire a spirit spouse and spirits that will help in his shamanizing by possessing his body and talking through his mouth, using animal cries or the languages of dead shamans, languages he does not know in his normal, waking life.

This ecstatic experience can be attained by sensory deprivation and/ or drugs. LSD, for example, produces "trips" quite similar to shamanic experiences. Mushrooms, narcotics, or decoctions of tobacco are all used to get the novice into the desired state of mind.[51] Ideally, however, it should be achieved without pharmacological aid. Among the Australian aborigines, for example, the novice knows he should become a shaman when he has a spontaneous ecstatic vision of the spirits. After he has been taught by an older shaman how to perform as a shaman, he is initiated. The teacher gathers herbs in the forest, which he rubs on the eyes of the novice in order to "make his sight clear," so he can see the spirits. The men sit opposite to each other, singing and ringing bells for three days and three nights. Neither can sleep until the novice's eyes are "clear." This is all repeated until the novice sees the spirits—when he embarks on his death and rebirth experience.

This ritual is amazingly similar to Scientology's TR-0, as described by Bainbridge. This fatigue-induced ecstasy may be Scientology's only strong similarity to shamanism, although the psychic powers claimed for clears are also reminiscent of shamanism. Scientologists, however, do not seem greatly interested in the cure or rescue of other people's souls. Spiritualism, on the other hand, is very like shamanism. Both the techniques and the effects are similar. A shaman, whether South American, Australian, African, or Siberian, is possessed by a spirit and becomes "the receptacle of a spirit that speaks through his mouth."[52] In short, he becomes a medium. A Goldi shaman, in Siberia, described his experience like this:

> When the "ayami" [the spirit that works through the shaman, his control or spirit guide, to use Spiritualism's terms] is within me, it is she who speaks through my mouth, and she does everything herself. When I am eating the "sukdu" [offering] and drinking the pig's blood [a taboo item], it is not I who eat and drink, it is my "ayami" alone.[53]

Just so might "Margery the Medium" have explained her sexual thrashings.

While in the trance, the shaman describes where he is with his helping spirits and what they are doing to rescue the lost soul of his patient, or to escort the sacrificial animal to heaven or the soul to the land of the dead. The personality speaking seems more active and aware than a medium is supposed to be, but it is hard to know which personality is speaking, the shaman or his helping spirits. Along with the shaman's narrative of his adventures, animal cries and the voices of dead shamans also come from his mouth—just as the voice of your dead Uncle Ernest will purportedly come from a medium's mouth.

How does such a séance differ from various psychotherapies? Lévi-Strauss, as we have seen, considered psychoanalysis a science, if only precariously perched on that high branch of human endeavor. The recent proliferation of therapies has tended to reduce the scientific appearance of any one therapy, and opinion has swung away from Lévi-Strauss. Various studies of the efficacy of various therapies have placed not only their claim to scientific status but even their claim to cure in doubt.

One such study was performed at the Kaiser Foundation Hospital in Oakland, California. One hundred and fifty patients were psychiatrically evaluated, and most were given therapy. Twenty-three had to be put on the waiting list—thus forming an ethically acceptable control group. All 150 patients were reevaluated after six months. It was found that the twenty-three waiting list patients had improved as much as the treated patients: "the therapy patients did not improve significantly more than did the waiting list controls."[54]

Comparisons, such as Lévi-Strauss's, between psychological therapies and shamanic séances have led to at least one study in which the two were directly compared. At the All-India Institute of Mental Health in Bangalor, Western-trained therapists compared the results of their methods of treating schizophenics with the results of the native Ayurvedic treatment. These results proved to be quite similar, the therapists getting an 85 percent improvement rating and the Ayurvedics getting 75 percent. Both seem to depend on spontaneous remission and on the patient's faith in a cure—the power of the placebo.[55]

Therapies provide a shared world view, a cosmology that maps the terra incognita of the mind and places the individual squarely in the center of that map. All this is equally true of religions, when they work, and, when faith in established religions wanes, of cults.

Therapies and scientifically oriented cults thus nourish the same essential part of human nature as priests and shamans, trying, like the alchemists, to reunite our sundered experiences, to achieve the spiritual gold of paradisiacally united body and spirit, the outer and inner sides of man. Our culture has long separated these joint sides of our nature, giving little importance to the organ of Veneration.

Does all this mean there is no difference between psychology and religion? No. There is one real difference. Religions deal with the soul and the Otherworld. The mystic's inner eye is set either on personal spiritual well-being or on the divine. Therapies try to instill the ability to deal with the external, day-to-day, empirical world of the senses. As we saw in considering The Power, when ultimate questions and the fate of the soul enter a therapy, the therapy becomes a cult.

The human mind has these two aspects, inner and outer experiences. There may well be a genetic predisposition towards various kinds of subjective religious experiences—based only on the evolutionary success of those experiences. Thus the real existence of religious feelings need not lead us to posit a real, externally existing god. We have no reason to believe that our impressions of the outer world are much more accurate than those of the frog. In Kant's terms, we can know only the phenomenal reality; noumenal, or real, reality forever eludes the grasp of our limited senses and minds. This leaves us with the ultimate question of human nature: Do we accept the phenomenal world as real, or do we seek ecstatically to know the unknowable noumena?

Whether you turn inward, to your inner self, or outward, to observe the world of sense perception, depends on your basic epistemological presuppositions about the nature of the world—the "real world" of the senses is either *maya*, illusion, or it is indeed real, existing independently of you. In traditional Western thought, the world exists. It may exist as scientific sense perception, as romantic evidence of God's great design, or as a diabolic temptation. In any case, it does exist. Of these three outlooks only the last leads one away from the world, the flesh, and the devil and on a journey either far inward, to the realization of the spiritual self, or far outward, to union with the godhead. This monastic, hermitic reaction is similar to Eastern mysticism. Both see the world as a testing ground where we are all too often seduced by the flesh and doomed to one or another hell, or to reincarnation as a lower animal. The other Western view of the world—whether romantic, deistic, or scientific—accepts this corporeal sphere as the rightful realm of the human soul, spirit, or mind, as well as of the body.

Since saints are rare, the worldly, scientific view has been the basic Western epistemology at least since the time of Locke and Hume, the great modern exponents of empiricism. In the classical world, empiricism goes back at least to Aristotle, who with Plato forms the fountainhead of Western thought. While there have been times when Platonism has been in the ascendant, empiricism has been the basis of Western civilization since the end of the Middle Ages. Any mystical, inward-looking cult, therefore, seems egotistical and self-centered to us. Since we accept the world of the senses as real, and on the whole as worthwhile, the mystical rejection of our world is in effect a rejection of our thoughts and attitudes, indeed of ourselves.

This clash of epistemological presuppositions, of ideas about what we know and how we know it, is the basic paradigmatic clash of human nature, the clash of belief and knowledge. Are we to believe what we can never scientifically know? Hamlet states the dilemma: "To sleep, perchance to dream. Aye, there's the rub." People feared the dark night of death and its attendant nightmares of hell long before Shakespeare's time. The fear, and the confusion, are still with us; "perchance" itself is the rub. To believe in the dreams and nightmares of others requires a leap of faith that does not come easily to the empirical mind. Scientologists and Spiritualists both have tried to cure this nagging rub by providing "scientific proof" of immortality—proof that many are eager to accept. Their systems still require belief, however, and are still religions rather than sciences. To believe is, by definition, to give credence to things beyond mortal ken, beyond even the possibility of human, sensory knowledge. To those who can believe, our everyday world can seem a drab sort of place at best, or, at worst, the den of demons ruled by the devil, a dark pit made terrible by fleshly temptations above which our souls must soar, or at least yearn to soar, if they are to survive.

This existential quandary may be, by our very nature, insoluble. All sorts of shamans are welcome in our search for a solution. Science tries to describe and explain the outer world. Religion tries to describe and explain the inner world. Psychology, being the attempt to describe and explain the inner world by using the techniques of science, is necessarily caught in the middle of different studies tending to go in different directions. Thus psychology may not be simply a science. Tending both inward and outward, psychology may well be the only way to chart the mind, which also tends both inward and outward.

Conclusion:

What Is Pseudoscience?

Is there such a thing as pseudoscience? The answer to this question has two aspects. The term "pseudoscience" is often used by critics to designate marginal scientific areas, using the criteria laid down by philosophers of science. These criteria do not work for the occult doubles of psychology that we have reviewed. We need to distinguish the public, formal criteria for pseudoscience that accusers say they are using from the functional meaning the term really has.

Since Popper's day, philosophers have worked to find a formal criterion that would distinguish science from pseudoscience, without reference to the content of the candidate for scientific status. Even before Popper's pioneering work, critics of historical fringe sciences shared this desire and usually accepted some formal philosophical demarcation criterion. Moreover, alleged pseudoscientists themselves believe that science is a formally definable, Popperian process. So parapsychologists today present arguments such as this:

> Science is not a collection of subjects "approved" for research.[1]
>
> *Science is defined by its established principles of method;* ways of designing and carrying out experiments, developing hypotheses, handling data, reporting results, and responding to the work of oth-

ers. . . . The subject matter of the research and the belief system of
the investigator or the reviewer, have no place in making such a
judgment.[2]

If a fact contradicts a theory, the theory must go. . . . This can be
said [to a critic] with an innocent air, adding, "I always thought
science works that way; doesn't it?"[3]

The answer to this innocent question is simply no. Christopher Jencks
counters the assertion quite baldly when he writes,

The chief value of parapsychology may after all be the light it
throws on the vagaries of the scientific method, and the support it
lends to the view that science is fundamentally a set of dogmas, not
a body of facts.[4]

Everyone involved in debates about pseudosciences, whether scientists or rejected self-styled scientists, thinks that science is an objective,
formally specifiable procedure by which one establishes facts and scientific laws. Kuhn, however, has shown that the formal view fails badly.
Science cannot be separated from substance. Normal science is guided
by a paradigm, a research program, a hard core—substantive sets of beliefs held partly consciously and partly unconsciously by the scientific
community. Findings that make no sense to the paradigm, or that seem
irrelevant, are dismissed as gibberish, as pseudoscience. "The subject
matter of the research" is relevant, for some subjects are senseless or
irrelevant to the dominant paradigm; "the belief system of the investigator" is relevant, for a finding may make sense in one belief system but
not in another. If a reviewer's paradigm clashes with the investigator's,
then the reviewer, with the power of the establishment, properly rejects
the work of the investigator. Science *is* a collection of subjects approved
for research.

Phrenologists, mesmerists, and psychical researchers got upset at this
state of affairs. They were horrified to find that, like a church, established science is built on dogmas and pronounces some ideas anathema.
Parapsychologists enjoy citing Kuhn against orthodox science.

To do so is naive, even if the underlying horror is genuine. For Kuhn,
normal science is the best science. As Lakatos pointed out, scientists
must be persistent in the face of the inevitable adverse results. Scientists
must hold firmly to their paradigm if they are going to find out how far it
will take them, how much it can achieve. Since any theory must con-

front inconsistent, apparently falsifying data, progress would be impossible without dogmatism. Each idea would soon seem disproved, and the next would fare no better. Results that do not fit in must, if normal progressive science is to continue, be denounced as making no sense.

What parapsychologists and other scientific rejectees fail to realize is that the same factors that result in the rejection of their papers by establishment journals also cause the rejection of papers that have absolutely nothing to do with the occult. In present-day experimental psychology, for example, a paper on anagram problem solving might be well written, theoretically well articulated, and methodologically impeccable—and be recognized as such by a journal editor—but be rejected because no one else is working in the area anymore. Rejection is the proper course here—a journal would ill-serve its readers if it did not exclude matter irrelevant to the present concerns of science, regardless of its methodological soundness. Similarly, a journal might reject a paper on clairvoyance not because the experiment was badly done or because the editor does not believe in E.S.P. but simply because the paper is irrelevant to the immediate research concerns of the editor and his audience. Rejection of all sorts of papers and their findings is often motivated by lack of interest in their content rather than hostility.[5]

Kuhn's puzzle-solving analogy is helpful here. A paradigm is like a sketchy drawing of the puzzle to be completed, providing general outlines to be filled in by the research of normal science. Normal science extends itself slowly from one area of the puzzle, or set of research problems, to another. The practitioner is always looking for the next piece adjacent to what has already been assembled—one consistent with the paradigm. In this way, normal science extends itself slowly, piece by piece, finding by finding.

So what is a scientist to do when someone aggressively comes in with a finding, or puzzle piece, that just does not fit into the current frontiers of research? Should he or she assume that all the hard-won successes of science so far are wrong? Of course not. He will dismiss the finding in some way—mildly, as a part of the puzzle not yet reached, or harshly, as a fraud. What the scientist believes, then, is determined more by content than by method. A discrepant fact is a fact because of the method used to find it. It is discrepant, however, because of its meaning, its content. Thus content rather than form or method determines which fields are considered to be pseudosciences.

This criterion of content is oddly revealed in the careers of phrenology and psychical research. Underneath the many objections made to phrenology was the recognition and fear of its latent materialism. To those who believed in an immortal soul possessing free will, phrenology's insistence that the brain was the organ of mind was an abomination. Phrenology was therefore rejected. But by the middle of the nineteenth century, as phrenology faded away, materialism became an established doctrine, Christianity's protests notwithstanding. Thus, when psychical researchers began to offer evidence of an immortal soul, their findings were rejected as inconsistent with the mechanics of modern science. In each case it was the content that earned a doctrine the label pseudoscience: in 1825 the occult doctrine was materialism; in 1882 it was spiritualism.

These considerations suggest that the nature of science is very different from what most of us think. We believe, scientists believe, pseudoscientists believe, that science produces Truth. We generally believe that sciences possess a certain set of procedures that, properly followed, must reveal True Facts—the laboratory-tested facts so dear to Scientology. So the pseudoscientist feels terribly hurt when he follows the procedures and unearths a bit of Truth, only to be called a fool and the new Truth nonsense.

Henry Veatch has suggested, however, that "the real thrust of the scientific enterprise is not aimed at anything like a knowledge of reality or the nature of things at all. . . . [Rather] it simply provides a convenient and useful ordering device . . . which the human mind or the mind of the scientist devises for the purpose of helping him get about, as it were, among the data. . . ." Thus science discloses not "the truth about things, but only what might be called the truth of our human predictions, manipulations, and devices for the control of nature. . . . The excellence of theories so conceived is not to be gauged by their approximation to the truth, or by the insights which they offer into the nature of reality, but only by what we might call in the crude sense their pragmatic consequences."[6]

In a Kuhnian view, Veatch describes science as pragmatic search for puzzle solutions. This makes the decision to call something a pseudoscience a pragmatic one rather than a formal one. If a field makes sense in terms of going ideas, it becomes a science; if it does not make sense, it is dismissed as false. Thus chemistry grew out of the theory of phlogiston and, having outgrown it, slew it, just as phlogiston had outgrown and slain alchemy. If its practitioners persist, the field becomes a pseudoscience. On rare occasions the outsider triumphs and joins the ranks of established science. Vaccination, for instance, was bitterly opposed by the medical establishment and was put into practice by politicians. If Kuhn and Veatch are correct, then, science is an odd affair indeed. Scientists must, if science is to work, adhere, with some, but not complete, dogmatism, to ideas that are not ultimately True.

In chapter 8 we saw how an initiate into The Power would be questioned repeatedly until an ''ultimate'' answer was given. Commenting, Bainbridge said, ''The sequence of questions and answers . . . shows the likelihood of a supernatural outcome in a therapy process that starts with obsessive assumptions and no supernatural bias. The sequence of questions forces the answerer to search for some ultimate response that can terminate the process. An answer that is less than ultimate will call forth another question.''

Here, it may be, is the the essential difference between science and other human activities, a difference pseudoscience tries to bridge and therefore is damned. If science is a pragmatic search for puzzle solutions, it does not ask, and cannot answer, ultimate questions. Paradigms are not questioned; rather they provide questions in the form of puzzles. The paradigm, quietly and surreptitiously, settles ultimate questions for the scientist; one day dualism is accepted, the next materialism. In any event, puzzles are posed that can profitably be pursued through research. But ultimate questions are avoided. The paradigm, then, may pose the puzzle, ''Where in the brain does the soul act?'' It will not, however, seek to show that there is, or is not, such an ultimate thing as a soul.

Much of our modern confusion arises because, since the nineteenth century, scientists have themselves misunderstood the pragmatic nature of science, arrogating to themselves the right to decide what is True. In 1874, John Tyndall, one of the most outspoken Victorian scientists, proclaimed that men of science

> claim, and . . . shall wrest from theology, the entire domain of cosmological theory. All schemes and systems which infringe upon the domain of science must, in so far as they do this, submit to its control and relinquish all thought of controlling it.[7]

With this attitude, however, we leave science, the search for solutions, and enter upon scientism, the faith that science can settle all questions, even ultimate ones. The Church of Scientology is a clear illustration of scientism. As Veatch points out, science is not the domain of Truth, which is more properly the domain of the humanities. Great philosophers such as Plato and great writers such as Shakespeare are still read and are considered classics because we still find in them valuable Truth about the nature of things. Religion, too, has claimed to reveal Truth to its believers. Scientism is a new religion that dismisses religion as superstition, the humanities as the idiosyncratic and outdated ramblings of artistic minds.

These idiosyncratic ramblings, however, may teach us more about human reality—within the mind or without—than science can ever hope to. Ultimate questions cannot be answered by science. Science brilliantly meets one human need, to find order in the universe. Science predicts, explains, controls. But science cannot meet another need, to find meaning in the order of the universe. The astronomer can say with great precision where the moon was at 6:27 A.M. on June 12, 1954; the astrologer claims to say what its position meant. Science succeeds as it does because it does not ask too many questions: it ends its dialogue with nature before it comes to an ultimate question.

But there seems to be something in human nature that demands answers to ultimate questions. Even the existentialist who says the universe is absurd, without meaning, has asked and answered, albeit gloomily, the ultimate question about the meaning of existence. The scientist never asks the question, knowing it to be empirically unanswerable.

In an age of scientism, however, there is nowhere to turn for ultimate answers but to science. Science has abandoned "obvious assumptions," but human nature has not. Pseudosciences arise to fill the gap between orthodox science and the need for meaning no longer provided by traditional religion: the need for meaning that Lévi-Strauss feared would turn psychoanalysis into a mystical pseudoscience; the need filled by shamans in many cultures that openly care about ultimate questions, and by mediums or therapists in cultures that do not.

Here, psychology plays a special role. Physicists and chemists, revered though they may be, cannot play the role of priest or shaman. It is the psychologist, the scientist concerned with human nature, who mediates between scientism's god and the layman. It is the psychologist who in popular forms such as *Psychology Today* and the *Bob Newhart Show* brings the most interesting knowledge—of oneself—to the masses. This double aspect of psychology is most evident in the job of the clinical psychologist who must be at once confessor and researcher. He is a new shaman mediating between the powers of the universe, now understood scientifically, and the needs of the client.[8] For those who cannot stand, or understand, our new, scientifically explained, ultimately absurd universe, the medium takes over from the psychologist, making the universe homey as it has not been in centuries. Fraudulent or not, mediums fill a need for a simple, down-home universe that scientific psychology cannot honestly provide.

Thus, caught as we are between science and religion, it is no wonder that occult doubles of psychology so easily shift from science to religion and back. Phrenology, which started as a science of brain, ended as a guidance counselor, offering a comprehensive world view that would unlock the secrets of character. Mesmerism began as a naturalistic theory of curing and ended as the window on the immaterial world, leaving as its heir Spiritualism, the religion of the New Age. Going the other way, psychical research began with the hopeful investigation of mediums and seems to be ending as a naturalistic science of unusual phenomena. Scientology and The Power began as therapies and ended as cults. All these movements attempted to bridge the gap between science and religious need—as alchemy and astrology did before them—but never really succeeded. Phrenology faded away; mesmerism was bifurcated into scientific hypnotism and occult Spiritualism; psychical research seems to be turning away from ultimate questions, retreating toward science and materialism; Scientology is regarded as a science fiction hoax (probably correctly); The Power broke up from internal bickering.

Since pseudosciences attempt to fill the religious void, we find that moral issues play a greater role in their proposal and acceptance than is the case elsewhere in science. Phrenology offered itself as a new world view supporting reform and enlightened morality; it was condemned for wicked materialism and for fostering irresponsibility and crime. Mesmerism proffered a new medical cure and a scientific basis for personal and social harmony; it was condemned as fraud tending toward sexual corruption. Psychical research hoped to prove the existence of the soul and establish the eternality of reward and punishment; it was condemned for fraud, scientific imposture, and subverting the gains of science. Areas that are commonly considered scientific, in contrast, do not make great moral or spiritual claims. A chemist may claim a new compound is useful, as a drug perhaps, but he does not claim that it, or chemistry, provides a new morality, expecting instead only solutions to some small puzzles.

Professional issues also arise to demarcate pseudosciences. As science got on a more sure footing in the nineteenth century, scientists began to organize themselves and set themselves off sharply from other groups, especially from the clergy.[9] Each of our pseudosciences was hurt by the professionalization process. Gall came along just as physiology was becoming a distinct, recognized, experimental science. Gall challenged the views of the emerging, respected leaders of the field such as Flourens, and his craniology was rejected. So, with Spurzheim and Combe phrenology moved to appeal, not to the scientists, but instead to the populace as a scientific world view, replacing the old Neoplatonic one. Similarly, mesmerism threatened to taint medicine with the occult just as it was emerging from its phase of crude empiricism into a scientifically based technology. Hypnotism was extracted, leaving behind a popular religion, Spiritualism. Psychical research began just as psychology was founded as an independent science. Parapsychologists' interest in ultimate questions, such as the existence of the soul, was an embarrassment to scientific psychologists striving for acceptance. So parapsychology had to go its own way, depending more on popular acceptance for its survival than on scientific approval.

In each case professional rejection was met with what we might call occult professionalism. The phrenologists established Phrenological Societies; the mesmerists established Societies of Harmony; the psychical researchers established the Society for Psychical Research, and the parapsychologists established the Parapsychology Association. Ironically, this meant that there were now occult establishments fighting off an even more unacceptable occult underground. "Orthodox" phrenologists denounced itinerant bump readers; "orthodox" mesmerists denounced stage mesmerists and false mediums; "orthodox" psychical researchers sought out fraud; "orthodox" parapsychologists fight to distance themselves from UFOs, the Bermuda Triangle, Big Foot, astrology, and mind control. Everyone winds up drawing the line somewhere.

What, finally, is pseudoscience? James Webb described the occult underground as a huge realm of beliefs rejected by orthodox society. Pseudoscience is a part of that underground—the part that follows the procedures of science and is captive to scientism. It is propelled by the unmet, deeply rooted human need for a universe of meaning, rather than one of mere order. Pseudosciences attempt to find meaning in many places—patterns in the sky, bumps on the skull, the speech of somnambules and mediums, patterns of card guesses. In each case, the phenomena are looked into scientifically, but in each case the motivation is to find something science cannot give—answers to the ultimate questions about the meaning, dignity, and endlessness of life. Obsessively pursued, these questions must lead away from science to the making of a pseudoscience. There is nothing unscientific about phrenology, mesmerism, or parapsychology—which conclusion does not make them sciences. They are not sciences because they try to delve deeper than any science can.

To say that they are not sciences is not to condemn them, except to the believer in scientism. If Veatch is correct, the searcher after Truth ought not go to science in the first place. Instead, the searcher should go to philosophy, art, literature, and religion. Not every human question has a scientific answer. Science can prolong life; it cannot tell us when life ought to be prolonged. Science can diagnose birth defects and abort babies; it cannot tell us which, if any, babies should be aborted. Science can build a laser; it cannot tell us where to aim it.

We cannot look to science for meaning and moral values. But we ought not infer from that that life has no meaning, that there are no moral values. Questions of meaning and morality must be asked; science may help us rule out certain answers. Ultimately, however, we must look elsewhere for Truth.

Notes

INTRODUCTION THE OCCULT MARKETPLACE

1. Elmer Kral, "The Teacher, the Student, and Reports of the Paranormal," *Skeptical Inquirer* 3, no. 4 (1979): 42.
2. Nat Freedland, *The Occult Explosion* (New York: G. P. Putnam's Sons, 1972), p. 11.
3. Ibid., p. 11.
4. William G. Roll, ed., *Research in Parapsychology* (Metuchen, N.J.: Scarecrow Press, 1979), p. 12.
5. David Marks and Richard Kammann, *The Psychology of the Psychic* (Buffalo, N.Y.: Prometheus Books, 1980), pp. 9–10.
6. Milbourne Christopher, *Mediums, Mystics and the Occult* (New York: Thomas Y. Crowell, 1975), p. 58.
7. Freedland, *Explosion*, pp. 91–92.

CHAPTER ONE PSEUDOSCIENCE AND PSYCHOLOGY

1. See Allen Janik and Stephen Toulmin, *Wittgenstein's Vienna* (New York: Touchstone Books, 1973).
2. The most illuminating, if informal, account of Popper's approach to science and pseudoscience is his 1953 lecture "Science: Conjectures and Refutations," printed in his *Conjectures and Refutations: The Growth of Scientific Knowledge* (New York: Harper Torchbooks, 1968). A more formal presentation is made in Popper's *The Logic of Scientific Discovery* (New York: Harper Torchbooks, 1965; orig. German ed., 1954).
3. Popper, "Conjectures," p. 35.
4. Ibid., p. 37.
5. The logical positivists; see Popper, "Conjectures," pp. 39–41.
6. See, e.g., David Willer and Judith Willer, *Systematic Empiricism: Critique of a Pseudoscience* (Englewood Cliffs, N.J.: Prentice-Hall, 1973), which applies a version of Popper's thought to modern sociology.
7. Imre Lakatos, "Falsification and the Methodology of Scientific Research Programs," in *Criticism and the Growth of Knowledge,* ed. Lakatos and A. Musgrave (Cambridge: At the University Press, 1970). A clear and simplified discussion of Lakatos's demarcation crite-

247

rion may be found in "Introduction: Science and Pseudoscience," in *The Methodology of Scientific Research Programs,* Volume 1 of Lakatos's collected philosophical papers, ed. J. Worrall and G. Currie (Cambridge: At the University Press, 1978).

8. Ibid., p. 102, italics deleted.

9. Ibid., p. 177. Lakatos described several examples of theories in the natural sciences, including Newtonian mechanics, that swam against a sea of "refuting" observations to ultimate triumph.

10. Ibid., p. 132, italics deleted.

11. Ibid., p. 175, italics deleted.

12. Ibid., p. 176.

13. Thomas S. Kuhn, *The Structure of Scientific Revolutions,* 2d ed. (Chicago: University of Chicago Press, 1970). See also his "Logic of Discovery or Psychology of Research" and "Reflections on my Critics" in *Criticism,* eds. Lakatos and Musgrave. In fact, Lakatos's methodology of research programs is an attempt to rationally reconstruct Kuhn's sociological proposals within a Popperian framework.

14. Kuhn, *Structure,* p. viii.

15. Kuhn, "Logic," p. 21.

16. Ibid., p. 5.

17. Ibid., p. 6.

18. Lynn Thorndike, *History of Magic and Experimental Science,* 8 vols. (New York: Columbia University Press, 1928–1958).

19. Kuhn, "Logic," p. 8.

20. Ibid., p. 9.

21. Kuhn does not state this explicitly.

22. Kuhn, "Logic," p. 9.

23. Ibid., pp. 9–10.

24. Lynn Thorndike, "The True Place of Astrology in the History of Science." *Isis* 46 (1955): 273–78.

25. Some very recent attempts to formulate more adequate demarcation criteria may be found in Part I of M. P. Hanen, M. J. Osler, and R. G. Weyant (eds.), *Science, Pseudoscience and Society* (Waterloo, Ontario, Canada: Wilfred Laurier University Press, 1980). But as these formulations are, as their authors concede, tentative and incomplete, they do not alter the general picture described here.

26. Richard Westfall, "The Role of Alchemy in Newton's Career," *Reason, Experiment, and Mysticism in the Scientific Revolution,* ed. M. L. Rhighini Bonelli and W. R. Shea (New York: Science History Pubns., 1975), p. 189. The other statements about Newton are also drawn from this source.

27. James Webb, *The Occult Underground* (LaSalle, Ill.: Open Court, 1974), and *The Occult Establishment* (LaSalle, Ill.: Open Court, 1976).

28. Skeptical Eye, "Paranormal Pentagon," *Discover,* March 1981, p. 15.

29. William S. Bainbridge, *Satan's Power: A Deviant Psychotherapy Cult* (Berkeley and Los Angeles: University of California Press, 1978).

Chapter Two   Doubles of Natural Science:
Alchemy and Astrology

1. Richard Westfall, "The Role of Alchemy in Newton's Career," in *Reason, Experiment, and Mysticism in the Scientific Revolution,* ed. M. L. Rhighini Bonelli and William R. Shea (New York: Science History Pubns., 1975), p. 189.

2. Ibid.

3. Ibid., pp. 195–96.

4. Thomas H. Leahey, *History of Psychology* (Englewood Cliffs, N.J.: Prentice-Hall, 1980), pp. 49–52.

5. Wayne Shumaker, *The Occult Sciences in the Renaissance* (Berkeley and Los Angeles: University of California Press, 1972), p. 179.

6. Frances A. Yates, *Giordano Bruno and the Hermetic Tradition* (London: Routledge and Kegan Paul, 1964), p. 63.
7. James Webb, *The Occult Underground* (LaSalle, Ill.: Open Court, 1974), p. 198.
8. B. Fingulus, *A Golden and Blessed Casket of Nature's Marvels* (London: Vincent Stuart, 1973), p. 259.
9. John Freccero, "Donne's 'Valediction: Forbidding Mourning,' " *English Literary History* 30 (1963): 363.
10. Kurt Seligmann, *The Mirror of Magic* (New York: Pantheon, 1948), p. 142.
11. Westfall, "Newton's Career," p. 203.
12. Kurt Seligmann, *Magic, Supernaturalism, and Religion* (New York: Pantheon, 1948), p. 83.
13. T. Burckhardt, *Alchemy* (London: Stuart and Walkins, 1967), p. 146.
14. Seligmann, *Mirror*, p. 129.
15. Shumaker, *Occult Sciences*, pp. 170–71.
16. The discussion of Newton draws heavily on Westfall, "Newton's Career," but we will footnote only direct quotations.
17. Westfall, "Newton's Career," p. 216.
18. Ibid., pp. 211–12.
19. Betty Jo Teeter Dobbs, *The Foundation of Newton's Alchemy* (Cambridge: At the University Press, 1975), p. vii.
20. Joseph A. Mazzeo, "Notes on John Donne's Alchemical Imagery," *Isis* 48 (1957): 120.
21. Burckhardt, *Alchemy*, p. 168.
22. Westfall, "Newton's Career," p. 229.
23. Ibid., pp. 224–25. Westfall develops this argument at length in "The Influence of Alchemy on Newton," *Science, Pseudoscience, and Society*, ed. M. Hanen, M. Osler, and R. Weyant (Calgary, Alberta, Canada: Wilfred Laurier University Press, 1980).
24. Ibid., p. 232.
25. John Donne, *The Complete Poetry of John Donne* (Garden City, N.Y.: Doubleday, Anchor Books, 1967), p. 44.
26. Ibid., pp. 96–97.
27. Ibid., p. 97, note 20.
28. Mazzeo, "Donne's Imagery," p. 120.
29. Freccero, "Donne's 'Valediction,' " pp. 337–38.
30. For further discussion of the transformation of alchemy in the seventeenth century, see Lynn Thorndike, *History of Magic and Experimental Science*, vols. 6–8 (New York: Columbia University Press, 1941–1958).
31. Webb, *Occult Underground*, p. 224.
32. Ibid., pp. 264, 275.
33. Ibid., pp. 274–75.
34. John Sladek, *The New Apocrypha* (London: Hart-David, MacGibbon, 1973), pp. 141–42.
35. Stephen F. Mason, *A History of the Sciences* (New York: Collier Books, 1962), p. 233.
36. Westfall, "Newton's Career," p. 204.
37. Dobbs, *Newton's Alchemy*, pp. 43–44.
38. Webb, *Occult Underground*, p. 216.
39. Ibid., pp. 214–16.
40. Westfall, "Newton's Career," p. 219.
41. *Bedazzled* (movie, 1967), screenplay by Peter Cooke.
42. James Joyce, *A Portrait of the Artist as a Young Man* (New York: Viking Press, 1964), p. 240.
43. Westfall, "Newton's Career," p. 189.
44. Alexander Marshack, *The Roots of Civilization* (New York: McGraw-Hill, 1972).
45. Jack Lindsay, *The Origins of Astrology* (New York: Barnes and Noble, 1971), pp. 26–27.
46. Ibid., p. 4.
47. Plato *Timaeus* 71E; *Republic* 8. 528E ff.
48. Claudius Ptolemy, *Tetrabiblos*, trans. F. E. Robbins (Cambridge, Mass.: Harvard University Press, 1964), p. 3.

49. Ibid., pp. 6–7.
50. Ibid., p. 13.
51. Ibid., pp. 14–15.
52. Ibid., pp. 21, 23.
53. Ibid., pp. 28–29.
54. Ellic Howe, *Astrology.* (New York: Walker, 1967); Herbert Leventhal, *In the Shadow of the Enlightenment* (New York: New York University Press, 1976), and Jon Butler, "Magic, Astrology and the Early American Religious Heritage," *American Historical Review* 84 (1979): 317–46.
55. Marcello Truzzi, "The Occult Revival as Popular Culture," *Sociological Quarterly* 13 (1972): 16–36; Truzzi, "Astrology as Popular Culture," *Journal of Popular Culture* 8 (1975): 906–11; Jacques Maitre, "The Consumption of Astrology in Contemporary Society," *Diogenes* 53 (1966): 82–98.
56. Derek and Julia Parker, *The Compleat Astrologer* (New York: McGraw-Hill, 1971), pp. 54–55.
57. "Objections to Astrology: A Statement by 186 Leading Scientists," *The Humanist* 35 (1975): 4–6; Bart J. Bok, "A Critical Look at Astrology," *The Humanist* 35 (1975): 609; Lawrence E. Jerome, "Astrology: Magic or Science?" *The Humanist* 35 (1975): 10–16. Subsequent issues of *The Humanist* continued the attack. During 1976 and 1977 the magazine presented articles defending and attacking the studies of Michel Gauquelin, who claims to have established planetary influences on human behavior, but without thereby supporting traditional astrology (see especially vol. 36, no. 1 (1976) and vol. 37, no. 6 (1977).) Since Gauquelin's work is technical, hotly controversial, and only marginally astrological, I will not consider it here. The interested reader should also consult *The Humanist's* offspring, *The Zetetic* (after 1979, vol. 2, *The Skeptical Inquirer*), which regularly denounces astrology and other occultisms.
58. The astrologer's reply, *The Humanist* 35 (1975): 24–26.
59. Howe, *Astrology,* chs. 6, 7.
60. Bernie Silverman, "Studies of Astrology," *Journal of Psychology* 77 (1971): 141–49; Silverman and Marvin Whitmer, "Astrological Indicators of Personality," *Journal of Psychology* 87 (1974): 89–95; Robert Pellegrini, "The Astrological 'theory' of Personality," *Journal of Psychology* 85 (1973): 21–28; Anthony Stauden, "Is There an Astrological Effect on Personality?" *Journal of Psychology* 89 (1975): 259–60; Pellegrini, "Birthdate Psychology: A New Look at Old Data," *Journal of Psychology* 89 (1975): 261–65; Nicholas Hume and Gerald Goldstein, "Is There an Association between Astrological Data and Personality?" *Journal of Clinical Psychology* 33 (1977): 711–13; C. R. Snyder, Daniel Larsen, and Larry Bloom, "Acceptance of General Personality Interpretations prior to and after Receipt of Diagnostic Feedback Supposedly Based on Psychological, Graphological and Astrological Assessment Procedures," *Journal of Clinical Psychology* 32 (1976): 258–65. See also C. R. Snyder, "Why Horoscopes are True," *Journal of Clinical Psychology* 30 (1974): 577–80.

CHAPTER THREE   PHRENOLOGY: THE THEORY AND ITS CRITICS

1. Lynn Thorndike, *A History of Magic and Experimental Science* (New York: Columbia University Press, 1923), 1:146.
2. The description of Costa's work is based on Thorndike, *History,* pp. 658–59.
3. For the development of faculty psychology during the Middle Ages and Renaissance, see Harry Wolfson, "The Internal Senses in Latin, Arabic, and Hebrew Philosophic Texts," *Harvard Theological Review* 28 (1935): 69–133; and E. Ruth Harvey, *The Inward Wits: Psychological Theory in the Middle Ages and Renaissance* The Warburg Institute, Survey VI (London: The Warburg Institute, 1975). For the history of brain function, see E. Clark and K. Dewhurst, *An Illustrated History of Brain Function* (Berkeley and Los Angeles: University of California Press, 1972).
4. Thorndike, *History,* 5:512.

5. Rene Descartes, "Meditations of First Philosophy," in *Philosophical Works of Descartes*, trans. E. Haldane and G. Ross (Cambridge: Cambridge University Press, 1972).

6. John Locke, *An Essay Concerning Human Understanding* (Oxford, England: At the Clarendon Press, 1972).

7. Etienne Bonnot de Condillac, *Treatise on Sensations*, 1754. Partially reprinted in *The Classical Psychologists*, ed. B. Rand (Gloucester, Mass.: Peter Smith, 1966). See also Isabel Knight, *The Geometric Spirit: The Abbé Condillac and the French Enlightenment* (New Haven: Yale University Press, 1968). Added in press: Hans Aarsleff in *From Locke to Saussure* (Minneapolis: University of Minnesota Press, 1982) has shown that this traditional description of Condillac is much mistaken. Whatever its sources, however, sensationalism was a widely held doctrine in Gall's time.

8. Thomas Reid, *Thomas Reid's Inquiry and Essays* (Indianapolis, Ind.: Bobbs-Merrill, 1975).

9. Dugald Stewart, *Elements of the Philosophy of the Human Mind* (London: A. Strahan and T. Caddell, 1792).

10. Franz Joseph Gall, *Outlines of the Science of Phrenology*, in a letter to Jos. Fr. de Retzer, 1798. Reprinted in N. Capen, *Reminiscences of Dr. Spurzheim and George Combe* (New York: Fowler and Wells, 1881).

11. *Dictionary of Scientific Biography*, s.v. "Gall, Franz Joseph."

12. Gall, *On the Functions of the Brain and Each of Its Parts*, trans. Winslow Lewis (Boston: Marsh, Capen and Lyon, 1835).

13. Ibid., 1:308, 55.

14. Ibid., 1:308.

15. Gall, *Outlines*, p. 74.

16. Robert M. Young, *Mind, Brain, and Adaptation in the Nineteenth Century* (Oxford: At the Clarendon Press, 1970), pp. 15–16.

17. Ibid., pp. 16–19.

18. Ibid., p. 18.

19. Ibid., p. 17.

20. Ibid., p. 36. Schematic chart reprinted with the permission of Oxford University Press.

21. Ibid., pp. 33–35.

22. Pierre Flourens, *Phrenology Examined* (Philadelphia: Hogan and Thompson, 1846).

23. See Erwin H. Ackernecht and Henri Vallois, *Franz Joseph Gall, Inventor of Phrenology and His Collection* (Madison: University of Wisconsin Medical School, 1956), or Owsei Temkin, "Gall and the Phrenological Movement," *Bulletin of the History of Medicine* 21 (1947): 275–321.

24. Based on Ackernecht and Vallois, *Gall*, pp. 24–26.

25. Imre Lakatos, "Falsification and the Methodology of Scientific Research Programs," in *Criticism and the Growth of Knowledge*, ed. I. Lakatos and A. Musgrave (Cambridge, Eng.: At the University Press, 1970).

26. Johann Spurzheim, *Phrenology*, rev. ed. from the 2d American ed. of 1833 (Philadelphia: J. B. Lippincott, 1908), p. 35.

27. Ibid., p. 36.

28. Ibid., p. 117.

29. Ibid., p. 156.

30. Ibid.

31. Ibid., p. 36. The term first appeared in 1805, when Benjamin Rush used it to designate mental science; it was independently used in 1815 by Thomas Forster; Spurzheim's independence is unclear. See Patricia Noel and Eric Carlson, "Origins of the Word 'Phrenology' " *American Journal of Psychiatry* 115 (1958–59): 535–38.

32. Spurzheim, *Outlines of Phrenology* (Boston: Marsh, Capen and Lyon, 1832).

33. Spurzheim, *Phrenology*, p. 149.

34. Ackernecht and Vallois, *Gall and His Collection*, p. 85–86.

35. Spurzheim, *Phrenology*, p. 148.

36. Ibid., p. 35.

37. Ibid., p. 138.

38. Ibid., pp. 35–36.

39. Ibid., p. 156, italics added.
40. Ibid., p. 156.
41. Ibid, p. 156. In the *Outlines* (p. 19) Spurzheim adds an eighth item to the list that does refer to organology, but it is clearly not a criterion, only a measure of certainty: "Its existence is placed beyond doubt, if its peculiar organ be made known by repeated observation."
42. Spurzheim, *Outlines* p. 156.
43. Ibid., p. 20.
44. Spurzheim also listed as "probable" propensities Desire to Live and Alimentiveness.
45. George Combe, "An Address Delivered at the Anniversary Celebration of the Birth of Spurzheim and the Organization of the Boston Phrenological Society, Dec. 31, 1839" (Boston: Marsh, Capen, Lyon & Webb, 1840; pamphlet), p. 11.
46. E.g., George Combe, *A System of Phrenology,* 2nd American from the 3rd Edinburgh ed. (Boston: Marsh, Capen and Lyon, 1834).
47. George Combe, *The Constitution of Man,* 9th American ed. from the latest English ed. (Boston: William Ticknor, 1839).
48. David de Giustino, *Conquest of Mind* (London: Croom Helm; Totowa, N.J.: Rowman and Littlefield, 1975), pp. 3–60.
49. Harriet Martineau, *Biographical Sketches,* new ed. (London: Macmillan, 1885), p. 265.
50. Combe, *Constitution,* pp. vii–viii.
51. Ibid., p. 4. Many works discuss evolution before Darwin. See, e.g., Peter Bowler, *Fossils and Progress* (New York: Science History Pubns., 1976); Loren Eiseley, *Darwin's Century* (Garden City, N.Y.: Doubleday, 1958); B. Glass, O. Temkin, and W. Straus (eds.), *Forerunners of Darwin: 1745–1859* (Baltimore: Johns Hopkins University Press, 1959); and J. C. Green, *The Death of Adam* (Ames, Iowa: Iowa State University Press, 1959).
52. Ibid., p. 6.
53. Ibid., p. 4.
54. Ibid., p. 12.
55. Ibid., p. 13.
56. Ibid., p. 37.
57. Combe's list of faculties is essentially the same as Spurzheim's (see Combe, *Constitution,* pp. 50–52), so we do not list Combe's system here.
58. Combe, *Constitution,* pp. 95–96.
59. Combe, "Address," p. 6.
60. Ibid., pp. 8–9.
61. Ibid., p. 7.
62. "Phrenological Quacks," *Phrenological Journal* (Edinburgh) 9 (Sept. 1834–March 1836): 517–19.
63. Orson Squire Fowler, "Practical Phrenology Defended," *American Phrenological Journal* 3 (1840–41): 570–71.
64. Orson Squire Fowler and Lorenzo Niles Fowler, *Phrenology Proved, Illustrated and Applied,* 4th ed. (Philadelphia: Fowler and Brevoort, 1839), p. 4. For the Fowlers' career, see *Heads and Headlines: The Phrenological* Fowlers by Madeleine B. Stern (Norman: University of Oklahoma Press, 1971).
65. See, e.g., L. N. Fowler, *The Principles of Phrenology and Physiology Applied to Man's Social Relations* (New York: L. N. and O. S. Fowler, 1842); O. S. Fowler, *Amativeness* (New York: Fowler and Wells, 1889); O. S. Fowler, *Love and Parentage,* 13th ed. (New York: Fowlers and Wells, 1850); O. S. Fowler, *Matrimony as Taught by Phrenology* (Boston: O. S. Fowler, c. 1859).
66. See, e.g., Jessie A. Fowler, *A Manual of Mental Science,* or *Childhood: Its Character and Culture* (New York: Fowler and Wells, 1897).
67. See, e.g., O. S. & L. N. Fowler, *Phrenology: A Practical Guide to Your Head* (New York: Chelsea House, 1969). Unfortunately, the reprint publisher does not give the original publishing information.
68. O. S. Fowler, "Elementary Phrenology," *American Phrenological Journal* 2 (1839–40): 321–34.
69. See, e.g., O. S. and L. N. Fowler, *Phrenology,* or J. Fowler, *Manual.*

70. O. S. and L. N. Fowler, *Phrenology Proved*, p. iii.
71. [O. S. Fowler], "Our Proposed Course," *American Phrenological Journal* 4 (1842): 1, 2, 5.
72. [O. S. Fowler], "Introductory Statement," *American Phrenological Journal* 1 (1838-39): 8.
73. "Progression a Law of Nature #2," *American Phrenological Journal* 7 (1845): 142-43. Almost all articles in the APJ were written by a Fowler, usually O. S. Fowler.
74. "Progression a Law of Nature #1," *American Phrenological Journal* 7 (1845): 75.
75. O. S. and L. N. Fowler, *Phrenology*, p. 67.
76. [O. S. Fowler], "Our Proposed Course," p. 7.
77. O. S. and L. N. Fowler, *Phrenology*, pp. 70-71.
78. George Henry Lewes, *The Biographical History of Philosophy*, vol. 2 (New York: D. Appleton, 1855).
79. John Shertzer Hittell, *A New System of Phrenology* (New York: C. Blanchard, 1857).
80. Ibid., p. 6.
81. Ibid.
82. Ibid., p. 54.
83. Ibid., pp. 13-14.
84. Ibid., p. 14.
85. Ibid., p. 16.
86. Ibid., p. 15-16.
87. Ibid., p. 11.
88. Ibid., p. 34.
89. Ibid., p. 5.
90. Ibid., p. 35.
91. Ibid., pp. 39-40.
92. Ibid., p. 49.
93. Ibid., p. 55.
94. Ibid., p. 56-57.
95. Ibid., p. 60.
96. Ibid., p. 66.
97. Ibid., pp. 68-72.
98. Ibid., p. 74.
99. [Thomas Brown], "Art. XV," *Edinburgh Review* 2 (1803): 147-60.
100. Ibid., p. 151.
101. Ibid., pp. 151-52.
102. Ibid., p. 152-53.
103. Ibid., p. 153.
104. Ibid., p. 153-54.
105. Ibid., p. 154.
106. Ibid., p. 155.
107. Ibid., pp. 156-57.
108. Ibid., p. 160.
109. Called "Cranioscopy," in earlier additions, it appeared as part of the seventh edition (1842) under a new title , "Phrenology": *Encyclopaedia Britannica*, 7th ed., (s.v. "Phrenology.")
110. Ibid.
111. Ibid.
112. Ibid.
113. Ibid.
114. Ibid.
115. Ibid.
116. Ibid.
117. Ibid. The specific example of Destructiveness is ours.
118. P. Flourens, *Phrenology Examined* (Philadelphia: Hogan and Thompson, 1846).
119. Ibid., pp. 34-35.
120. Ibid., p. 728; Gall's discoveries are reviewed on pp. 143-44.
121. Ibid., p. 28.

122. Ibid., p. 96.
123. Ibid., pp. 47, 57.
124. Ibid., p. 53.
125. Ibid., p. 58.
126. Ibid, pp. 58–59.
127. Ibid., p. 61.
128. Ibid., p. 62.
129. Ibid., p. 95.
130. Alexander Bain, *On the Study of Character, Including an Estimate of Phrenology* (London: Parker, Son, and Bourne, 1861).
131. Ibid., pp. v–vi.
132. Ibid., p. 49.
133. Ibid., pp. 90–93.
134. Ibid., pp. 171–72.
135. Ibid., pp. 177–90; quotes on pp. 182 and 189.
136. "Phrenologists," *Times* (London) 16 January 1824, p. 2, col. 3.
137. *Times* (London), 2 February 1824, p. 2, col. 5.
138. "Phrenological Transactions," *Times* (London), 11 March 1824, p. 3, cols. 2–3.
139. "Phrenology and Dr. Spurzheim," *Times* (London), 16 March 1825, p. 3, col. 3.
140. "Phrenology," *Times* (London), 28 December 1827, p. 3, col. 3.
141. "Phrenology," *Times* (London), 30 December 1835, p. 2, col. 3.
142. "Phrenology," *Times* (London), 15 August 1837, p. 2, col. 4.
143. Richard Chevenix, "Gall and Spurzheim, Phrenology," *Foreign Quarterly Review,* 2 (1828): 1–59.
144. George Henry Lewes, "Phrenology in France," *Blackwood's Magazine* 82 (1857): 665–674.
145. Lewes, *History,* 749–768.
146. George Henry Lewes, *The Study of Psychology* (Boston: Houghton, Osgood and Co., 1879).
147. "Phrenology," *The North American Review* 37 (1833): 59–83.
148. "Review of George Combe's *Constitution of Man,*" *The Knickerbocker* 1 (1833): 315–16.
149. Timothy Flint, "Phrenology," *The Knickerbocker* 2 (1833): 103–10. Other favorable articles in *The Knickerbocker* are "Phrenology Made Easy," 11 (1838): 523–27, and Caleb Ticknor, "Popular Objections to Phrenology," 13 (1838): 308–15.
150. "The Editor's Table, Increase of Crime." *Harper's Magazine* 6, no. 31 (1852): 125–28.
151. David Reese, *Phrenology Known by Its Fruits* (New York: Howe and Bates, 1836).
152. Edward Hungerford, "Poe and Phrenology," *American Literature* 2 (1930–31): 209–31.
153. [Edgar Allan Poe], "Phrenology," *Southern Literary Messenger* 2 (1835–36): 286–87. See Combe on Phrenology, *Southern Literary Messenger,* 5 (1839): 393–97; 459–64; 567–70; 602–5; 667–70; 766–70; 810–13.
154. A Phrenologist, "On Rights and Government," *The United States Magazine and Democratic Review* 9 (1841): 459–76, 568–83.
155. It is also clear that some people, such as the writers of the *Times,* simply found phrenology laughable. But the resulting ridicule cannot be considered a rational criticism.
156. D. L. Emblem, *Peter Mark Roget: The Word and the Man* (New York: Thomas Y. Crowell, 1970), pp. 143–47; Andrew Combe, "Cranioscopy, by Dr. Roget," *The Phrenological Journal* 17 (1823): 165–76. George Combe's own reply is in his *System of Phrenology,* pp. 584–600, but it is directed against critics in general. Andrew's article includes George's rebuttals and adds his own.
157. See, e.g., G. Combe, *System of Phrenology,* p. 600.
158. *Encyclopaedia Britannica,* s.v. "Phrenology."
159. Ibid.
160. Emblem, *Roget,* pp. 150–52.
161. Quoted by Bernard Hollander in *The Mental Functions of the Brain* (New York: G. P. Putnam's Sons, 1901), p. 417.
162. "Cruelty to animals—Sir William Hamilton's Experiments," *Phrenological Journal* 7 (1831–32), 427–33.
163. George Combe, "On the Nature of the Evidence by Which the Functions of the Different Parts of the Brain May Be Established," *The Phrenological Journal* 10 (1836–37): 563–64.

164. Ibid., p. 561.
165. Ibid., p. 558.
166. Ibid., p. 559.
167. Ibid., pp. 560–61. Other phrenological critiques of physiologists' methods and findings may be found in O. S. and L. N. Fowler, *Phrenology Proved*, pp. 354 ff. and pp. 376 ff., and Johann Spurzheim, *Anatomy of the Brain* (Boston: Marsh, Capen and Lyon, 1834), pp. 236 ff.
168. "Phrenology: Its Scientific Claims, Its Investigation," *American Phrenological Journal* 8 (1846): 8; O. S. and L. N. Fowler, *Phrenology Proved*, p. 8.
169. See, e.g., Spurzheim, *Anatomy*, pp. 222 ff., L.E.G.E., "Fact against Fancy," *The Zoist* 9 (1845): 4; or O. S. and L. N. Fowler, *Phrenology Proved*, pp. 360 ff.
170. See Johann Spurzheim, *Phrenology*, 5th American ed. (New York: Harper and Brothers, 1855), pp. 94–98 and 107–14, and *Outlines*, pp. 73 ff.; Combe, *Constitution*, pp. 1–26, and *System*, pp. 593 ff.; O. S. and L. N. Fowler, *Phrenology Proved*, practically every page, but see especially pp. 380 ff.
171. O. S. and L. N. Fowler, *Phrenology Proved*, p. 388.
172. L.E.G.E., "Cerebral Physiology," *The Zoist* 1 (1843–44): 16.
173. Ibid., p. 17.
174. Ibid., pp. 16–17.
175. Ibid., pp. 13, 17.
176. L.E.G.E., "Fact against Fancy," *The Zoist* 3 (1845–46): 21–22.

CHAPTER FOUR   PHRENOLOGY: SUCCESS AND FAILURE

1. Both quotes in John D. Davies, *Phrenology: Fad and Science* (New Haven, Conn.: Yale University Press, 1955), p. 165.
2. R. J. Cooter, "Phrenology and British Alienists, c. 1825–1845; Part II, Doctrine and Practice," *Medical History* 20 (1976): 138.
3. L.E.G.E., "Cerebral Physiology," *The Zoist* 1 (1843–44): 13.
4. For Britain, see J. F. C. Harrison, *The Early Victorians* (New York: Praeger, 1971). For America, see Ronald G. Walters, *American Reformers 1815–1860* (New York: Hill and Wang, 1978).
5. [Orson Squire Fowler], "Our Proposed Course," *American Phrenological Journal* 4 (1841): 7; L.E.G.E., "Cerebral Physiology," p. 13.
6. E.g., O. S. Fowler and Lorenzo Niles Fowler, *Phrenology: A Practical Guide to Your Head* (Reprint, New York: Chelsea House, 1969). For example, to cultivate Spirituality "Muse and meditate on divine things . . ."; to restrain it "Cultivate the terrestrial more and the celestial less . . ." (p. 132).
7. E.g., O. S. Fowler, *Matrimony as Taught by Phrenology* (Boston: O. S. Fowler, c. 1859) or *Love and Parentage*, 13th ed. (New York: Fowlers and Wells, 1850); Alexander Smart, "On the Application of Phrenology in the Formation of Marriages," *Phrenological Journal* (Edinburgh) 8 (1832–34): 464–75; and L.E.G.E., "Fact against Fancy," *The Zoist* 3 (1845–46): 20.
8. "Physical Puritanism," *Westminster Review* 57 (1852): 409.
9. A. Cameron Grant, "New Light on an Old View," *Journal of the History of Ideas* 29 (1968): 293–301.
10. J. F. C. Harrison, *Quest for the New Moral World* (New York: Charles Scribner's Sons, 1969), 239–43.
11. George Combe, "Phrenological Remarks on the Relation between the Natural Talents and Dispositions of Nations, and the Development of Their Brains," appendix to Samuel George Morton, *Crania Americana* (Philadelphia: J. Dobson, 1839), pp. 271–73.
12. Combe, "Phrenological Remarks," p. 282. Combe's views were not idiosyncratic. Similar views and analyses of "national heads" may be found throughout the *American Phrenological Journal;* e.g., on Chinese heads, vol. 4 (1842).
13. John S. Haller and Robin M. Haller, *The Physician and Sexuality in Victorian America* (Urbana: University of Illinois Press, 1974), pp. 48–61.

14. Quoted by David de Giustino, *The Conquest of Mind* (London: Croom Helm; Totowa, N.J.: Rowman and Littlefield, 1975), p. 72.
15. L. N. Fowler, *The Principles of Phrenology and Physiology Applied to Man's Social Relations* (New York: L. N. & O. S. Fowler, 1842), p. 132.
16. "Woman—Her Character, Influence, Sphere and Consequent Duties and Education," *American Phrenological Journal* 7 (1845): 8–12.
17. Harrison, *Early Victorians,* p. 135.
18. Ibid., p. 135.
19. Smart, "Formation of Marriages," pp. 464–65.
20. Ibid., pp. 466–67. Given the probable audience of the Edinburgh *Phrenological Journal,* it is significant to notice that the editor considered Smart's portrait of the nobility overgeneralized and "too strongly drawn" (p. 467).
21. Ibid., p. 468.
22. Ibid., pp. 468–72. Smart anticipates here Francis Galton's program of positive eugenics. Cf. Galton, *Hereditary Genius* (London: Macmillan, 1925), p. 1, and *Inquiries into the Human Faculty and Its Development* (London: J. M. Dent, 1907), p. 47.
23. Ibid., pp. 472–75.
24. Richard S. Westfall, "Newton and the Fudge Factor," *Science* 179: (1973): 751–58.
25. See especially Owsei Temkin, "Gall and the Phrenological Movement," *Bulletin of the History of Medicine* 21 (1947): 275–321; and David Bakan, "The Influence of Phrenology of American Psychology," *Journal of the History of the Behavioral and Social Sciences* 2 (1966): 200–220. Spiritualists, too, revered the Baconian ideal of facts before theory. See Logie Barrow, "Socialism in Eternity: The Idealogy of Plebian Spiritualists, 1853–1913," *History Workshop Journal* 9 (1980): 59.
26. Richard Chevenix, "Gall and Spurzheim—Phrenology," *Foreign Quarterly Review* 2 (1828): 8–9; Orson Fowler, "Practical Phrenology Defended," *American Phrenological Journal* 3 (1841): 570; [Orson Fowler], "Our Proposed Course," *American Phrenological Journal* 4 (1841): 7.
27. This is the best-documented aspect of phrenology. See especially Cooter, "Phrenology and Alienists"; Davies, *Phrenology: Fad and Science,* and de Giustino, *Conquest of Mind.* For differing views on the centrality of application in phrenological thought, see the exchange in *Annals of Science* 32 (1975) between G. N. Cantor, author of "The Edinburgh Phrenology Debate: 1803–1828" (pp. 195–218), who maintained that application was only a late concern of the phrenologists, and Steven Shapin, author of "Phrenological Knowledge and the Social Structure of Early Nineteenth-Century Edinburgh" (pp. 219–43), who maintained that application was the central issue in the debate. Cantor replied in "Critique of Shapin's Social Interpretation of the Edinburgh Phrenology Debate" (245–56). Shapin continued his program in "The Politics of Observation: Cerebral Anatomy and Social Interests in the Edinburgh Phrenology Disputes," in *On the Margins of Science: Social Construction of the Paranormal,* ed. R. Wallis, *Sociological Review Monographs* 27 (1979): 139–78. An additional social analysis of phrenology's appeal and rejection, alternative to both ours and Shapin's, may be found in Roger Cooter, "Deploying Pseudoscience: Then and Now," in *Science, Pseudoscience and Society,* ed. M. Hanen, M. Osler, and R. Weyant (Calgary, Alberta, Canada: Wilfrid Laurier University Press, 1980). While these sources and our chapter focus on Great Britain and the United States, phrenology passed through the same stages and had the same appeals in France. See Angus McLaren, "A Prehistory of the Social Sciences: Phrenology in France," *Comparative Studies in Society and History* 23 (1981): 3–22.
28. Auguste Comte, *The Positive Philosophy,* trans. Harriet Martineau (New York: C. Blanchard, 1855; reprint, New York: AMS Press, 1974), pp. 381–82.
29. For England, see J. F. C. Harrison, *Quest for the New Moral World* (New York: Charles Scribner's Sons, 1969); for America, see Perry Miller, *The Life of the Mind in America* (New York: Harcourt, Brace and World, 1965).
30. See Harrison, *Quest,* pp. 91–138.
31. "Introductory Statement," *American Phrenological Journal* 1 (1838): 8.
32. For a good broad treatment of nineteenth-century scientism, see Franklin L. Baumer, *Modern European Thought* (New York: Macmillan, 1977), pp. 305–13.

33. "Phrenology: Its Scientific Claims, Its Investigation," *American Phrenological Journal* 8 (1846): 7–8.

34. Peter Gay, *The Enlightenment: An Interpretation* (New York: W. W. Norton, 1969), ch. 4, especially pp. 174–86.

35. Quoted by Angus McClaren, "Phrenology: Medium and Message," *Journal of Modern History* 46 (1974): 86, 91. Phrenology's materialist supporters were especially vocal in France; see McClaren, "Prehistory," 5–13.

36. These techniques and ideas are discussed thoroughly in Haller and Haller, *Physician and Sexuality*, especially chapter 1.

37. Lewis Perry, " 'Progress, Not Pleasure Is Our Aim': The Sexual Advice of an Antebellum Radical," *Journal of Social History* 12 (1979): 358.

38. Haller and Haller, *Physician and Sexuality,* p. 201.

39. Undated dedication on the flyleaf of a copy of Jessie A. Fowler, *A Manual of Mental Science for Teachers and Students* (New York: Fowler and Wells, 1897), now in the possession of the Virginia State Library, Richmond, Virginia.

40. Merle Curti, *The Growth of American Thought* (New York: Harper and Row, 1964), p. 333.

41. Harrison, *Early Victorians,* p. 139.

42. Orson Fowler, "Proposed Course," pp. 2, 5.

43. Harrison, *Early Victorians,* p. 138.

44. Orson Fowler, "Phrenology, Its Scientific Claims," p. 9.

45. L.E.G.E., "Cerebral Physiology," pp. 8–9.

46. Shapin, "Phrenological Knowledge" (footnote 27), pp. 237, 241.

47. Quoted by Davies, *Phrenology: Fad and Science,* pp. 26–27.

48. Harrison, *Early Victorians,* pp. 137–43.

49. Richard Sennett, *The Fall of Public Man* (New York: Vintage Books, 1978), p. 24.

50. Quoted by Pierre Flourens, *Phrenology Examined* (Philadelphia: Hogan & Thompson, 1846), p. 94.

51. "Signs of Character," *American Phrenological Journal* 8 (1846): 13–19.

52. Robert Chambers, *Vestiges of the Natural History of Creation* (London: John Churchill, 1845), p. 348.

53. L.E.G.E. "Fact Against Fancy," *The Zoist* 3 (1845–46): 11.

54. T. M. Parssinen, "Popular Science and Society: The Phrenology Movement in Early Victorian Britain," *Journal of Social History* 8 (1974): 1–20.

55. For the later development of the brain sciences, including the new phrenology, see Robert M. Young, *Mind, Brain and Adaptation in the Nineteenth Century* (Oxford: Clarendon Press, 1970). In the early years of the century the "new phrenology" itself was quite controversial; see, e.g., Shepard Ivory Franz, "A New Phrenology," *Science* 35 (1912): 321–28, and the reply, F. H. Pike, "A Defense of the 'New Phrenology'," *Science* 35 (1912): 619–22. The leader in trying to make the new phrenology an active revival of Gall was Bernard Hollander; e.g., *The Mental Functions of the Brain* (New York: G. P. Putnam's Sons, 1901).

56. See de Giustino, *Conquest of Mind,* chs. 5 ("Transmission and Schism") and 6 ("The Ungodly Error").

57. Richard S. Westfall, "Newton and the Fudge Factor," *Science* 179 (1973): 751–58; David L. Hull, "Scientific Bandwagon or Traveling Medical Show?" In *Sociobiology and Human Nature,* ed. Michael S. Gregory, Anita Silvers, and Diane Sutch (San Francisco: Jossey-Bass, 1978), pp. 136–63.

58. Ralph Holloway, "The Casts of Fossil Hominid Brains," *Scientific American* 231 (1974), 106–15; Harry Jerison, "Should Phrenology Be Rediscovered?" *American Anthropologist* 18 (1977): 744–46.

59. Richard Dawkins, *The Selfish Gene* (New York: Oxford University Press, 1976); Lionel Tiger, "Optimism: The Biological Roots of Hope," *Psychology Today* 12 (January 1979): 18–30, 33; Edward O. Wilson, *Sociobiology: The New Synthesis* (Cambridge, Mass.: Harvard University Press, 1975); and Edward O. Wilson, *On Human Nature* (New York: Bantam Books, 1978).

60. John McFie, "Recent Advances in Phrenology," *Lancet* 7 (Aug. 12, 1962): 360, 363.

61. Macdonald Critchley, "Phrenology in Medicine," *Lancet* 10 (Dec. 5, 1964), 1227.

62. Hull, "Scientific Bandwagon," p. 162.
63. Andrew Wilson, "The Old Phrenology and the New," *Popular Science Monthly* 14 (1879): 475, 476.
64. M. Allen Starr, "The Old and the New Phrenology," *Popular Science Monthly* 35 (1889): 748.
65. "Scientific Phrenology," *Science* 9 (1889): 299.
66. Edwin G. Boring, *A History of Experimental Psychology*, 2d ed. (New York: Appleton-Century-Crofts, 1950), ch. 3.
67. "Temkin, Gall and the Phrenological Movement," *Bulletin of the History of Medicine* 21 (1947): 275–321; Ackernecht and Vallois, *Franz Joseph Gall* (Madison: University of Wisconsin Medical School, Department of the History of Medicine, 1956). The recovery of phrenology as an important social movement began with Davies, *Phrenology: Fad and Science*.
68. For a survey of the new phrenological studies, see R. J. Cooter, "Phrenology: Provocation of Progress," *History of Science* 14 (1976): 211–34.

CHAPTER FIVE   MESMERISM

1. Article reprinted from the *Foreign Quarterly Review* by the *Select Journal* 3 (1834): 145.
2. Franz Anton Mesmer, *Dissertation on the Discovery of Animal Magnetism* (1779), trans. Maurice M. Tinterow and reprinted in his *Foundations of Hypnosis* (Springfield, Ill.: Charles C Thomas, 1970), p. 34.
3. Account of Mesmer's dissertation based on Tinterow, *Foundations*, pp. 34–35 and Vincent Buranelli, *The Wizard from Vienna* (New York: Coward, McCann and Geoghegan, 1975), pp. 34–37.
4. Mesmer, *Discovery*, p. 40.
5. Ibid., p. 41.
6. Ibid., pp. 41–45.
7. Lynn Thorndike, *History of Magic and Experimental Science*, vol. 8 (New York: Columbia University Press, 1958), p. 176.
8. Mesmer, *Discovery*, pp. 45–46.
9. Robert Darnton, *Mesmerism and the End of the Enlightenment in France* (Cambridge, Mass.: Harvard University Press, 1968), ch. 1.
10. Buranelli, *Wizard*, pp. 93–95.
11. Mesmer, *Discovery*, p. 54.
12. Ibid., pp. 54–56. Courtesy of Charles C Thomas, Publisher, Springfield, Illinois.
13. Ibid., pp. 56–57.
14. Buranelli, *Wizard*, 161–62.
15. Tinterow, *Foundations*, p. 82. Account of the commission's findings based on Tinterow's reprint, pp. 82–128.
16. Reprinted in *The Nature of Hypnosis*, ed. Ronald E. Shor and Martin T. Orne (New York: Holt, Rinehart, & Winston, 1965), pp. 5–7.
17. Reprinted in ibid., Shor and Orne, *Nature of Hypnosis*, pp. 8–23.
18. Buranelli, *Wizard*, p. 167.
19. Darnton, *Mesmerism*, pp. 85–88.
20. Ibid., p. 66.
21. Ibid., p. 70.
22. Ibid., p. 74.
23. Ibid., pp. 79–80.
24. Ibid., p. 101.
25. Account of Bergasse's ideas drawn from Darnton, *Mesmerism*, pp. 112–25.
26. Contemporary description of Puységur's magnetized tree quoted by Frank Podmore in *From Mesmerism to Christian Science* (New Hyde Park, N.Y.: University Books, 1963), p. 76. Published by arrangement with Lyle Stuart, Inc.
27. Henri Ellenberger, *The Discovery of the Unconscious* (New York: Basic Books, 1970), p. 71.

28. Quoted by Buranelli in *Wizard*, p. 118.
29. Ibid.
30. Quoted by Podmore in *From Mesmerism*, p. 73.
31. Quoted by Ellenberger in *Unconscious*, p. 72.
32. M. F***, *Essay on the Probabilities of Magnetic Somnambulism* (1785), reprinted by Tinterow in *Foundations*, p. 131.
33. See, e.g. "Is the State of Hypnosis a Unique State of Consciousness? —Yes, Ernest R. Hilgard (*Psychology Today*, November 1974) —No, Theodore X. Barber (*Psychology Today*, July 1970)," *Taking Sides: Clashing Views on Controversial* Psychological *Issues*, ed. Joseph Rubin and Brent Slife (Guilford, Conn.: Dushkin, 1980), pp. 275–88.
34. Buranelli, *Wizard*, p. 205.
35. Account of the Lyons group based on Buranelli, *Wizard*, pp. 169–72, and Darnton, *Mesmerism*, pp. 68–69.
36. Podmore, *From Mesmerism*, pp. 197–98.
37. Darnton, *Mesmerism*, p. 133.
38. Ibid., p. 137. Account of spiritual mesmerism draws heavily from Darnton.
39. William Gregory, *Animal Magnetism*, 3d ed. (1909; reprint, New York: Arno Press, 1976), ch. 6.
40. Ibid., pp. 89–90.
41. Ibid., p. 119.
42. James Braid, *Neurypnology* (1843; reprint, New York: Arno Press, 1976), ch. 6.
43. Account of French Mesmerism to 1840 based on Podmore, *From Mesmerism*, chs. 5–6.
44. Account of the Nancy and Salpêtrière schools based largely on Ellenberger, *Unconscious*, pp. 85–102.
45. Favorable notice is given of the opening in London of a mesmeric clinic by a French female disciple of Mesmer on November 30, 1785, p. 2, col. 3.
46. By 1791 the *Times* was disclosing the mesmerist's secrets (January 12, p. 2, col. 4) and observing its "sinking into contempt" (March 24, p. 2, col. 4). Following Dupotet's visit the *Times* turned actively hostile, for example welcoming the stopping of Elliotson's demonstrations (June 25, 1838, p. 7, col. 2).
47. Account of Elliotson's career based largely on Harley Williams, *Doctors Differ* (London: Jonathon Cape, 1946), pt. 2.
48. Ibid., p. 69.
49. E. G. Boring, *A History of Experimental Psychology*, 2d ed. (New York: Appleton-Century-Crofts, 1950), p. 126.
50. Reprinted from the only surviving copy, his own, by Tinterow in *Foundations*, pp. 318–30.
51. Braid, *Neurypnology*, pp. 19–20.
52. Braid, *The Power of the Mind over the Body*, partially reprinted in Tinterow, *Foundations*, pp. 331–64.
53. Braid, *The Critics Criticized*, partially reprinted in Tinterow, *Foundations*, pp. 375–89.
54. Ibid., p. 389.
55. Ellenberger, *Unconscious*, p. 78.
56. Account of seeress based on Ellenberger, *Unconscious*, pp. 78–81, and Podmore, *From Mesmerism*, pp. 214–15.
57. Podmore, *From Mesmerism*, pp. 200–204.
58. Ibid., pp. 172–83.
59. Gregory, *Animal Magnetism*, chs. 4, 5, 9, 14; Joseph Haddock, *Somnolism and Psycheism* (1851; reprint, New York: Arno Press, 1975), chs. 6 and 9.
60. N.E.E.N., "Spirit Rapping." *The Zoist* 11 (1853–54): 86–96.
61. J. W. Jackson, "Table-Moving, Rappings, and Spiritual Manifestations," pt. 1, *The Zoist* 11 (1853–54): 412–29; pt. 2, *The Zoist* 12 (1854–55): 1–17.
62. Darnton, *Mesmerism*, p. 127.
63. Ellenberger, *Unconscious*, pp. 74, 188–89.
64. Darnton, *Mesmerism*, p. 151.
65. Ibid., pp. 143–45.
66. Ibid., p. 151, quoting Théophile Gautier.
67. Ibid., pp. 148–59; Ellenberger, *Unconscious*, pp. 158–70.

68. James Wyckhoff, *Franz Anton Mesmer: Between God and Devil* (Englewood Cliffs, N.J.: Prentice-Hall, 1975), which tries to defend the fluidic theory.
69. See, e.g., Peter W. Sheehan and Campbell W. Perry, *Methodologies of Hypnosis* (Hillsdale, N.J.: Erlbaum, 1976).
70. Barber, "State of hypnosis unique?—No," p. 288.

CHAPTER SIX   SPIRITUALISM

1. M. Lamar Keene, *The Psychic Mafia* (New York: St. Martin's Press, 1976), pp. 60, 76, 132, 133–34. Reprinted by permission of St. Martin's Press, Inc. Macmillan & Co., Ltd.
2. Ibid., p. 159.
3. Ibid., p. 74.
4. Ibid., p. 65.
5. Ibid., p. 73.
6. Ibid., p. 99.
7. Ibid., pp. 100–102.
8. Ibid., p. 51.
9. Howard Kerr, *Mediums, and Spirit-Rappers, and Roaring Radicals* (Urbana: University of Illinois Press, 1972), pp. 4–5.
10. James Webb, *The Occult Underground* (La Salle, Ill.: Open Court, 1974), p. 22.
11. Kerr, *Mediums,* pp. 5–6.
12. Webb, *Underground,* pp. 26–29.
13. Ibid., p. 31.
14. Ibid., p. 32.
15. A. F. Tyler, *Freedom's Ferment,* 1944, reprint (New York: Harper and Row, 1962), pp. 68–75.
16. Webb, *Underground,* p. 118.
17. Ibid., p. 44.
18. Ibid., p. 12.
19. Ibid., p. 16.
20. T. H. Huxley, a letter of January 29, 1869, included in London Dialectical Society, *Report on Spiritualism* (London: Longman's Green, Reader and Dyer, 1871) p. 229.
21. Webb, *Underground,* pp. 35–36.
22. Ibid., p. 34.
23. W. B. Gibson and M. N. Young, eds., *Houdini on Magic* (New York: Dover, 1953), pp. 122–23.
24. Ibid., pp. 124–27.
25. Kerr, *Mediums,* p. 12.
26. Milbourne Christopher, *Mediums, Mystics, and the Occult* (New York: Thomas Y. Crowell Co., 1975), pp. 192–93.
27. Keene, *Mafia,* pp. 108–11, 120.
28. Kerr, *Mediums,* p. 109.
29. James Webb, *The Occult Establishment* (La Salle, Ill.: Open Court, 1976), pp. 23–24.
30. J. B. Priestley, *English Journey* (London: William Heinemann, 1934), pp. 158–59, 161. Reprinted by permission of William Heinemann Ltd.
31. Webb, *Establishment,* p. 24.
32. W. Y. Evans-Wentz, *The Fairy-Faith in Celtic Countries,* 1911, reprint (New Hyde Park, N.Y.: University Books, 1966), pp. vi-viii.
33. Ibid., pp. xxiv-xxv.
34. Ibid., pp. 21–22.
35. Ibid., p. 32.
36. Ibid., p. 365.
37. Ibid., p. 514.
38. Harry Price, *Confessions of a Ghost Hunter* (New York: Causeway Books, 1974), p. 329.
39. This analysis of Norse customs and beliefs draws heavily on two books by H. R. Ellis-

Davidson, *The Road to Hel* (Cambridge, Eng.: Cambridge University Press, 1943) and *Gods and Myths of Northern Europe* (Baltimore: Penguin, 1964).

40. Ellis, *Hel*, p. 192.
41. Ibid., p. 115.
42. Ellis-Davidson, *Gods*, pp. 93–94.
43. Ellis, *Hel*, pp. 139–41.
44. Ibid., p. 139.
45. Ibid.
46. Ibid., p. 149.
47. Magnus Magnusson and Hermann Palsson, eds., *The Vinland Sagas* (Baltimore: Penguin, 1965), pp. 81–83.
48. Ellis-Davidson, *Gods*, p. 120.
49. Magnussan and Palsson, *Vinland Sagas*, pp. 81–83. Reprinted by permission of Penguin Books Ltd.
50. Ellis, *Hel*, pp. 160–62. Reprinted by permission of Cambridge University Press.
51. Eugene G. d'Aquili, "The Neurological Bases of Myths and Concepts of Deity," *Zygon* 13 (1978): 257–75.
52. Margret Boden, *Artificial Intelligence and Natural Man* (New York: Basic Books, 1978): pp. 106–7.
53. d'Aquili, "Neurological Bases," p. 265.
54. J. Y. Lettvin, H. R. Maturana, W. S. McColloch, and W. Pitts, "What the Frog's Eye Tells the Frog's Brain," *Proceedings of the I.R.E.* 47 (1959): 1940–51.
55. Wolfgang Kohler, *The Mentality of Apes*, 1925, reprint (New York: Liveright, 1976).
56. N. D. Sundberg, "The Acceptability of 'Fake' versus 'Bona Fide' Personality Test Interpretations," *Journal of Abnormal and Social Psychology* 50 (1975): 145–57. Many similar results are reprinted by David Marks and Richard Kammann, *The Psychology of the Psychic* (Buffalo, N.Y.: Prometheus Books, 1980), chapter 12.
57. C. R. Snyder and R. J. Shenkel, "The P. T. Barnum Effect," *Psychology Today* 8 (1975): 52–54. Copyright 1975, Ziff-Davis Pub. Co.
58. Ray Hyman, " 'Cold Reading': How to Convince Strangers You Know All about Them," *The Zetetic* 1, 2 (1979): 27.
59. Keene, *Mafia*, p. 46.
60. Hyman, "Cold Reading," p. 26.
61. Keene, *Mafia*, p. 140.
62. Ibid., p. 150.

CHAPTER SEVEN   PSYCHICAL RESEARCH

1. There are many histories of psychic research. The classic early work is Frank Podmore, *Mediums of the Nineteenth Century* 2 vols., 1902, reprint (New Hyde Park, N.Y.: University Books 1963). The general intellectual climate that nourished the founders of psychical research is admirably detailed by Frank Turner in *Between Science and Religion* (New Haven, Conn.: Yale University Press, 1974), although his scope is much broader than psychical research. For the founding of the S.P.R., see Alan Gauld, *The Founders of Psychical Research* (New York: Schocken Books, 1968). Two more controversial books are D. Scott Rogo, *Parapsychology: A Century of Inquiry* (New York: Dell, 1975) and R. Laurence Moore, *In Search of White Crows* (New York: Oxford University Press, 1977). Rogo is himself a parapsychologist, and his book should be read with that in mind; nor has it received uniformly favorable reviews from other parapsychologists. Moore is a historian, and in parapsychological quarters his book, which covers spiritualism, psychical research, and modern parapsychology, has been read as an attack on the field (e.g., J. G. Pratt, "Obituary for Parapsychology," *Journal of the A.S.P.R.* 72 (1978): 257–66). The professionalization of the field by Rhine is fully presented by Seymour Mauskopf and Michael McVaugh, *The Elusive Science: Origins of Experimental Psychical Research* (Baltimore: Johns Hopkins University Press, 1980), who make extensive use of unpublished material.

2. Lewis Perry, " 'Progress, Not Pleasure, Is Our Aim': The Sexual Advice of an Antebellum Radical," *Journal of Social History* 12 (1979): 354–66. See also Moore, *White Crows*, pt. 1.

3. "Movements of Spiritualists," *New York Times*, October 14, 1858, p. 4, col. 4. During this period the *Times* regularly associated spiritualism with free love.

4. J. F. C. Harrison, *Quest for the New Moral World* (New York: Charles Scribner's Sons, 1969), pp. 250–52. The intertwining of political reform movements and spiritualism is explored by Logie Barrow, "Socialism in Eternity: The Ideology of Plebeian Spiritualists, 1853–1913, *History Workshop Journal* 9 (1980): 37–69.

5. Frederic Myers, *Human Personality and Its Survival of Bodily Death* (London: Longmans, Green, 1903), vol. 2, p. 279.

6. Ibid., pp. 79, 279.

7. William James, "What Psychical Research Has Accomplished," a lecture and essay given in various forms, 1890–97, reprinted from its final form in James' *Will to Believe* (1897) in *William James on Psychical Research*, ed. G. Murphy and R. Ballou (New York: Viking, 1960), pp. 25–47.

8. William James, "Spiritualism New and Old," *Atlantic Monthly* 29 (1872): 358–62.

9. James, "Psychical Research," p. 28.

10. "The Society for Psychical Research," *Science* 4 (11 July 1885): 40–43; boxed editorial, *Scientific American* 126 (Jan. 1922): 60.

11. Andrew Lang, "Psychical Research," *Harper's Magazine* 109 (1904): 878–82.

12. Joseph Jastrow, "The Problem of 'Psychic Research,' " *Harper's Magazine* 79 (1889): 76–82; and the "Psychology of Spiritualism," *Science* 8 (17 Dec. 1886): 567–68.

13. Joseph Banks Rhine, *New Frontiers of the Mind* (New York: Farrar and Rinehart, 1937) pp. 25–26. As early as 1888, British Spiritualists aimed at "converting the supernatural into the natural," Barrow, "Socialism in Eternity," p. 54.

14. Ibid., pp. 4–5.

15. Editorial: "The Change in Editorship and the New Program," *Journal of Parapsychology* 6 (1942): 4.

16. Editorial: "Whose Field Is Parapsychology?" *Journal of Parapsychology* 6 (1942): 82.

17. J. B. Rhine, "Impatience with Scientific Methods in Parapsychology," *Journal of Parapsychology* 11 (1947): 283–95.

18. J. B. Rhine, "Why National Defense Overlooks Parapsychology," *Journal of Parapsychology* 21 (1957): 245–58. In their Afterword to Mauskopf and McVaugh, *Elusive Science*, Joseph and Louisa Rhine reiterate that their desire to find more in man than "just his physical, sensorimotor side" was the "great ideal" that launched them on their way and kept them going "with or without more general recognition" (p. 309).

19. Samuel Moss and Donld C. Butler, "The Scientific Credibility of ESP," *Perceptual and Motor Skills* 46 (1978): 1064, 1077.

20. R. A. McConnell, "A Parapsychological Dialogue," *Journal of the A.S.P.R.* 71 (1977): 429–35.

21. J. G. Pratt, "Parapsychology, Normal Science and Paradigm Change," *Journal of the A.S.P.R.* 73 (1979): 24. There is at present a movement afoot to rename, or reorient, parapsychology by transforming it into a perhaps more acceptable "Anomalistic Psychology." See Leonard Zusne and Warren Jones, *Anomalistic Psychology: A Study of Extraordinary Phenomena of Behavior and Existence* (Hillsdale, N.J.: Lawrence Erlbaum, 1981).

22. *Times* (London), July 4, 1838, p. 4, col. 3, and Sept. 11, 1838, p. 4, col. 5.

23. Prize announcment in *Scientific American* 127 (Dec. 1922): 389. Committee announced in *Scientific American* 128 (Jan. 1923): 6–7, 61, 67.

24. Moore, *White Crows*, p. 177.

25. J. Malcolm Bird, "Our Psychic Investigation," *Scientific American*, 130 (1924): 236, 291–92, 294.

26. Bird, "Our Next Psychic," *Scientific American* 131 (July 1924): 28–29, 70; and "The Margery Mediumship—I," *Scientific American* 131 (August 1924): 88–89, 132.

27. E. E. Free, the editor of *Scientific American*, reported a preliminary canvass of the committee in *Scientific American* 131 (1924): 304; MacDougall was unavailable at that time.

28. *Scientific American* 131 (1925): 229.

29. Search opened, *Scientific American* 164 (April 1941): 210–11; closed, *Scientific American* 168 (April 1943): 147.

30. Hudson Hoagland, "Science and the Medium," *Atlantic Monthly* 136 (1925): 666–81.

31. In defense, see L. R. G. Crandon, "The Margery Mediumship"; on the other side, reporting Rhine's disillusionment, see Wolber Franklin Prince, "A Review of the Margery Case." Both in Carl Murchison (ed.) *The Case For and Against Psychical Belief*, 1927. Reprint. New York: Arno, 1975).

32. George Price, "Science and the Supernatural," *Science* 122 (August 26, 1955): 359–67. Replies appear in *Science* 123 (January 6, 1956): 7–19. Price's apology is in a short letter in *Science* 175 (January 28, 1972): 359.

33. C. E. M. Hansel, *ESP: A Scientific Evaluation* (New York: Charles Scribner's Sons, 1966), and *ESP and Parapsychology: A Critical Re-evaluation* (Buffalo, N.Y.: Prometheus Books, 1980). The revision includes references and replies to Hansel's many parapsychological critics.

34. For example, Russell Targ and Harold E. Puthoff, *Mind Reach* (New York: Delacorte Press, 1977).

35. For example, Ray Hyman, "Review of the Geller Papers," *The Zetetic* 1, no. 1 (1976): 73–80; or David Marks and Richard Kammann, "The Non-Psychic Powers of Uri Geller," *The Zetetic* 1, no. 2 (1977): 9–17. A touching personal account of belief and disillusionment in Geller is given by psychedelic enthusiast Andrew Weil, "Parapsychology: Andrew Weil's Search for the True Geller, Part I," *Psychology Today* 8, no. 11 (1974): 45–60; "Part II," *Psychology Today* 8, no. 12 (1974): 74–78, 82. An extensive critique of Geller may be found in David Marks and Richard Kammann, *The Psychology of the Psychic* (New York: Prometheus Books, 1980), chapters 6–10.

36. J. B. Rhine, "A New Case of Experimenter Unreliability," *Journal of Parapsychology* 39 (1975): 306–25.

37. Hansel, *Reevaluation*, pp. 164–65; see also *Parapsychological Review* 10, no. 1 (1979): 27.

38. For a general account of scientific fraud, see Deena Weinstein, "Fraud in Science," *Social Science Quarterly* 59 (1979) 639–52. Very recent frauds in science are found in Philip J. Hilts, "Research Results Falsified," *Washington Post*, February 17, 1981, p. A1 and p. A4.

39. Lawrence Le Shan, "On Dealing with Our Critics," *Parapsychology Review* 10, no. 1 (1979): 7–8.

40. J. G. Pratt, "Parapsychology, Normal Science and Paradigm Changes," *Journal of the A.S.P.R.* 73 (1979): 24. Le Shan (note 39) is directly replied to by Peter Phillips, "Some Traps in Dealing with Our Critics," *Parapsychology Review* 10, no. 4 (1979): 7–8.

41. R. A. McConnell, "Areas of Agreement between the Parapsychologist and the Skeptic," *Journal of the A.S.P.R.* 70 (1976): 303.

42. Henry Margenau and Lawrence LeShan. Unpublished letter to *Science*, printed as an addendum to Theodore Rockwell, "Heresy and Excommunication in American Science," *Association of Humanistic Psychologists Newsletter*, Nov. 1979, p. 13. See also Theodore Rockwell, "Parapsychology and the Integrity of Science," *Washington Post*, Aug. 26, 1979, p. D8. LeShan also takes this position in "Dealing with our Critics" (note 39) and is rebutted by Phillips, "Some Traps" (note 40).

43. See, e.g., Charles Tart, "Information Processing Mechanisms and ESP," invited address at the annual meeting of the American Psychological Association, Toronto, Canada, Aug. 31, 1978; and Arthur Koestler, *The Roots of Coincidence* (London: Hutchinson, 1972).

44. Donald O. Hebb, "The Role of Neurological Ideas in Psychology," *Journal of Personality* 20 (1951): 45.

45. Targ and Puthoff, *Mind Reach*, p. 169.

46. *New York Times*, editorial, Feb. 18, 1859, p. 4, col. 3.

47. Cyril Burt, *ESP and Psychology* (New York: John Wiley and Sons, 1975), p. 70.

48. J. Godfrey Raupert, "The Other Side of Psychical Research," *New York Times*, March 21, 1909, sec. 5 (magazine), p. 8.

49. There are two useful collections of papers regarding psychical research and philosophy. One is Peter A. French (ed.) *Philosophers in Wonderland* (Saint Paul, Minn.: Llewellyn Pubns., 1975); the other is Jan Ludwig (ed.) *Philosophy and Parapsychology* (Buffalo, N.Y.: Pro-

metheus Books, 1978). There is remarkably little overlap between these books; French's is concerned with technical philosophical issues (e.g. the idea of "survival"), while Ludwig's leans more toward philosophy-of-science problems (e.g. fraud, precognition).

50. Rhine, *New Frontiers*, pp. 20–21. Reprinted by permission of Louisa E. Rhine.
51. John Beloff, "Parapsychology and Its Neighbors," *Journal of Parapsychology* 34 (1970): 131; McConnell, "Parapsychological dialogue," *Journal of the A.S.P.R.* 71 (1977): 435.
52. J. B. Rhine, "The Shifting Scene in Parapsychology," *Journal of Parapsychology* 26 (1962): 293–307, and "Comments: Psi Methods Reexamined," *Journal of Parapsychology* 39 (1975): 38–57; Robert Thouless, "A Program of Parapsychology," *Journal of Parapsychology* 12 (1948): 113–19, and *From Anecdote to Experiment in Psychical Research* (London: Routledge & Kegan Paul, 1972); LeShan, "Dealing with Our Critics."
53. R. Ramakrishna Rao, "On the Nature of Psi," *Journal of Parapsychology* 41 (1977): 294–351.
54. Robert Thouless, "Parapsychology during the Last Quarter of a Century," In *Progress in Parapsychology*, ed. J. B. Rhine (Durham, N.C.: Parapsychology Press, 1971): 232.
55. Moss and Butler, "Scientific Credibility of ESP," pp. 1069–70.
56. Ibid., p. 1070.
57. The main period of statistical controversy over ESP was 1934-41. See Dorothy A. H. Pope and J. G. Pratt, "The ESP Controversy," *Journal of Parapsychology* 6 (1942): 174–89. A recent study of the debate was made by Seymour H. Mauskopf and Michael R. McVaugh, "The Controversy over Statistics in Parapsychology 1934–1938," in *The Reception of Unconventional Science*, ed. S. H. Mauskopf (Boulder, Colo: Westview Press, for the American Association for the Advancement of Science, 1979), pp. 105–24. A recent attack is Persi Diaconis, "Statistical Problems in ESP Research," *Science* 201 (1978): 131–36.
58. This view of parapsychology is considered and rejected by John Beloff, "Explaining the Paranormal," reprinted in Ludwig, *Philosophy and Parapsychology*, 353–70.
59. Moss and Butler, "Scientific Credibility of ESP," p. 1077.
60. H. M. Collins and J. J. Pinch, "The Construction of the Paranormal: Nothing Unscientific Is Happening," in *On the Margin of Science*, ed. Roy Wallis. Sociological Review Monograph 27 (1979): 255–56.
61. R. A. McConnell, "Parapsychology and the Occult," *Journal of the A.S.P.R.* 67 (1973): 225–43.
62. See, for example, James H. Hyslop, *Science and a Future Life* (Boston: Small, Maynard Co., 1910), or French, *Philosophers in Wonderland*, pp. 289–344. The declining interest in the spirit-hypothesis is observed by J. B. Rhine, "Some Present Impasses in Parapsychology," *Journal of Parapsychology* 19 (1955): 103–5.
63. See, for example, J. B. Rhine, "Telepathy and Clairvoyance Reconsidered," *Journal of Parapsychology* 7 (1945): 176–93; "Telepathy: Will History Repeat Itself?" *Journal of Parapsychology* 7 (1946): 1–4.
64. J. G. Pratt, "Prologue to a Debate: Some Assumptions Relevant to Research in Parapsychology," *Journal of the A.S.P.R.* 72 (1978): 129. The general features of the new approach are outlined by Lawrence LeShan and Henry Margenau, "An Approach to a Science of Psi," *Journal of the S.P.R.* 50 (1980): 273–83. It was Rhine himself who, despite his early pronouncements, first edged away from the revolutionary view of parapsychology; see Rhine, "Parapsychology and Scientific Recognition," *Journal of Parapsychology*, 16 (1952): 225–32, where he seems to advocate adopting camouflage for psi's inherent antimaterialism.
65. Pratt, "Prologue," passim. See also his "Parapsychology: Normal Science and Paradigm Change," pp. 25–26; also John Beloff, "Could There Be a Physical Explanation for Psi?" [He argues no.] *Journal of the S.P.R.* 50 (1980): 263–72. We should note that not all the young parapsychologists have abandoned the search for the soul. See Donald McBurney (a skeptic), "The Persistence of Parapsychology," paper presented at the annual meeting of the American Psychological Association, Montreal, Sept. 1980.
66. George M. Beard, "The Psychology of Spiritism," *North American Review* 129 (1879): 65–66. An early ambition of Rhine's, before his parapsychology work, was to establish an "Institution for Experimental Religion." See Mauskopf and McVaugh, *Elusive Science*, 86–87.

67. The materialistic tendencies of psychical research were early decried by Wilhelm Wundt, "Spiritualism as a Scientific Question," *Popular Scientific Monthly* 15 (1879): 557–93. The young James voiced similar misgivings: William James, "Spiritualism New and Old," *Atlantic Monthly* 29 (1872): 358–62.

68. Theodore Rockwell, "Parapsychology and the Integrity of Science," p. D8. See also Rockwell's feud with *The Humanist*. Theodore Rockwell, Robert Rockwell, and W. Teed Rockwell, "Irrational Rationalists," *Journal of the A.S.P.R.* 72 (1978): 23–34; the editor of *The Humanist*, Paul Kurtz, replied in *A.S.P.R. Journal* 72 (1978), 349–57, followed by a rebuttal by the Rockwells, 357–64.

69. "The Conversion of Kübler-Ross: From Thanatology to Séances and Sex." *Time*, November 12, 1979, p. 81.

CHAPTER EIGHT   CONTEMPORARY THERAPEUTIC CULTS

1. William Simms Bainbridge, *Satan's Power* (Berkeley and Los Angeles: University of California Press, 1978), p. 14. Copyright 1978 by The Regents of the University of California. Published by the University of California Press.

2. See Thomas Robbins and Dick Anthony, "The Sociology of Contemporary Religious Movements," *Annual Review of Sociology* 5 (1979): 75–89; and Vernon Padgett, "Cults vs. Religions: What's the Difference?" unpublished ms., Ohio State University, 1979.

3. Claude Levi-Strauss, "The Sorcerer and His Magic," *Magic, Witchcraft, and Curing*, ed. John Middleton (Garden City, N.Y.: Natural History Press, 1967), pp. 39–40.

4. Ibid., p. 38.

5. Frank Cioffi, "Was Freud a Liar?" British Broadcasting Corporation Radio 3, no date. For a discussion, see Thomas Leahey, *A History of Psychology* (Englewood Cliffs, N.J.: Prentice-Hall, 1980), pp. 220–21.

6. This discussion of Dianetics is based largely on L. Ron Hubbard, *Dianetics: The Modern Science of Mental Health* (New York: St. Hill Press, 1950), and Roy Wallis, *The Road to Total Freedom* (London: Heinemann, 1976).

7. Hubbard, *Dianetics*, p. 16.

8. Ibid., pp. 10–11.

9. Ibid., p. 13.

10. Wallis, *Road*, p. 31.

11. Hubbard, *Dianetics*, pp. 107–8.

12. Ibid., p. 133.

13. John Sladek, *The New Apocrypha* (London: Hard-Davis, McGibbon, 1973), p. 248.

14. Hubbard, *Dianetics*, p. 263.

15. Wallis, *Road*, p. 53.

16. Ibid., p. 71.

17. Roy Wallis, "Poor Man's Psychoanalysis? Some Observations on Dianetics," *The Zetetic*, 1 (1976): 18.

18. Wallis, *Road*, pp. 77–78.

19. Ibid., p. 103–4.

20. James Webb, *The Occult Establishment* (La Salle, Ill.: Open Court, 1976), p. 505.

21. Ibid, p. 505.

22. Bainbridge, *Power*, pp. 30–31. Bainbridge calls Hubbard Rogers and Scientology Technianity. For convenience we will use the Scientological names.

23. Wallis, *Road*, p. 107–8.

24. Ibid.

25. Bainbridge, *Power*, pp. 30–31.

26. Ibid., p. 205.

27. Ibid.

28. Ibid., p. 208.

29. Hubbard, *Dianetics*, p. 129.

30. Bainbridge, *Power*, p. 32. The names "The Power," Edward de Forest, and Kitty McDougle are all pseudonyms employed by Bainbridge.

31. Ibid., p. 33.
32. Ibid., p. 215.
33. Ibid., p. 179.
34. Ibid., p. 170.
35. Ibid., p. 181.
36. Ibid., p. 193.
37. Ibid., p. 192.
38. Ibid., p. 18.
39. Ibid., pp. 220–21.
40. Ibid., pp. 203–4.
41. Ibid., pp. 219–20. Note the similarity to ELIZA.
42. Ibid., pp. 219–20.
43. This discussion of TM is based on Eric Woodrun, "The Development of the Transcendental Movement," *The Zetetic,* 1 (1976): 38–48.
44. Woodrun, "Development," p. 40.
45. Ibid., p. 39.
46. Robert Greenfield, *The Spiritual Supermarket* (New York, E.P. Dutton, Saturday Review Press, 1975), p. 60.
47. E. O. Wilson, *On Human Nature* (New York: Bantam, 1979), pp. 184–85.
48. Mircea Eliad, *Shamanism: Archaic Techniques of Ecstasy* (Princeton, N.J.: Princeton University Press, 1964).
49. Ibid., p. 228.
50. Milbourne Christopher, *Mediums, Mystics, and the Occult* (New York: Thomas Y. Crowell, 1975), pp. 52–56.
51. Eliad, *Shamanism,* p. 221.
52. Ibid., pp. 82–83.
53. Ibid., pp. 72–73.
54. Martin L. Gross, *The Psychological Society* (New York: Simon & Schuster, 1978), p. 18.
55. Ibid., p. 40. Similarities of psychiatrists and shamanic healers is discussed at length by E. Fuller Torrey, *The Mind Game: Witchdoctors and Psychiatrists* (New York: Emerson Hall, 1972).

CONCLUSION

1. Ted Rockwell, "Parapsychology and the Integrity of Science," *Washington Post*, August 26, 1979, p. D8.
2. Theodore Rockwell, "Pseudoscience or Pseudocriticism?" *Journal of Parapsychology* 43 (1979): 229.
3. Lawrence LeShan, "On Dealing with Our Critics," *Parapsychology Review* 10, no. 1 (1979): 7.
4. Christopher Jencks, "Beyond the Five Senses," *New Republic* 144 (Jan. 2, 1961): 18.
5. For a study of the editorial process of scientific journals, see Duncan Lindsey, *The Scientific Publication System in Social Science* (San Francisco: Jassey-Bass, 1978).
6. Henry B. Veatch, "Science and Humanism," 1972, reprinted in *Theories in Contemporary Psychology*, ed. M. H. Marx and T. E. Goodson, 2d ed. (New York: Macmillan, 1976), pp. 65–66.
7. Quoted by Frank M. Turner, "The Victorian Conflict between Science and Religion: A Professional Dimension," *Isis* 69 (1978): 373.
8. Sometimes psychologists themselves recognize their new role. See George W. Albee, "The Protestant Ethics, Sex, and Psychotherapy," *American Psychologist* 32 (1977): 150–61.
9. See ibid., passim.

Bibliography

PSEUDOSCIENCE AND PSYCHOLOGY

Andreski, Stanislav. *Social Sciences as Sorcery.* London: Andre Deutsch, 1972.

Ashworth, C. E. "Flying Saucers, Spoon-Bending and Atlantis: A Structural Analysis of New Mythologies." *Sociological Review* 28 (1980): 353–76.

Barnes, Barry. *Scientific Knowledge and Sociological Theory.* London: Routledge and Kegan Paul, 1974.

Barzun, Jacques. *Science: The Glorious Entertainment.* New York: Harper and Row, 1964.

Crawshay-Williams, Rupert. *The Comforts of Unreason.* 1947. Reprint. Westport, Conn.: Greenwood Press, 1970.

DeMille, Richard. *Castaneda's Journey.* Santa Barbara, Calif.: Capra Press, 1976.

Dodds, E. R. *The Greeks and the Irrational.* Berkeley and Los Angeles: University of California Press, 1951).

Feyerabend, Paul K. *Against Method.* London: New Left Books, 1975.

Gibson, Walter B., and Litzka, R. *The Complete Illustrated Book of the Psychic Sciences.* Garden City, N.Y.: Doubleday, 1966.

Goran, Morris. *Fact, Fraud and Fantasy.* Cranbury, N.J.: A. S. Bernes, 1979.

Greeley, Andrew. *The Sociology of the Paranormal.* New York: Sage Pubns., 1975.

Kearney, Hugh. *Science and Change.* New York: World University Library, 1971.

Laudan, Larry. *Progress and Its Problems*. Berkeley and Los Angeles: University of California Press, 1977.

Mulkay, Michael. *Science and the Sociology of Knowledge*. London: George Allen and Unwin, 1979.

Rachleff, Owen S. *The Occult Conceit*. New York: Bell, 1971.

Ravetz, Jerome S. *Scientific Knowledge and Its Social Problems*. Oxford: Clarendon Press, 1971.

Stegmüller, Wolfgang. *The Structure and Dynamics of Theories*. New York: Springer-Verlag, 1976.

Tiraykin, Edward, ed. *On the Margin of the Visible*. New York: John Wiley and Sons, 1974.

Yates, Frances A. *Giordano Bruno and the Hermetic Tradition*. London: Routledge and Kegan Paul, 1964.

Yates, Frances A. *The Rosicrucian Enlightenment*. Boulder, Colo.: Shambala, 1978.

ALCHEMY AND ASTROLOGY

Allen, Don Cameron. *The Star-Crossed Renaissance*. London: Frank Cass and Co., 1966.

Debus, Allen G. *The English Paracelsians*. London: Oldbourne, 1965.

French, Peter J. *John Dee: The World of an Elizabethan Magus*. London: Routledge and Kegan Paul, 1972.

Gauquelin, Michel. *Dreams and Illusions of Astrology*. (Buffalo, N.Y.: Prometheus Books, 1979).

McCann, H. Gilman. *Chemistry Transformed*. Norwood, N.J.: Ablex Pub. Corp., 1978.

Pachter, Henry M. *Magic into Science*. New York: Henry Schuman, 1951.

Paracelsus. *Selected Writings*. New York: Pantheon, 1951.

Parker, Derek. *Familiar to All: William Lilly and Astrology in the Seventeenth Century*. London: Jonathan Cape, 1975.

Read, John. *Prelude to Chemistry*. 1936. Reprint. Cambridge, Mass.: M.I.T. Press, 1966.

Redgrove, H. Stanley. *Alchemy: Ancient and Modern*. 1911. Reprint. New York: Barnes and Noble, 1977.

"Scientific Astrology?" *Zetetic Scholar* 1, no. 3 and 4 (combined) (1979): 71–106.

Stillman, John M. *The Story of Alchemy and Early Chemistry,* 1924. Reprint. New York: Dover, 1960.

Thorndike, Lynn. "The Place of Astrology in the History of Science," *Isis* 46 (1955): 273–78.

PHRENOLOGY

Bailey, P. "The Great Psychiatric Revolution." *American Journal of Psychiatry* 113 (1956): 387–406.

Bakan, David. "Is Phrenology Foolish?" *Psychology Today* 1, no. 12 (May 1968): 44–50.

Bentley, Madison. "Psychological Antecedents of Phrenology." In *Studies in Social and General Psychology*, edited by M. Bentley. *Psychological Monographs* 21, no. 92 (1916): 102–15.

Butler, Jon. "Magic, Astrology and the Early American Religious Heritage, 1600–1766." *American Historical Review* 84 (1979): 317–46.

Capen, Nahum. *Reminiscences of Dr. Spurzheim and George Combe.* New York: Fowler & Wells, 1881.

Carlson, Eric T. "The Influence of Phrenology on Early American Psychiatric Thought." *American Journal of Psychiatry* 115 (1958–59): 535–38.

Chambers. Howard. *Phrenology for the Millions.* 1968. Reprint. New York: Award Books, 1970.

Collins, Philip. "The First Science of the Mind." *Times Literary Supplement,* April 25, 1975, 455–56.

Dallenbach, Karl. "The History and Derivation of the Word Function as a Systematic Term in Psychology." *American Journal of Psychology* 27 (1915): 473–84.

De Giustino, David. "Reforming the Commonwealth of Thieves." *Victorian Studies* 15 (1972): 439–62.

Denton, George. "Early Psychological Theories of Herbert Spencer." *American Journal of Psychology* 32 (1921): 5–15.

Erickson, Paul. "Phrenology and Physical Anthropology: The George Combe Connection." *Current Anthropology* 18 (1977): 92–93.

Fyvie, John. "The Ethological Society and the Revival of Phrenology." *The Nineteenth Century and After* 57 (1907): 957–70.

Grant, A. Cameron. "George Combe and American Slavery." *Journal of Negro History* 45 (1960): 259–69.

Grant, A. Cameron. "Combe on Phrenology and Free Will." *Journal of the History of Ideas* 26 (1965): 141–47.

Hungerford, Edward. "Walt Whitman and His Chart of Bumps." *American Literature* 2 (1930–31): 350–84.

Jefferson, Geoffrey. "The Contemporary Reaction to Phrenology." In his *Selected Papers.* Springfield, Ill.: Charles C Thomas, 1960.

Jerison, Harry. "Should Phrenology Be Rediscovered?" *Current Anthropology* 18 (1977): 744–46.

Krech, David. "Cortical Localization of Function." In *Psychology in the Making,* edited by Leo Postman. New York: Alfred A. Knopf, 1962.

Lesky, Erna. "Structure and Function in Gall." *Bulletin of the History of Medicine* 44 (1970): 297–314.

"Phrenology and Animal Magnetism." *The Knickerbocker* 15, no. 2 (1840): 98–101.

"Review of Thomas Sewall's *An Examination of Phrenology.*" *North American Review* 45 (1837): 505–8.

Riegel, Robert. "Early Phrenology in the United States." *Medical Life* 37 (1930): 361–76.

Riegel, Robert. "The Introduction of Phrenology to the United States." *American Historical Review* 39 (1933): 73–78.

Risse, Guenter. "Vocational Guidance in the Depression: Phrenology vs. Applied Psychology." *Journal of the History of the Behavioral Sciences* 12 (1976): 130–40.

Rosenberg, Charles. *No Other Gods.* Baltimore: The Johns Hopkins University Press, 1976.

Sampson, Marmaduke. *Rationale of Crime.* 3d ed. 1846. Reprint. Montclair, N.J.: Patterson Smith, 1973.

"Scientific Phrenology." *Science* 9 (1887): 299.

Starkman, Miriam. "Quakers, Phrenologists and Jonathan Swift." *Journal of the History of Ideas* 20 (1959): 403–12.

Walsh, Anthony. "Is Phrenology Foolish?" *Journal of the History of the Behavioral Sciences* 6 (1970): 358–61.

Walsh, Anthony. "George Combe: A Portrait of a Heretofore Generally Unknown Behaviorist." *Journal of the History of the Behavioral Sciences* 7 (1971): 269–78.

Webster, William. "The Phreno-Magnetic Society of Cincinnati." *The American Journal of Clinical Hypnosis* 18 (1976): 277–81.

Wilson, John. "Phrenology and the Transcendentalists." *American Literature* 28 (1956–57), 220–25.

Wrobel, Arthur. "Orthodoxy and Resectability in Nineteenth-Century Phrenology." *Journal of Popular Culture* 9 (1975): 38–50.

MESMERISM

Baudouin, Charles. *Suggestion and Autosuggestion.* London: George Allen and Unwin, 1920.

Cahagnet, Louis. *The Celestial Telegraph.* 1850. Reprint. New York: Arno Press, 1976.

Colquhoun, J. C. *Report of the Experiments on Animal Magnetism.* 1833. Reprint. New York: Arno, 1975.

DuPotet de Sennevoy, Jules. *An Introduction to the Study of Animal Magnetism.* 1838. Reprint. New York: Arno, 1976.

Esdaile, James. *Natural and Mesmeric Clairvoyance.* 1852. Reprint. New York: Arno, 1975.

Goldsmith, Margaret. *Franz Anton Mesmer.* Garden City, N.Y.: Doubleday, 1934.

Kaplan, Fred. " 'The Mesmeric Mania:' The Early Victorians and Animal Magnetism." *Journal of the History of Ideas* 35 (1974): 691–702.

Kaplan, Fred. *Dickens and Mesmerism.* Princeton, N.J.: Princeton University Press, 1975.

Parker, Gail. *Mind Cure in New England.* Hanover, N.H.: University Press of New England, 1973.

"Phrenology and Animal Magnetism. How They Served an Individual." *The Knickerbocker* 15 (1940): 98–101.

Quen, Jacques. "Case Studies in Nineteenth Century Scientific Rejection." *Journal of the History of the Behavioral Sciences* 11 (1975): 149–56.

Thornton, E. M. *Hypnotism, Hysteria and Epilepsy.* London: William Heinemann Medical Books, 1976.

Tomlinson, D. M. "Mesmerism in New Orleans." *American Journal of Psychiatry* 13 (1974): 1402–4.

Walmsley, D. M. *Anton Mesmer.* London: Robert Hale, 1967.

Webb, R. K. *Harriet Martineau. A Radical Victorian.* London: Heinemann, 1960.

Zweig, Stefan. *Mental Healers.* Garden City, N.Y.: Garden City Pub. Co., 1932.

SPIRITUALISM

Capron, Eliab W. *Modern Spiritualism.* 1855. Reprint. New York: Arno Press, 1917.

Goodall, Jane van Lawick. *In the Shadow of Man.* New York: Dell, 1972.

Grimm, Jacob. *Teutonic Mythology,* 4 vols, 1883. Trans. by James S. Stallybrass. Reprint. New York: Dover, 1966.

Kirk, Robert. *The Secret Common-wealth*, 17th century. Reprint. Cambridge: D. S. Brewer, 1976.

Morris, William, trans. *Volsunga Saga.* New York: Macmillan, 1967.

Podmore, Frank. *The Newer Spiritualism.* 1910. New York: Arno, 1975.

Tyler, Alice Felt. *Freedom's Ferment.* 1944. Reprint. New York: Harper, Torchbooks, 1962.

Underhill, A. Leah. *The Missing Link in Modern Spiritualism,* 1885. Reprint. New York: Arno, 1976.

Wimberly, Lowry C. *Folklore in the English and Scottish Ballads.* 1928. Chicago: University of Chicago Press, 1928.

Yeats, W. B. *Irish Folk Stories and Fairy Tales.* New York: Grosset and Dunlap, n.d.

PSYCHICAL RESEARCH

Beloff, John. *New Directions in Parapsychology*. London: Elek Science, 1974.

Coover, John E. *Experiments in Psychical Research*. New York: Arno, 1917.

Douglas, Alfred. *Extra-Sensory Perception*. London: Victor Gallancz, 1976.

Gudas, Fabian, ed. *Extrasensory Perception*. 1961. Reprint. New York: Arno, 1975.

Mackenzie, Brian, and MacKenzie, S. Lynn. "Whence the Enchanted Boundary? Sources and Significance of the Parapsychological Tradition?" *Journal of Parapsychology* 44 (1981): 125–66.

CULTS

Anthony, Dick, and Robbins, Thomas. "Religious Movements and the 'Brainwashing' Issue." Paper presented at the annual meeting of the American Psychological Association, New York, September, 1979.

Balch, Robert, and Taylor, David. "Seekers and Saucers: The Role of the Cultic Milieu in Joining a U.F.O. Cult." *The American Behavioral Scientist* 20 (1977): 839–860.

Eliade, Mircea. *Occultism, Witchcraft and Cultural Fashions*. Chicago: University of Chicago Press, 1976.

Evans, Christopher. *Cults of Unreason*. New York: Delta, 1973.

Festinger, Leon, Riecker, H., and Schachter, S. *When Prophecy Fails*. New York: Harper, Torchbooks, 1956.

Robbins, Thomas. "Cults and the Therapeutic State." *Social Policy*, June, 1974, pp. 42–46.

Torrey, E. Fuller. *The Mind Game: Witchdoctors and Psychiatrists*. New York: Emerson Hall, 1972.

Wallis, Roy, ed. *Sectarianism: Analyses of Religious and Non-religious Sects*. London: Peter Owen, 1975.

Index